MAKE-A-MIX

KARINE ELIASON, NEVADA HARWARD & MADELINE WESTOVER

FISHER
er
BOOKS™

Publishers: Bill Fisher
               Helen Fisher
               Howard Fisher

Editors: Helen Fisher
               Sarah Smith

Book
Production: Deanie Wood
               Paula Peterson

Art Director: B. Josh Young

Published by Fisher Books
4239 West Ina Road, Suite 101
Tucson, AZ 85741
(520) 744-6110

©1995 Fisher Books
ISBN 1-55561-073-0 (paper)
ISBN 1-55561-107-9 (hardback)

Printed in the U.S.A
Printing 10 9 8 7 6 5 4 3 2 1

TABLE OF CONTENTS

Introduction 1 ~ 12

Master Mixes
Dry & Semi-dry Mixes 13 ~ 37
Freezer, Refrigerator 38 ~ 65
Special Mixes 66 ~ 81

Appetizers & Snacks 82 ~ 92
Soups & Salads 93 ~ 114
Vegetables & Side Dishes 115 ~ 125

Main Dishes
Beef Dishes 126 ~ 148
Chicken Dishes 149 ~ 169
Mexican & Italian Dishes 170 ~ 188
Main Dishes ~ Other 189 ~ 209

Breakfast & Brunch 210 ~ 228
Yeast Breads & Quick Breads 229 ~ 247
Muffins & Rolls 248 ~ 271
Cakes 272 ~ 292
Pies 293 ~ 310
Desserts 311 ~ 328

Index 329 ~ 332

MEET THE AUTHORS

Nevada Harward, Madeline Westover, Karine Eliason

When you have some of the answers to a problem shared by millions of people—especially the working woman or busy mom—you want to share your knowledge. This is what Karine Eliason, Nevada Harward and Madeline Westover have been doing for the 16 years since their first book, *Make-A-Mix Cookery*, was published.

This is their sixth book. Their books have sold over two-million copies. The "mix" ladies have added new mixes, revised many old ones, and lowered fat and cholesterol in many recipes.

The authors have long praised the joys of making and using mixes as they lectured extensively throughout the United States, appearing on TV and demonstrating before large groups. Busy mothers and working women have said that the mix books have been a lifesaver in the kitchen.

All three authors are active volunteers. With their busy schedules and large families (they have 18 children and 20 grandchildren) everyone gets involved. Their married children have created mixes that are shared in this book.

MASTER MIXES

Here they are—the starting points for hundreds of breads, main dishes, appetizers, side dishes, desserts and beverages! With these mixes in your pantry, refrigerator and freezer, you can offer a different menu every day of the year with a minimum of preparation time.

There are three types of Master Mixes:

Dry Mixes contain only dry ingredients and will keep 6 to 8 months in your cupboard. Shake or stir them before using, as they may have settled during storage. Dry mixes include HOT ROLL MIX, SNACK CAKE MIX and a variety of seasoning mixes.

Semi-dry Mixes contain shortening, butter or margarine. Be sure to follow storage instructions because some of these should be refrigerated. Favorites include QUICK MIX and WHITE SAUCE MIX. These mixes will generally stay fresh for 10 to 12 weeks.

Freezer-Refrigerator Mixes are moist and require cold storage. They keep well for 3 months or more, and range from FIVE-WAY BEEF MIX to PINTO BEAN MIX to CREAM-CHEESE PASTRY MIX.

Be certain to familiarize yourself with the different kinds of **Master Mixes** and the many potential uses for each. We've included our favorite recipes in the following chapters and listed their page numbers following the corresponding master-mix recipe. Of course, we expect you to experiment and create your own master-pieces.

A few **Special Mixes,** such as CHILI SEASONING MIX, HOT CHOCOLATE MIX and the salad-dressing mixes are designed primarily for one recipe. In this case the recipe is included with the mix instructions.

In addition to making life easier at home, mixes are a wonderful convenience when camping. With an ample supply of your own mixes, food can be prepared quickly and cooperatively at the campsite.

Creative gift-giving is one of the most popular uses of homemade mixes. A new bride will be grateful for such a creative gift—especially when you include a copy of *Make-A-Mix* as part of the gift. Adapt your gift-giving creativity to the holiday season by including a cookie cutter with COOKIE MIX packed in a pretty jar.

Whether for gifts or for your own use, be sure to label all containers clearly with the contents and date.

BAKING & COOKING WITH MIXES

The **Magic of Mixes**—One quick look at your cupboard shelves will tell you that mixes have become an essential part of today's cooking. Our busy lifestyle has created a major trend toward the use of time-saving convenience foods, and mixes are the popular choice for many of our cooking needs. Because the time-consuming part of cooking is assembling supplies and equipment and measuring ingredients, it is easy to see why mixes are so valuable to every cook.

Mixes Are Easy—With your own mixes you save almost three-fourths the time you spend preparing food. This is because you prepare for several meals at one time. Whether your family has 2 or 22 members, you can make the right amount for each meal. Dinners are better planned, delicious and nutritious—even when there's little time. Children can make most of the recipes.

Mixes Are Economical—Commercial mixes are generally advertised as time-savers rather than money-savers. Their prices increase regularly with rising labor and packaging costs. Why not save those extra dollars by providing the labor and packaging yourself? Compare the cost per cup of commercial mixes with homemade mixes and you'll discover your mixes cost less than half. Save more by watching for specials on items such as flour, sugar and shortening.

Mixes Are Nutritious—There's a special satisfaction in choosing your own ingredients to cook with and knowing what is in your foods. If you want to reduce the preservatives and additives you consume, making your own mixes is the way to start. You can also reduce the fat and substitute other ingredients as you wish.

When you make meals from your own mixes, you'll notice the fresher flavor. Most of the mix recipes in this book contain ingredients chosen for their health value as well as taste appeal.

Mixes Are Versatile—The extent to which mixes can be used is almost limitless. QUICK MIX, which makes dozens of different recipes can be substituted for any recipe that calls for commercially prepared biscuit mixes.

Depending on the type of storage space available, you can keep COOKIE MIX on your pantry shelf or SLICE & BAKE COOKIES in your freezer. Both can be used to make a variety of cookies. Pies are quick and easy when you keep FREEZER PIE-CRUST MIX on hand.

Some mixes are seasonings to complement specific recipes. Make individual packets of TACO SEASONING MIX, HOME-STYLE DRESSING MIX, CHILI SEASONING MIX and our other "special" mixes and you're ready for any occasion! They're better than those you can buy. Some are so unusual you can't even buy them in stores.

Mixes Can Be Personalized—Use a salt or sugar substitute or whole grains, eliminate MSG or reduce fats and sugars, thus meeting your own personal preferences and needs.

Ingredients

THE INGREDIENTS

Always use fresh, high-quality products when you're making your own mixes. The foods you prepare are only as good as their contents.

It is important to know what each ingredient offers to a recipe. Here are some tips to help you make mixes and meals everyone will remember.

Flours—All-purpose flour is best in most dry mixes. It is a blend of hard and soft wheat flours. Either bleached or unbleached flour can be used, but unbleached flour has higher nutritional value. There are also flours milled specifically for baking breads. Check the labels. Because moisture content varies in wheat flours, some yeast-bread recipes indicate an approximate measurement. Always begin with a small amount of flour and add more until the desired texture is reached.

Whole-wheat flour can be used instead of all-purpose flour. Use 1 to 2 tablespoons less per cup of flour called for in the recipe and increase the leavening (yeast almost doubled, baking powder and baking soda increased by one-third). Whole-wheat flour mixes should be refrigerated to retain maximum nutrition.

Fats—Butter and margarine are used interchangeably in most recipes. However, butter produces a different texture and flavor than margarine and should be used in those recipes where specified. Mixes containing either butter or margarine must be refrigerated.

Vegetable oils are pressed from seeds, fruits and nuts. Canola oil and olive oil are preferred because they are lower in saturated fat. Hydrogenated vegetable shortening is used in some recipes because of its storage properties. (Mixes containing vegetable shortening may be covered and stored in a cool, dry place for 3 months or more.) You may use vegetable oils in all your mixes by omitting the shortening from the dry ingredients and adding the vegetable oil when you prepare the recipe. Of course, there will be a slight change in texture and taste. Caution: Vegetable oils do not store for extended periods of time so DO NOT include them in the mix. Add the oil when you make the recipe using the mix.

Fresh eggs are a boost to every recipe because they have a much better texture and taste than eggs that have been stored a while. Use large eggs, about 2 ounces in weight. Eggs at room temperature produce more volume. Replacing fresh eggs with egg substitutes works well in most recipes. Or use 2 egg whites in place of 1 whole egg for lower fat and cholesterol.

Leavening Agents—We want to stress the importance of using fresh baking ingredients. Active dry yeast is convenient for mixing purposes. Yeast is comprised of living organisms that feed on sugars and produce alcohol and carbon dioxide. Be certain the liquid you add to the yeast is lukewarm, about 110F (45C)—not any hotter. To eliminate guesswork, instant-read thermometers are now available. If you plan to make yeast breads and rolls on a regular basis, buy yeast in bulk rather than in individual packets. After opening the yeast, store it in the refrigerator or freezer, otherwise it loses its strength—giving poor results.

Baking powder generally starts to work when it is combined with liquid, but its impact on a product is increased when the product is heated. Double-action baking powder is preferred for its availability and consistency. Do not use baking powder that is older than the expiration date on the bottom of the can. If it is, discard it and buy fresh.

Baking soda alone has no leavening properties, but when used in combination with acidic ingredients such as sour milk, buttermilk or molasses, it produces a tender crumb texture.

Sugar—Sugars contribute sweetness and tenderness to foods. In breads, sugar aids in producing a golden-brown crust. Small pinches of sugar added to certain vegetables increase their flavor. Granulated sugar is usually used in our recipes. Use powdered sugar, brown sugar, honey and molasses only when specified. They are *not* interchangeable with granulated sugar.

Spices—Sometimes the difference between an outstanding and a mediocre dish is the seasoning. Our recipes allow you to use a wide variety of herbs, seasonings and spices. For best results, use recently purchased, high-quality spices, because spices lose their flavor in a short time. When fresh spices and herbs are available, they are preferred to dried spices and herbs, but the amounts should be increased three to four times.

Vegetables, Meats and Poultry—Use care in preparing vegetables, meats and poultry for storage. It is essential to use fresh, clean, top-quality ingredients. Follow directions carefully for preparing and storing frozen mixes.

Instant Nonfat Dry Milk—With milk solids added to a dry mix, you have the option of adding water to the recipe instead of milk. Adding milk gives extra enrichment and nutrition. Dried buttermilk powder can be used in some dry mixes, too.

TIPS FOR LOWERING FAT

In baked items substitute 2 egg whites for each whole egg.

Use egg substitute instead of egg.

Use skim milk in recipes calling for milk.

Use nonfat or lowfat plain yogurt to replace some or all of oil in recipes.

Use applesauce instead of oil in some baked breads or cakes.

Use water or lowfat broth instead of oil for sautéing.

Use vegetable cooking sprays instead of oil to brown meats and vegetables.

Use lowfat or fat-free mayonnaise, sour cream and salad dressings.

Substitute lowfat, plain yogurt for sour cream.

Use more spices and herbs instead of butter and salt to flavor foods.

Cut back on shortening and oil in breads. Usually you can get by with less without sacrificing quality.

Use ground turkey or chicken instead of ground beef, but be sure to check the fat content. If it is ground with the skin on, that will make it almost as fat as beef. If you are unsure, have the butcher grind it for you without the skin. Fresh ground turkey or chicken must be used within 2 days of purchase or frozen for later use.

Use leaner cuts of beef or pork.

After browning ground beef, drain it in a colander and rinse it with hot water.

Use lowfat or part-skim milk cheese in place of higher-fat cheese.

Buy lowfat or fat-free versions of such foods as chicken or beef broth, refried beans, sauces, etc.

Read labels carefully. Often foods tagged as *lite* or *healthy* are not really lowfat. According to experts, for a food to be considered lowfat, it should get 30% or less of its calories from fat.

EQUIPMENT & PROCEDURES

Cooking with Make-a-Mix recipes is very similar to the way you cook now. You probably already have all the equipment you need for measuring, mixing and storing the ingredients. You will spend a little extra time preparing your mixes, but you'll save much more time in the final preparation of recipes. Make up several mixes at a time. Because you're working mainly with dry ingredients, the clean-up will be minimal. In a short time, you can fill your shelves with an abundance of mixes that will make cooking more enjoyable for weeks to come.

Measuring—Accuracy in measuring ingredients is necessary to ensure satisfactory results in your cooking. You should have:

    set of dry measuring cups
    liquid measuring cup with pouring spout
    set of measuring spoons
    straight-edged spatula
    rubber scraper

Dry ingredients should be measured in a cup with a flush rim for leveling. Lightly spoon ingredients into a cup and level with a straight-edged spatula.

Liquid ingredients require a transparent measuring cup with markings and a pouring spout. Measure liquid ingredients at eye level.

Moist ingredients such as brown sugar, soft breadcrumbs, grated cheese, coconut and raisins should be firmly packed so they hold the shape of the cup when turned out.

Solid ingredients such as shortening should be pressed firmly into the measuring cup or spoon so no air pockets remain. Level with a straight-edged spatula. Use a rubber scraper to get all the shortening out of the measure.

Mixing—A real convenience in preparing mixes is a heavy-duty mixer. A small electric mixer or pastry blender will produce the same results but will require more effort. If you do not have a pastry blender, use 2 knives to distribute dry ingredients and fats evenly.

You will definitely need an extra-large mixing bowl. If you do not have a bowl large enough to hold about 35 cups (9 quarts) of mix, a round-bottom dishpan is an alternative.

For dry mixes, stir all ingredients together until evenly distributed.

For semi-dry mixes, evenly distribute the dry ingredients, then cut in shortening, butter or margarine until the mixture resembles cornmeal in texture.

Storing—For maximum freshness, store dry mixes in airtight containers in a cool, dry and dark place. For freezer storage use containers allowing at least 1/2-inch expansion. Lightweight plastic bags and cottage-cheese cartons are not suitable for freezer use. Frozen mixes should be thawed in the refrigerator or microwave oven, and used immediately after thawing.

Consider two methods of storing dry mixes. Large-Canister Storage lets you store your mixes in one or several large containers. This is especially useful for QUICK MIX, HOT ROLL MIX and other mixes that make a large number of recipes using different amounts. You can use large coffee cans lined with heavy plastic bags, large screw-top jars or airtight plastic containers or canisters.

Premeasured Storage keeps just the amount you'll use in a specific recipe, so you won't have to measure it later. This is a good way to store meat mixes, seasoning mixes, SNACK CAKE MIX, MUFFIN MIX and any other mix that uses the same amount of mix in each recipe. Use plastic containers such as margarine tubs, drink-mix cans or any metal can with a lid, glass jars or heavy-duty-foil packets.

Labeling—Before you place a mix on the shelf or in the freezer, make sure it is properly labeled. Resist the urge to store a mix, then label it later, because later the mixes may all look alike! On each container, write the name of the mix and the date by which it should be used. In most instances the mixes can be stored longer than the specified time, but at the risk of loss in flavor and nutrients. You may also want to write down the amount of mix in each container, particularly if you have divided the mix into premeasured amounts.

1. Airtight canisters, jars and cans are useful for storing mixes. Freezer containers should allow for expansion of frozen mixes.

2. On each mix container write the name and date by when mix should be used. Also record the amount of mix and recipe page number.

BREADMAKER MIX

This mix can also be made by substituting whole-wheat flour for half of the white flour.

13 cups bread flour
2 tablespoons salt
1/2 cup sugar
1/2 cup instant nonfat dry milk

Combine all ingredients in a large bowl. Stir together to distribute evenly. Label and package in six (2-1/4-cup) containers, if using a 1-pound-loaf breadmaker, or in four (3-1/3-cup) containers for larger capacity bread makers. Store in a cool, dry place. Use within 6 months. Makes about 14 cups BREADMAKER MIX.

TO MAKE SMALL LOAF
1-1/2 teaspoons active dry yeast
2-1/4 cups BREADMAKER MIX
1 tablespoon butter or vegetable oil
3/4 cup warm water

TO MAKE LARGE LOAF
2 teaspoons active dry yeast
3-1/3 cups BREADMAKER MIX
1-1/2 tablespoons butter or vegetable oil
1-1/4 cups warm water

Mix and bake on LIGHT setting per breadmaker instructions.

Variations

Cinnamon Raisin—To the basic recipe add 1/2 cup raisins and 1-1/2 teaspoons ground cinnamon. Glaze with powdered-sugar glaze, if desired, while still warm.

French Bread—Eliminate the butter or vegetable oil.

Sweet Bread—Add 1 tablespoon of sugar with dry ingredients. Break 1 egg into measuring cup, fill cup with water to amount called for in recipe.

Herb Bread—Add 1-1/2 teaspoons dry herbs (rosemary, basil, dill, etc.)

BROWNIE MIX

This has become a "best of all" recipe by the Ricks family. And as we demonstrate throughout the country, many others share that opinion.

6 cups all-purpose flour
4 teaspoons baking powder
4 teaspoons salt
8 cups sugar
1 (8-oz.) can unsweetened cocoa powder

BROWNIE MIX makes:

Chewy Chocolate Cookies,
    page 316
Our Best Brownies, page 314
Texas Sheet Cake, page 291
Brownie Alaska, page 315
Mississippi Mud, page 286

In a large bowl, combine flour, baking powder, salt, sugar and cocoa. Stir with a wire whisk until evenly distributed. Put in a large airtight container. Label with date and contents. Store in a cool, dry place. Use within 10 to 12 weeks. Makes about 15 cups BROWNIE MIX.

CORN BREAD MIX

Corn bread baked in glass, cast-iron or a dark-metal pan develops a golden-brown crust.

4 cups all-purpose flour
4 cups yellow cornmeal
**2 cups instant nonfat milk
  powder or dry buttermilk
  powder**
2/3 cup granulated sugar
4 tablespoons baking powder
1 tablespoon salt
1 tablespoon baking soda

CORN BREAD MIX makes:
Corn Dogs, page 206

CORN BREAD
1 egg, beaten
1/2 cup water
2 tablespoons butter, melted
1-1/4 cups CORN BREAD MIX

In a large bowl, combine all ingredients. Stir with a wire whisk until evenly distributed. Pour into a 10-cup container with a tight-fitting lid. Seal container. Label with date and contents. Store in a cool, dry place. Use within 10 to 12 weeks. Makes about 10 cups CORN BREAD MIX.

CORN BREAD
Preheat oven to 425F (220 C). Butter a 5" x 3" loaf pan. In a bowl beat together, egg, water and butter. Stir in CORN BREAD MIX until moistened. Batter will be lumpy. Pour into prepared pan. Bake 20 to 25 minutes. Makes 1 loaf.

GRAHAM-CRACKER-CRUST MIX

*With this mix, you'll crumb
enough crackers for six crusts.*

1 (2-lb.) box graham crackers
1 cup granulated sugar
2 teaspoons ground cinnamon

*GRAHAM-CRACKER-CRUST MIX
makes:*

Chocolate-Peppermint Supreme,
   page 326
Orange-Light Dessert, page 323
Our Favorite Cheesecake,
   page 320
Banana-Split Cake, page 275
Lemonade Ice Cream Dessert,
   page 327

Process 6 or 7 crackers in blender or
food processor fitted with the metal
blade to make fine crumbs. Pour crumbs
into a large bowl. Repeat with remaining
crackers. Or use a rolling pin to crush
crackers between 2 sheets of waxed
paper or in a plastic bag. Stir in sugar
and cinnamon. Pour into a 10-cup
container with a tight-fitting lid. Seal
container. Label with date and contents.
Store in a cool, dry place. Use within 6
months. Makes about 9 cups GRAHAM-
CRACKER-CRUST MIX.

GRAHAM-CRACKER CRUST
1-1/2 cups GRAHAM-CRACKER-
   CRUST MIX, above
1/3 cup melted butter or
   margarine

GRAHAM-CRACKER CRUST
To make crust for 9-inch pie plate,
springform pan or baking dish:
Combine GRAHAM-CRACKER-CRUST
MIX with melted butter or margarine.
Press mixture over bottom and sides of
pie plate or springform pan. Refrigerate
45 minutes before filling. If baking crust,
preheat oven to 375F (190C). Bake 6
to 8 minutes in preheated oven; cool
completely before adding filling. Fill as
desired. Makes one 8- or 9-inch crust.

HOT ROLL MIX

Fix this ahead and you're ready to roll!

5 lb. (20 cups) all-purpose flour
1-1/4 cups sugar
4 teaspoons salt
1 cup instant nonfat dry milk

Combine all ingredients in large bowl. Stir together to distribute evenly. Put in a large airtight container. Label with date and contents. Store in a cool, dry place. Use within 6 to 8 months. Makes about 22 cups HOT ROLL MIX.

HOT ROLL MIX makes:

Swedish Cinnamon Twists, page 216
Tatonuts, page 266
Cinnamon Rolls, page 213
Cream-Cheese Swirls, page 257
Butterscotch Butter Balls, page 212
Pluckit, page 215
Mary's Honey-Walnut Swirl, page 234
French Bread, page 230
Pan Rolls, page 262
Orange Butterflake Rolls, page 261
Crescent Rolls, page 258
Savory Tomato-Rosemary Bread, page 232
Bread Basket Bowls, page 244

Homemade White Bread, page 231
Big Soft Pretzels, page 92
Hamburger Buns, page 260
Pizza Crust, page 267
Squash Rolls, page 263
Bagels, page 264
English Muffins, page 259

Variation

Use 9 cups whole-wheat flour and 8 cups all-purpose flour instead of 20 cups all-purpose flour. Decrease sugar to 1 cup.

*We prefer to refriger-
ate this mix if we are
not going to use it
immediately.*

WHOLE-WHEAT HOT-ROLL MIX

Get extra fiber with this mix.

9 cups whole-wheat flour
**8 cups unbleached or all-
    purpose flour**
**1 cup instant nonfat milk
    powder**
4 teaspoons salt
**1 cup packed brown sugar
    or 1 cup granulated sugar**

*WHOLE-WHEAT HOT-ROLL MIX
makes:*

Swedish Rye Bread, page 233
Country French Bread, page 247
Whole-Wheat Cinnamon Rolls,
    page 214

In a large bowl, combine whole-wheat flour, unbleached or all-purpose flour, milk powder and salt. Stir with a wire whisk until evenly distributed. Press brown sugar through a coarse sieve to remove any lumps. Stir brown sugar or granulated sugar into flour mixture. Pour into an 18-cup container with a tight-fitting lid. Attach lid. Label container with date and contents. Store in a cool, dry place and use within a week, in a refrigerator 10 to 12 weeks or in a freezer up to 6 months. Makes about 18 cups WHOLE-WHEAT HOT-ROLL MIX.

MUFFIN MIX

One of our favorite mixes. There is no end to the variety of tempting muffins you can make from this one mix. See our Lowfat Tips section, page 9 for ways to make these nearly fat-free.

8 cups all-purpose flour
3 cups sugar
3 tablespoons baking powder
2 teaspoons salt
2 teaspoons ground cinnamon
2 teaspoons ground nutmeg

MUFFIN MIX makes:

Melt-in-Your-Mouth Muffins with
    variations, page 250
Molasses Bran Muffins,
    page 251
Apple Muffins, page 271
Lemon-Poppy Seed Muffins,
    page 249
Cranberry Cakes with Butter
    Sauce, page 281
Zucchini Muffins, page 253
Gran Muffins, page 271

In a large bowl, combine flour, sugar, baking powder, salt, cinnamon and nutmeg. Mix well. Put in a large airtight container. Label with date and contents. Store in a cool, dry place. Use within 6 to 8 months. Makes about 11 cups of MUFFIN MIX.

SWEET QUICK-BREAD MIX

Always pack brown sugar into a cup to ensure a full measure. This is one of the most popular "gift" mixes.

12 cups all-purpose flour
2 tablespoons baking powder
2 tablespoons baking soda
1 tablespoon salt
3 cups granulated sugar
3 cups brown sugar, firmly packed

SWEET QUICK-BREAD MIX makes:

Banana-Nut Bread, page 236
Carrot-Orange Loaf, page 237
Cranberry Bread, page 241
Date-Nut Bread, page 240
Pumpkin Bread, page 243
Spicy Applesauce Bread, page 245
Zucchini Bread, page 246
Poppy Seed-Lemon Bread, page 242

In a large bowl, stir flour, baking powder, baking soda, salt, granulated sugar and brown sugar with a large wire whisk until blended. Spoon into a 24-cup container with a tight-fitting lid. Seal container. Label with date and contents. Store in a cool, dry place. Use within 6 months. Makes about 20 cups SWEET QUICK-BREAD MIX.

QUICK MIX

The most versatile of all mixes.

8-1/2 cups all-purpose flour
4 tablespoons baking powder
1 tablespoon salt
2 teaspoons cream of tartar
1 teaspoon baking soda
1-1/2 cups instant nonfat dry
  milk or dry buttermilk
  powder
2-1/4 cups vegetable
  shortening

QUICK MIX makes:

Super-Duper Doughnuts,
    page 269
Sunshine Coffee Cake,
    page 218
Morning Muffins, page 252
Quick Pancakes, page 221
Golden Corn Bread, page 238
Crispy Breadsticks, page 253
Biscuits, page 255
Never-Fail Rolled Biscuits,
    page 256
Curried Shrimp Rounds,
    page 83
Self-Crust Cheese Tart,
    page 208

In a large bowl, sift together all dry ingredients. Blend well. With pastry blender or heavy-duty mixer, cut in shortening until mixture resembles cornmeal in texture. Put in a airtight container. Label with date and contents. Store in a cool, dry place. Use within 10 to 12 weeks. Makes about 13 cups of QUICK MIX.

Variation

Use 4-1/4 cups all-purpose flour and
    4-1/4 cups whole-wheat flour.
    Increase baking powder to 5 table-
    spoons.

Tuna-Cheese Swirls, page 197
Molasses Cookies, page 317
Caramel-Nut Pudding Cake,
    page 277
Hot-Fudge Pudding Cake,
    page 280
Pineapple Upside-Down Cake,
    page 288
Impossible Pie, page 298
Sunday Shortcake, page 290
Apple-Walnut Cobbler,
    page 312
English Griddle Scones, page 270

Master Mixes

ALL-PURPOSE CAKE MIX

Use this mix as you would a packaged cake mix.

10 cups all-purpose flour
6-1/4 cups sugar
1 cup cornstarch
5 tablespoons baking powder
1 tablespoon salt
2-1/2 cups vegetable shortening

ALL-PURPOSE CAKE MIX makes:

Lemon Pound Cake, page 285
Yellow Cake, page 289
White Cake, page 289
Mom's Spumoni Cake,
    page 282

In a large sifter, combine flour, sugar, cornstarch, baking powder and salt. Sift, in batches, into a large bowl. Use a pastry blender or a heavy-duty mixer to blend in shortening until mixture resembles cornmeal in texture. Spoon into a 20-cup container with a tight-fitting lid. Seal container. Label with date and contents. Store in a cool, dry place. Use within 10 to 12 weeks. Makes about 17 cups ALL-PURPOSE CAKE MIX.

SNACK CAKE MIX

Pre-measuring this mix into individual containers gives you all the convenience of a commercial mix at a fraction of the cost.

8-3/4 cups all-purpose flour
2 tablespoons baking soda
1 tablespoon salt
5-1/4 cups granulated sugar

SNACK CAKE MIX makes:

Applesauce Snack Cake,
    page 273
Banana-Walnut Snack Cake,
    page 274
Carrot Snack Cake, page 278
Date-Chocolate-Chip Snack
    Cake, page 292
Gingerbread Snack Cake,
    page 284
Oatmeal Spice Cake, page 287
Peach Cobbler, page 313
Double-Chocolate Snack Cake,
    page 279

In a large bowl, combine all ingredients. Stir with a wire whisk until blended. Divide mixture into six portions, about 2-1/3 cups each. Store in containers with tight-fitting lids. Label with date and contents. Store in a cool, dry place. Use within 10 to 12 weeks. Makes 6 packages or about 13-1/2 cups SNACK CAKE MIX.

BUTTERMILK PANCAKE & WAFFLE MIX

Your family will kiss the cook when you serve them these delicious morning treats.

2 cups dry buttermilk powder
8 cups all-purpose flour
1/2 cup sugar
8 teaspoons baking powder
4 teaspoons baking soda
2 teaspoons salt

BUTTERMILK PANCAKE & WAFFLE MIX makes:

Aebleskivers, page 268
Buttermilk Pancakes, page 222
Buttermilk Waffles, page 220
Monte Cristo Sandwiches,
    page 190
Puff Pancake, page 223

In a large bowl, combine all ingredients. Stir with a wire whisk until evenly distributed. Pour into a 12-cup container with a tight-fitting lid. Seal container. Label with date and contents. Store in a cool, dry place. Use within 6 months. Makes about 10-1/2 cups BUTTERMILK PANCAKE & WAFFLE MIX.

WHOLE-GRAIN PANCAKE MIX

*Grated apple makes a great
addition to these pancakes.*

3-1/2 cups whole-wheat flour
3-1/4 cups white flour
3/4 cup sugar
1 tablespoon baking soda
1 tablespoon salt

*WHOLE-GRAIN PANCAKE MIX
makes:*

Whole-Grain Pancakes,
    page 221
Whole-Grain Waffles, page 220

In a large bowl, combine all ingredients.
Stir with a wire whisk until evenly distributed. Pour into a 10-cup container with
a tight-fitting lid. Seal container. Label
with date and contents. Store in a cool,
dry place. Use within 6 months. Makes
about 7-1/2 cups WHOLE-GRAIN
PANCAKE MIX.

CHOCOLATE PUDDING & PIE-FILLING MIX

After you've used a wire whisk, you'll wonder how you ever got along without one.

1-1/2 cups plus 2 tablespoons unsweetened cocoa powder, sifted

3-1/4 cups granulated sugar

1-1/3 cups cornstarch

1/2 teaspoon salt

CHOCOLATE PUDDING & PIE-FILLING MIX makes:

Chocolate Cream Pie,
    page 296

CREAMY CHOCOLATE PUDDING

1 cup CHOCOLATE PUDDING & PIE-FILLING MIX

2-3/4 cups milk

2 tablespoons butter or margarine

1-1/2 teaspoons vanilla extract

In a large bowl, combine all ingredients. Stir with a wire whisk until evenly distributed. Pour into a 6-cup container with a tight-fitting lid. Seal container. Label with date and contents. Store in a cool, dry place. Use within 3 to 4 months. Makes about 6 cups CHOCOLATE PUDDING & PIE-FILLING MIX.

CREAMY CHOCOLATE PUDDING
In a saucepan combine CHOCOLATE PUDDING & PIE-FILLING MIX and milk. Cook and stir until mixture thickens. Remove from heat, stir in butter and vanilla. Pour into 6 serving bowls. Makes 6 servings.

LEMON PIE-FILLING MIX

Tart and refreshing for a sauce or filling. One of our favorite uses is as a topping on hot gingerbread.

2-1/2 cups presweetened powdered lemonade mix

1 cup plus 2 tablespoons cornstarch

1-1/4 cups sugar, more for sweeter flavor

1 teaspoon salt

LEMON PIE-FILLING MIX makes:

Hot Lemon Sauce, page 322
Luscious Lemon Pie, page 299

In a medium bowl, combine lemonade mix, cornstarch, sugar and salt. Mix well. Put in a 1-quart airtight container. Label with date and contents. Store in a cool, dry place. Use within 6 to 8 months. Makes about 4-1/4 cups LEMON PIE-FILLING MIX.

VANILLA PUDDING & PIE-FILLING MIX

Puddings and pies made from this cornstarch-based mix will be smoother and clearer than those made from flour-based mixes. Shake or stir mix before measuring to make recipes.

2-1/3 cups granulated sugar
1-3/4 cups cornstarch
3/4 teaspoon salt

VANILLA PUDDING & PIE-FILLING MIX makes:

Boston Cream Pie, page 276
Creamy Vanilla Pudding,
    page 324
Layered Vanilla Cream,
    page 325
Sour Cream & Raisin Pie,
    page 301
Vanilla Cream Pie, page 302

In a large bowl, combine all ingredients. Stir with a wire whisk until blended. Pour into a 4-cup container with a tight-fitting lid. Seal container. Label with date and contents. Store in a cool, dry place. Use within 4 months. Makes about 4 cups VANILLA PUDDING & PIE-FILLING MIX.

COOKIE MIX

Package this mix in a gift container and attach a cookie cutter with a bow.

8 cups all-purpose flour
2-1/2 cups granulated sugar
2 cups brown sugar, packed
4 teaspoons salt
1-1/2 teaspoons baking soda
3 cups vegetable shortening

COOKIE MIX makes:

Tropic Macaroons, page 319
Snickerdoodles, page 319
Chocolate-Chip Cookies,
    page 316
Banana-Coconut Delights,
    page 328
Peanut-Butter Cookies,
    page 318

In a large bowl, combine flour, granulated sugar, brown sugar, salt and baking soda until well-blended. With a pastry blender or heavy-duty mixer, cut in shortening until mixture resembles cornmeal in texture. Put in a large airtight container. Label with date and contents. Store in a cool, dry place. Use within 10 to 12 weeks. Makes about 16 cups COOKIE MIX.

CRISP COATING MIX

A crunchy flavorful coating you'll find very useful.

**3 cups cornflake crumbs
   (about 8 cups cornflakes)**
1 cup wheat germ
1/2 cup sesame seeds
**4 teaspoons dried parsley
   leaves, crushed**
1 tablespoon paprika
2 teaspoons salt
1 teaspoon dry mustard
1 teaspoon celery salt
1 teaspoon onion salt
1/2 teaspoon ground pepper

CRISP COATING MIX makes:

Chicken & Ham Foldovers,
   page 156
Crunchy-Crust Chicken,
   page 154
Crunchy Fish Bake, page 209
Baked Pork Chops, page 200

In a large bowl, combine all ingredients. Stir with a wire whisk until evenly distributed. Pour into a 5-cup container with a tight-fitting lid. Seal container. Label with date and contents. Store in a cool, dry place. Use within 2 months. Makes about 4-1/2 cups CRISP COATING MIX.

GRANOLA MIX

Try it as a topping on pancakes, yogurt or ice cream—what a treat!

10 cups old-fashioned oats
1 cup wheat germ
1/2 lb. shredded coconut
2 cups raw sunflower seeds
1 cup sesame seeds
3 cups chopped almonds,
   pecans or walnuts
1-1/2 cups brown sugar, packed
1-1/2 cups water
3/4 cup vegetable oil
1/2 cup honey
1/2 cup molasses
1-1/2 teaspoons salt
2 teaspoons ground cinnamon
3 teaspoons vanilla extract
Raisins or other dried fruits, if
   desired

GRANOLA MIX makes:

Gran Muffins, page 271
Energy Bars, page 317

Preheat oven to 300F (150C). In a large bowl combine oats, wheat germ, coconut, sunflower seeds, sesame seeds and nuts. Blend well.

In a large saucepan, combine brown sugar, water, oil, honey, molasses, salt, cinnamon and vanilla. Heat until sugar is dissolved, but do not boil. Pour syrup over dry ingredients and stir until well-coated. Spread into five 13" x 9" baking pans or cookie sheets with sides.

Bake 20 to 30 minutes, stirring occasionally. Bake 15 minutes longer for crunchier texture. Cool. Add raisins or other dried fruit, if desired. Put in airtight containers. Label with date and contents. Store in a cool, dry place. Use within 6 months. Makes about 20 cups GRANOLA MIX.

Pour honey mixture over dry ingredients and stir to coat well.

HERBED STUFFING MIX

Keep this handy on the shelf for meat or poultry stuffing or tossed salad croutons!

30 slices firm-textured bread, cut in 1/2-inch cubes
2/3 cup cooking oil
3 tablespoons instant minced onion
3 tablespoons dried parsley flakes
2 teaspoons garlic salt
3/4 teaspoon ground sage
1/2 teaspoon seasoned pepper

HERBED STUFFING MIX makes:

Chicken Oahu, page 160
Supper Stuffing, page 125
Chicken Strata, page 163
Zucchini Casserole, page 120
Scallop Casserole, page 194
Sausage-Cheese Breakfast
   Strata, page 224

Preheat oven to 300F (150C). Put bread cubes in two 13" x 9" baking pans. Toast bread cubes in oven for 45 minutes, stirring occasionally. Remove from oven and cool slightly. Stir in oil, onion, parsley flakes, garlic salt, sage and seasoned pepper. Lightly toss bread cubes with seasonings to coat cubes. Put in a large airtight container. Label with date and contents. Store in a cool, dry place. Use within 3 to 4 months. Makes about 12 cups HERBED STUFFING MIX.

MUESELI OATMEAL MIX

This popular European cereal which originated in Switzerland is showing up on breakfast tables across America.

8 cups quick-cooking oats
1/2 cup brown sugar, packed
2 teaspoons salt
2-1/2 teaspoons ground cinnamon
1-1/2 teaspoons ground nutmeg
1-1/2 cups dried apple pieces or raisins

MUESELI OATMEAL MIX makes:

Swiss Porridge, page 228

Combine all ingredients in a large bowl. Stir with a wire whisk until evenly distributed. Pour into a 10-cup container with a tight-fitting lid. Label with date and contents. Store in a cool, dry place. Use within 6 months. Makes about 10 cups MUESELI OATMEAL MIX.

ONION SEASONING MIX

Check your bulk foods or whole-sale stores for instant bouillon granules and spices—you'll save even more on this mix. Use this mix whenever your recipe calls for dry onion soup mix.

4 teaspoons instant beef-bouillon granules

8 teaspoons dried minced onion

1 teaspoon onion powder

1/4 teaspoon Bon Appetit Seasoning®

ONION SEASONING MIX makes:

Apricot Chicken, page 169
Baked Beef Brisket,
    page 127
French Onion Soup Gratiné,
    page 96
Meat & Potato Pie, page 141
No-Fuss Swiss-Steak Stew,
    page 134
Onion Pot Roast, page 128

Cut a 6-inch square of heavy-duty foil. Place all ingredients in center of foil. Fold foil to make an airtight package. Label with date and contents. Store in a cool, dry place. Use within 6 months. Makes 1 package ONION SEASONING MIX.

Combine 2 tablespoons seasoning mix with 1 cup sour cream to make a tasty dip for chips and vegetables.

TACO SEASONING MIX

This is a hot and spicy mix. If you prefer a milder mix, reduce the red pepper.

2 teaspoons instant minced onion
1 teaspoon salt
1 teaspoon chili powder
1/2 teaspoon cornstarch
1/2 teaspoon crushed dried red pepper
1/2 teaspoon instant minced garlic
1/4 teaspoon dried oregano leaves
1/2 teaspoon ground cumin

TACO SEASONING MIX makes:

Taco Supreme, page 175
Soft Chicken Taco, page 176

TACO FILLING
1-1/2 lb. lean ground beef
1/2 cup water
1 pkg. TACO SEASONING MIX, above

Combine all ingredients in a small bowl until evenly distributed. Spoon mixture onto a 6-inch square of aluminum foil and fold to make airtight. Label with date and contents. Store in a cool, dry place. Use within 6 months. Makes 1 package or about 2 tablespoons TACO SEASONING MIX.

TACO FILLING
Brown ground beef in a medium skillet over medium-high heat. Drain excess grease. Add water and TACO SEASON-ING MIX. Reduce heat and simmer 10 minutes, stirring occasionally. Makes filling for 8 to 10 tacos.

DRIED CALICO BEAN SOUP MIX

Substitute garbanzo or another favorite for any of the beans in the mix. Great to have on hand for those cold wintry nights.

2 cups dried pinto beans
2 cups dried kidney beans
2 cups Great Northern beans
2 cups pea or navy beans
2 cups dried black-eyed peas
2 cups lentils or split peas

DRIED CALICO BEAN SOUP MIX makes:

Calico Bean Soup, page 114

In a large bowl, combine all ingredients and mix well to distribute ingredients evenly. Package in 2-cup containers or bags. Label and store in a cool, dry place. Makes about 12 cups DRIED CALICO BEAN SOUP MIX.

ALL-PURPOSE GROUND-MEAT MIX

*Use this mix in most casseroles
that call for a meat mixture.*

**5 lb. lean ground beef, turkey
  or chicken**
1 tablespoon salt
2 cups chopped celery
2 cups chopped onion
1 cup diced green pepper

In a large pot or Dutch oven, brown ground meat, stirring to break up meat. Drain excess grease. Stir in salt, celery, onion and green pepper. Cover; simmer until vegetables are crisp-tender, about 10 minutes. Remove from heat; set aside.

Ladle into six 2-cup freezer containers with tight-fitting lids, leaving 1/2-inch space at top of each. With a knife cut through mixture in each container several times to remove air pockets. Attach lids. Label with date and contents. Store in freezer. Use within 3 months. Makes 6 packages or about 12 cups ALL-PURPOSE GROUND-MEAT MIX.

GROUND-MEAT MIX makes:

Best-Ever Minestrone Soup,
    page 103
Dinner in a Pumpkin, page 138
Hearty Chowder, page 112
Saturday Stroganoff, page 132
Enchilada Casserole, page 136
Hurry-Up Curry, page 139
Mexican Delight, page 91
Oriental-Style Skillet Dinner,
    page 143
Quick Chow Mein, page 204
Slumgullion, page 148
Spaghetti Casserole, page 179
Taco Salad, page 111
Quick Taco Dip, page 85
Mexican Haystack, page 142

Skillet Enchiladas, page 133
Country Casserole, page 137

CHICKEN MIX

We prefer using 12 to 14 whole boneless chicken breasts instead of fryers. It reduces the fat and is a whole lot easier to make.

**11 lb. chicken (4 medium
    fryers), cut up**
4 qt. cold water
3 tablespoons parsley flakes
4 carrots, peeled and chopped
4 teaspoons salt
1/2 teaspoon pepper
2 teaspoons dried basil leaves

Combine all ingredients in a large pot or Dutch oven. Cover and cook over high heat until water boils. Simmer until chicken is tender about 1-1/2 hours. (Less time is required, if you are using boneless chicken breasts). Remove from heat. Strain broth and refrigerate until fat can be skimmed.

Cool chicken, remove and discard bones and skin. Put chicken into six 1-pint freezer containers, leaving 1/2-inch space at top. Pour skimmed chicken broth into six more 1-pint containers, with 1/2-inch space at top. Seal and label with date and contents. Freeze. Use within 3 months. Makes 6 pints of CHICKEN MIX. Makes 6 pints of CHICKEN BROTH.

CHICKEN MIX makes:

Chicken Burgers, page 151
Hawaiian Haystack, page 158
Mexican Haystack, page 142
Sweet & Sour Chicken,
    page 164
Chicken Continental, page 153
Club Chicken Casserole,
    page 152
Creamy Chicken Enchiladas,
    page 155
Mexican Chicken Bake,
    page 168
Cream-of-Chicken Soup,
    page 100
Tuna-Cheese Swirls, page 197

Soft Chicken Taco, page 176
White Chili, page 166
Chicken à la King, page 157
Hot Chicken Salad, page 106
Oriental Chicken Noodle Salad,
    page 107
Strawberry-Spinach Salad, page 108
Gayle's Chicken Salad,
    page 105
Corn-Tortilla Chicken Soup, page 94
Taco Salad, page 111
Chicken-Zucchini Casserole, page 120
Dinner in a Pumpkin, page 138

FIVE-WAY BEEF MIX

Delicious by itself. For special meals, refer to the recipes below.

5 lb. lean beef cubes or lean ground beef
4 onions, chopped, or 1 cup dried chopped onions
About 1 cup water, if using beef cubes
8 cups diced peeled potatoes
6 cups diced peeled carrots
1/3 cup cornstarch
1/2 cup cold water
1 (24-oz.) pkg. frozen peas, partially thawed
4 teaspoons seasoning salt
2 teaspoons ground sage
1 teaspoon salt
1 teaspoon pepper

FIVE-WAY BEEF MIX makes:

Bread Basket Stew, page 130
Deep-Dish Pot Pie, page 147
Grandma's Hamburger Soup,
    page 109
Swiss Hamburger Soup,
    page 113
Vegetable-Cheese Casserole,
    page 135

Spray vegetable cooking spray in skillet; add beef cubes and onions. Cook until browned. Add about 1 cup water to browned beef cubes. Cover and simmer until tender, about 1 hour, adding more water if needed. Or: Brown ground beef and onions in a large skillet; drain excess grease.

Place potatoes and carrots in a 5-quart Dutch oven. Add water to cover. Bring to a boil. Simmer vegetables until crisp-tender, about 15 minutes. Stir cornstarch into 1/2 cup cold water. Stir into vegetable mixture until slightly thickened. Stir in remaining ingredients. Stir in browned-beef mixture. Cool.

Ladle mix into four 6-cup freezer containers with tight-fitting lids, leaving 1/2-inch space. Stir to remove air pockets. Attach lids. Label with date and contents. Store in freezer. Use within 2 months. Makes 4 packages or about 24 cups FIVE-WAY BEEF MIX.

ITALIAN COOKING SAUCE MIX

Superb, savory and simple. We use this mix as a pizza topping.

2 (14.5-oz.) cans stewed tomatoes, puréed
4 (8-oz.) cans tomato sauce
2 cups water
2 (6-oz.) cans tomato paste
2 tablespoons dried minced onion
2 tablespoons parsley flakes
1 tablespoon salt
2 tablespoons cornstarch
4 teaspoons dried green-pepper flakes
1 teaspoon instant minced garlic
1 tablespoon sugar
1-1/2 teaspoons Italian seasoning.

ITALIAN COOKING SAUCE MIX makes:

Stuffed Manicotti Shells, page 182
Veal Parmigiana, page 205
Chicken Cacciatore, page 151
Last-Minute Lasagna, page 207
Spaghetti Casserole, page 179

Combine all ingredients in a large pot or Dutch oven. Simmer 15 minutes. Cool. Put into six 2-cup freezer containers, leaving 1/2-inch space at top. Seal and label containers. Freeze. Use within 6 months. Makes about 6 pints ITALIAN COOKING SAUCE MIX.

ITALIAN-STYLE MEAT MIX

An Italian friend shared this recipe with us and it's one of our favorites. Pork bones truly make a difference.

3 lb. sweet Italian sausage, cut in 2-inch lengths

2 (28-oz.) cans tomato purée

1 (28-oz.) can peeled tomatoes

1-1/2 teaspoons dried sweet-basil leaves, crushed

1-1/4 teaspoons dried parsley leaves, crushed

1 teaspoon granulated sugar

1/4 teaspoon pepper

1/2 teaspoon garlic powder

5 teaspoons grated Romano cheese

6 cups water

1-1/2 lb. pork bones

1 qt. MEATBALL MIX, page 44

ITALIAN-STYLE MEAT MIX makes:

Cathy's Meatball Sandwiches, page 177
Eggplant Parmesan, page 178
Green Peppers Mediterranean-Style, page 123
Spaghetti Royale, page 180
Italian-Style Zucchini, page 124
Last-Minute Lasagna, page 207

In a large skillet or Dutch oven, brown Italian sausage, stirring occasionally. Simmer 20 to 25 minutes longer until meat is no longer pink. Drain, reserving 2 tablespoons drippings in skillet. Stir in tomato purée, tomatoes, basil, parsley, sugar, pepper, garlic powder, Romano cheese, water and pork bones. Cover; simmer 30 minutes.

Spoon MEATBALL MIX into tomato mixture. Bring to a boil. Cover; simmer 5 to 6 hours until thickened. Remove pork bones. Cool meat mixture in skillet on a rack. Spoon into freezer containers in amounts shown in recipes listed below. Leave 1/2-inch space at top of each container. Attach lids. Label containers with date, contents and quantity. Store in freezer. Use within 6 months. Makes about 16 cups ITALIAN-STYLE MEAT MIX.

MEAT LOAF MIX

For variety, shape some of this mix into individual meat loaves or into a ring before freezing.

4 eggs, beaten

2-1/4 cups milk

6 tablespoons dried onion flakes

6 tablespoons dried parsley flakes

1 tablespoon salt

1-1/2 teaspoons ground sage

4-1/2 lb. lean ground beef

1-1/2 cups bread crumbs

MEAT LOAF MIX makes:

Meat Loaf with Tangy Topper
  Sauce, page 185
Stuffed Green Peppers,
  page 186

Cut three 15" x 12" pieces of plastic wrap or heavy-duty foil. Combine eggs, milk, onion flakes, parsley flakes, salt and sage. Stir in ground beef and bread crumbs.

Divide meat-loaf mixture into three equal portions. Shape each portion into a meat loaf. Place on plastic wrap or heavy-duty foil. Wrap each meat loaf airtight. Label with date and contents. Store in freezer. Use within 3 months. Makes 3 packages MEAT LOAF MIX.

MEATBALL MIX

Now our children are creating their own mixes. Thanks, Shelly.

4 lb. lean ground beef
2 eggs, slightly beaten
1 cup dry bread crumbs
1/2 cup finely chopped onion
1 tablespoon salt
1 teaspoon pepper
2 cups milk

MEATBALL MIX *makes:*

Swedish Meatballs, page 196
Meatball Stew, page 183
Cocktail Meatballs, page 88
Sweet & Sour Meatballs,
   page 184

Preheat oven to 375F (190C). Combine all ingredients. Blend well. Shape mixture into 1-1/2-inch balls. Place meatballs on ungreased baking sheet and bake 25 to 30 minutes, until browned.

Remove immediately and drain on paper towels. When cooled, put about 20 meatballs each into four 1-quart freezer containers, leaving 1/2-inch space at top. Seal and label with date and contents. Freeze. Use within 3 months. Makes about 80 MEATBALLS.

MEAT SAUCE MIX

For a chunky texture, coarsely chop the carrots and celery. To disguise the texture of the carrots and celery, chop finely in food processor

4 medium onions, sliced

3 garlic cloves, finely chopped, or 1/2 teaspoon dried minced garlic

2 cups finely chopped celery

2 to 3 chopped carrots, if desired

5 lb. lean ground beef

5 teaspoons salt

1/2 teaspoon pepper

3 tablespoons Worcestershire sauce

1 (28-oz.) bottle ketchup

6 drops hot pepper sauce

MEAT SAUCE MIX makes:

Speedy Pizza, page 87

Rancher's Sloppy Joes, page 187

Hamburger Trio Skillet, page 188

Hamburger-Noodle Skillet, page 188

Three-Layer Casserole, page 145

Chili Con Carne, page 187

Grease large skillet with vegetable cooking spray. Sauté onions, garlic, celery and carrots until onions are golden. Add ground beef, cook until browned. Drain excess fat. Add salt, pepper, Worcestershire sauce, ketchup and hot pepper sauce. Cover and simmer 20 minutes. Cool.

Put into five 2-cup freezer containers, leaving 1/2-inch space at top. Cut through mixture with a knife several times to remove air pockets. Seal and label containers with date and contents. Freeze. Use within 3 months. Makes about 5 pints MEAT SAUCE MIX.

Cook until the meat is browned, then add Worcestershire sauce, ketchup and hot pepper sauce.

MEXICAN MEAT MIX

We have tried a lot of Mexican Meat Mixes, but this is the best.

5 lb. beef roast or combination of beef and pork roasts
3 onions, chopped
1 (4-oz.) can chopped green chiles
2 (7-oz.) cans green-chile salsa
1/4 teaspoon garlic powder
4 tablespoons all-purpose flour
4 teaspoons salt
1 teaspoon ground cumin

MEXICAN MEAT MIX makes:

Green-Chile Burros, page 174
Chalupa, page 171
Chimichangas, page 172
Sour-Cream Enchiladas, page 173
Taco Supreme, page 175
Mini-Chimis, page 89
Taco Salad, page 111
Chili Con Carne, page 187

Preheat oven to 275F (135C). Place roasts in large roasting pan or Dutch oven. Do not add salt or water. Cover with a tight lid and roast 8 to 10 hours, until well done. Or cook with 1 cup water in pressure cooker 35 to 40 minutes. Drain meat, reserving juices. Cool meat, then remove bones. Shred meat, and set aside.

Spray a large skillet with vegetable cooking spray. Sauté onions and green chiles 1 minute. Add green-chile salsa, garlic powder, flour, salt and cumin. Reduce heat and cook 1 minute. Stir in reserved meat juices and meat. Cook 5 minutes until thickened. Cool.

Put about 3 cups mix into three 1-quart freezer containers, leaving 1/2-inch space at top. Seal and label containers with date and contents. Freeze. Use within 6 months. Makes about 9 cups MEXICAN MEAT MIX.

CUBED PORK MIX

This "other white meat" is now healthier than in the past.

5 lb. boneless lean pork, cubed
3 medium onions, sliced
3/4 cup all-purpose flour
About 3-1/2 cups water
4 teaspoons instant chicken-
 bouillon granules or 4
 chicken-bouillon cubes
2-1/2 teaspoons salt
1/2 teaspoon pepper

CUBED PORK MIX makes:

Hurry-Up Curry, page 139
Pork Chow Mein, page 202
Quick Chow Mein, page 204
Sweet & Sour Pork, page 203
Won Tons, page 90
Oriental Noodle Soup,
 page 102

Heat a large skillet, add pork cubes. Cook until lightly browned, stirring occasionally. Drain and reserve drippings. Add onions. Cook, stirring 10 to 15 minutes until onions are golden.

Sprinkle flour over pork mixture. Stir gently until flour is absorbed, about 1 minute. Add water to drippings to make 4 cups liquid. Stir liquid, bouillon granules or bouillon cubes, salt and pepper into pork mixture. Bring to a boil, stirring occasionally. Cover; cook over low heat 2 hours longer or until pork is tender.

Remove from heat. Cool. Ladle mixture into five 2-cup freezer containers with tight-fitting lids, leaving 1/2-inch space at top of each. Attach lids. Label with date and contents. Store in freezer. Use within 6 months. Makes 5 packages or 10 cups CUBED PORK MIX.

Spoon into five 2-cup containers, leaving 1/2-inch space at top. Label and store in freezer.

NAVY BEAN MIX

This mix is a great meal by itself or you can add a ham bone or diced ham for a heartier flavor.

**2 lb. (4-1/2 cups) dried navy
  or small white beans**
Soaking water
10 cups water
1 large onion, diced
2 tablespoons butter, optional
1 tablespoon salt
1/2 teaspoon pepper

NAVY BEAN MIX makes:

Molasses-Baked Beans,
    page 116
Pasta e Fagioli, page 97
White Chili, page 166

Wash and sort beans. In a large pot or Dutch oven, combine beans and enough water to cover. Bring to a boil. Boil 2 minutes. Remove from heat. Cover and let stand 1 hour.

Drain and discard soaking water from beans. Rinse beans and return to cooking pot. Add 10 cups water, onion, butter, if desired, salt and pepper. Bring to a boil. Reduce heat and simmer about 2 hours until beans are tender. Set aside and cool.

Ladle into 3- or 4-cup freezer containers with tight-fitting lids. Leave 1/2-inch space at top of each. Cut through mixture with a knife several times to remove air pockets. Label with date and contents. Store in freezer. Use within 6 months. Makes about 12 cups NAVY BEAN MIX.

PINTO BEAN MIX

Bean mixes in your freezer put you minutes away from delicious, lowfat meals.

**6 cups dried pinto beans
  (about 3 lb.)**
Soaking water
10 cups water
3 large onions, chopped
**2 garlic cloves, minced or
  1 teaspoon garlic powder**
2 tablespoons butter, optional
2 tablespoons salt
1/2 teaspoon pepper

PINTO BEAN MIX makes:

Wintry-Day Chili, page 146
South of the Border Vegetarian
  Bake, page 192
Whole-Bean Veggie Burros,
  page 198
Fat-free Refried Beans,
  page 119
Chalupa, page 171
Enchilada Casserole, page 136
Mexican Haystack, page 142

Wash and sort beans. In a large pot or Dutch oven, combine beans and enough water to cover. Bring to a boil. Boil 2 minutes. Remove from heat; cover and let stand 1 hour.

Drain and discard soaking water from beans. Rinse beans and return to cooking pot. Add 10 cups water, onions, garlic, butter, if desired, salt and pepper. Bring to a boil. Reduce heat and simmer about 2 hours until beans are tender. Cool.

Ladle into 3- or 4-cup freezer containers with tight-fitting lids. Leave 1/2-inch space at top of each. Cut through mixture with a knife several times to remove air pockets. Label with date and contents. Store in freezer. Use within 6 months. Makes about 14 cups PINTO BEAN MIX.

CREAM-CHEESE PASTRY MIX

Thaw dough completely before you roll it out. Thaw overnight in the refrigerator or in a few hours on the countertop.

4 (3-oz.) pkgs. cream cheese, softened
1 lb. butter or margarine, softened
5 cups all-purpose flour

CREAM-CHEESE PASTRY MIX makes:

Cream-Cheese Pastry, page 308
Almond Kringle, page 211
Chess Tarts, page 303
Mini Fruit Tarts, page 307
Lime Tarts Supreme, page 304
Pecan Tarts, page 305

Cut eight 12-inch squares of plastic wrap and heavy-duty foil; set aside. In a bowl, beat cream cheese and butter or margarine until blended. Add flour all at once. Knead in flour until evenly distributed. Shape into a large ball. Divide into 8 smaller balls. Slightly flatten each ball. Wrap each flattened ball in a piece of plastic wrap. Place 1 wrapped ball on each piece of foil. Fold foil tightly against dough, making an airtight seal.

Label each package with date and contents. Store in freezer. Use within 6 months. Makes 8 packages CREAM-CHEESE PASTRY MIX, enough for 8 single-crust pies, 4 double-crust pies or 80 tart shells.

FREEZER PIE-CRUST MIX

Tender pie crusts are now "easy as pie" to make.

6 cups all-purpose flour
2 teaspoons salt
1 (1-lb.) can vegetable shortening (2-1/3 cups)
1-1/4 to 1-1/2 cups cold water

FREEZER PIE-CRUST MIX makes:

Freezer Pie Crust, page 309
Cherry-Almond Pie, page 297
Chocolate Cream Pie,
    page 296
Deep-Dish Pot Pie, page 147
Fresh Peach Pie, page 300
Meat & Potato Pie, page 141
All-American Apple Pie,
    page 294
Simplified Quiche, page 227
Luscious Lemon Pie, page 299
Sour Cream & Orange Pie,
    page 310
Spanish Cheese Pie, page 193
Turkey Dinner Pie, page 165
Vanilla Cream Pie, page 302
Sour Cream & Raisin Pie,
    page 301

Cut seven 12-inch squares of plastic wrap and heavy-duty foil; set aside. In a bowl, combine flour and salt. With pastry blender or heavy-duty mixer, cut in shortening until mixture resembles cornmeal in texture. Add 1-1/4 cups water all at once. Mix lightly with a fork until water is absorbed and mixture forms a ball. If necessary add additional water.

Divide dough into 7 portions. Shape into balls. Flatten each ball slightly. Wrap each flattened ball in 1 piece of plastic wrap. Place 1 wrapped ball on each piece of foil. Fold foil tightly against ball, making an airtight seal.

Label each package with date and contents. Store in freezer. Use within 10 months. Makes 7 packages of FREEZER PIE-CRUST MIX, enough for seven 8- or 9-inch single-crust pies. If you use a 10-inch pie plate, divide the dough into 6, instead of 7 balls.

MARIE'S FRUIT COCKTAIL MIX

When summer fruits are at their peak, prepare this mix for future use.

4 cups sugar

2 qt. water

1 (6-oz.) can frozen orange-juice concentrate

1 (6-oz.) can frozen lemonade concentrate

I watermelon, cut in balls

2 cantaloupes, cut in chunks

2 crenshaw melons, cut in chunks

3 lb. green grapes

3 lb. peaches, cut in chunks

1 lb. blueberries, fresh or frozen

In a saucepan bring sugar and water to a boil, stirring constantly. Stir in frozen orange-juice concentrate and frozen lemonade concentrate. In a bowl combine watermelon, cantaloupes, crenshaw melons, grapes, peaches and blueberries.

Put mixed fruit in 12 1-pint freezer containers, leaving 1/2-inch space at top. Pour hot juice syrup over top. Seal and label containers with date and contents. Freeze. Use within 6 to 8 months. Makes about 12 pints MARIE'S FRUIT COCKTAIL MIX.

MARIE'S FRUIT COCKTAIL

1 pint MARIE'S FRUIT COCKTAIL MIX, above.

1 pint ginger ale

MARIE'S FRUIT COCKTAIL
Partially thaw MARIE'S FRUIT COCKTAIL MIX. Spoon into serving bowls or fruit cups. Pour ginger ale over top. Makes 4 servings.

FRUIT SLUSH MIX

A quick, cool, refreshing drink—right from your freezer.

4 cups sugar
4 cups water
1 (6-oz.) can frozen orange-juice concentrate
1/2 cup lemon juice
1 (46-oz.) can pineapple juice

Combine sugar and water in a medium saucepan. Heat until sugar is dissolved. Add orange-juice concentrate, lemon juice and pineapple juice. Fill 6 or 7 ice cube trays with mixture. Freeze until firm. Remove cubes from freezer trays and store in freezer bags. Label with date and contents. Use within 6 months. Makes about 100 small cubes.

Vatiation

Add 5 to 6 mashed bananas to mixture before freezing.

FRUIT SLUSH
FRUIT SLUSH MIX cubes, above
Ginger ale
Orange wedges for garnish

FRUIT SLUSH
Fill a glass with FRUIT SLUSH MIX cubes. Add ginger ale to cover. Let stand 15 minutes. Garnish with orange wedges on a skewer. Makes 1 serving.

FREEZER CHEESE-SAUCE MIX

A nice complement to most vegetables. Try it as a hot dip with raw vegetables.

3/4 cup all-purpose flour
1-1/2 teaspoons salt
1/4 teaspoon ground nutmeg
3/4 cup butter or margarine
4 cups milk
2 cups condensed chicken broth
1 cup half-and-half
4 egg yolks, beaten
12 oz. (3 cups) shredded Cheddar cheese

FREEZER CHEESE-SAUCE MIX makes:

Cauliflower Fritters in Cheese Sauce, page 117
Cheese Fondue, page 86
English Poached Eggs & Ham, page 225
Old-Fashioned Vegetable Platter, page 122
Puffy Omelet, page 226

In a small bowl, combine flour, salt and nutmeg; set aside. In a heavy large saucepan, melt butter or margarine over medium heat. Gradually stir in flour mixture, milk and chicken broth until smooth. Cook and stir until smooth and slightly thickened, about 2 minutes. Remove from heat.

In a medium bowl, stir half-and-half into egg yolks. Blend in about half of the hot sauce. Stir egg mixture into remaining sauce. Cook and stir over medium heat about 2 minutes; do not boil. Remove from heat. Stir in cheese until melted. Cool to room temperature.

Refrigerate sauce until cooled. Pour about 1-1/3 cups sauce into each of 6 freezer containers with tight-fitting lids. Leave 1-inch space at top of each container. Attach lids. Label with date and contents. Store in freezer. Use within 6 months. Makes 6 packages or about 8 cups FREEZER CHEESE-SAUCE MIX.

SLICE & BAKE CHOCOLATE-CHIP COOKIES

If you wet your hands first it is easier to shape rolls.

2 cups butter or margarine

1-1/3 cups granulated sugar

1-2/3 cups brown sugar, packed

1 tablespoon vanilla extract

4 eggs

5-1/2 cups all-purpose flour

2 teaspoons salt

2 teaspoons baking soda

2 cups semisweet chocolate chips

1 cup chopped nuts

CHOCOLATE-CHIP COOKIES
1 roll frozen cookie dough, above, slightly thawed

Shape into four 8- to 10-inch rolls. Wrap in waxed paper or plastic wrap.

Cut four 14" x 12" pieces of waxed paper or plastic wrap. In a bowl, cream butter or margarine, granulated sugar and brown sugar. Beat in vanilla and eggs until light and fluffy. In a bowl, combine flour, salt and baking soda. Stir flour mixture into egg mixture until blended. Add chocolate chips and nuts.

Divide dough into 4 pieces. Shape each piece into an 8- to 10-inch roll. Wrap rolls in waxed paper or plastic wrap. Place in a plastic freezer container with a tight-fitting lid, or wrap airtight in a 14" x 12" piece of heavy-duty foil. Label with date and contents. Store in freezer. Use within 6 months. Makes 4 rolls of dough or about 12-dozen cookies.

CHOCOLATE-CHIP COOKIES
Preheat oven to 350F (175C). Cut dough into 1/4-inch slices. Arrange cut pieces on an ungreased baking sheet about 1-1/2 inches apart. Bake 10 minutes until browned around edges. Remove and cool.

SLICE & BAKE CHOCOLATE-WAFER COOKIES

Use these cookies to make ice-cream sandwiches or a Chocolate-Wafer Pie Crust.

2 cups butter or margarine

2-1/2 cups granulated sugar

3 eggs

2 teaspoons vanilla extract

5 cups all-purpose flour

1 teaspoon baking soda

1-1/4 cups unsweetened cocoa powder

CHOCOLATE-WAFER COOKIES

1 roll frozen cookie dough, above, slightly thawed

Place rolls in freezer container or wrap airtight in heavy-duty foil.

Cut four 14" x 12" pieces of waxed paper or plastic wrap; set aside. In a bowl, cream butter or margarine, sugar, eggs and vanilla until light and fluffy. In a bowl, combine flour, baking soda and cocoa powder. Stir flour mixture into sugar mixture until evenly distributed.

Divide dough into 4 pieces. Shape each piece into an 8- to 10-inch roll. Wrap each roll in waxed paper or plastic wrap. Place in plastic freezer container with a tight-fitting lid, or wrap airtight in a 14" x 12" piece of heavy-duty foil. Label with date and contents. Store in freezer. Use within 6 months. Makes 4 rolls of dough or about 12-dozen cookies.

CHOCOLATE-WAFER COOKIES
Preheat oven to 350F (175C). Lightly grease 2 large baking sheets. Slice dough into 1/4-inch slices. Arrange slices on prepared baking sheets about 1/2 inch apart. Bake 8 to 10 minutes until cookies are set on edges and slightly firm on top. Remove cookies and cool on wire racks. Makes about 36 cookies.

SLICE & BAKE GINGERSNAP COOKIES

These can also be thawed, rolled out and cut into gingerbread boys. Brush with powdered-sugar glaze and decorate.

2 cups vegetable shortening

3 cups sugar

3 eggs

3/4 cup molasses

6 cups all-purpose flour

2 tablespoons baking soda

1 teaspoon salt

2 tablespoons ground ginger

1 tablespoon ground cinnamon

GINGERSNAP COOKIES

1 roll frozen cookie dough, above, slightly thawed

Granulated sugar

Cut four 14" x 12" pieces of waxed paper or plastic wrap; set aside. In a bowl, cream shortening and sugar. Beat in egg and molasses; set aside. In a bowl, combine flour, baking soda, salt, ginger and cinnamon. Gradually stir flour mixture into egg mixture until blended.

Divide dough into four pieces. Shape each piece into a 8- to 10-inch roll. Wrap rolls in waxed paper or plastic wrap. Place in a plastic freezer container with a tight-fitting lid, or wrap airtight in a 14" x 12" inch piece of heavy-duty foil. Label with date and contents. Store in freezer. Use within 6 months. Makes 4 rolls of dough, or about 12-dozen cookies.

GINGERSNAP COOOKIES
Preheat oven to 350F (175C). Cut slightly thawed dough into 1-1/3-inch-thick slices. Cut each slice into fourths. Roll each piece into a ball. Roll each ball in granulated sugar. Place balls on an ungreased baking sheet about 1-1/2 inches apart. Bake 8 to 10 minutes until set around edges with cracked tops. Don't overbake. Remove cookies from baking sheets and cool on wire racks. Makes about 30 to 36 cookies.

SLICE & BAKE OATMEAL COOKIES

Chocolate chips are a nice addition, either in place of or in addition to the raisins.

2 cups butter or margarine
2 cups granulated sugar
2 cups brown sugar, packed
4 eggs
2 teaspoons vanilla extract
4 cups all-purpose flour
5 cups rolled oats
1 teaspoon salt
2 teaspoons baking soda
2 teaspoons baking powder
3/4 cup chopped nuts
1 to 2 cups raisins

OATMEAL COOKIES
1 roll frozen cookie dough, above, slightly thawed

Cut four 14" x 12" pieces of waxed paper or plastic wrap. Cream butter or margarine, granulated sugar and brown sugar in a large bowl until smooth. Beat in eggs and vanilla until light and fluffy. In a medium bowl, combine flour, oats, salt, baking soda and baking powder. Stir flour mixture into egg mixture until blended. Stir in nuts and raisins.

Divide dough into 4 pieces. Shape each piece into an 8- to 10-inch roll. Wrap each roll in 1 piece of waxed paper or plastic wrap. Place in a plastic freezer container with a tight-fitting lid, or wrap airtight in a 14" x 12" piece of heavy-duty foil. Label with date and contents. Store in freezer. Use within 6 months. Makes 4 rolls of dough or about 12-dozen cookies.

OATMEAL COOKIES
Preheat oven to 375F (190C). Lightly grease 2 large baking sheets; set aside. Cut dough into 1/4-inch slices. Place slices about 1 inch apart on prepared baking sheets. Bake 10 to 12 minutes until edges are light brown and centers are slightly set. Cool about 2 minutes on baking sheet. Remove cookies and cool on wire racks. Makes about 36 cookies.

SLICE & BAKE PEANUT-BUTTER COOKIES

Use a whisk to stir flour and baking soda together evenly.

2 cups vegetable shortening
2 cups granulated sugar
2 cups brown sugar, packed
2 cups creamy or chunky-style
   peanut butter
2 teaspoons vanilla extract
4 eggs
5 cups all-purpose flour
4 teaspoons baking soda

PEANUT-BUTTER COOKIES
1 roll frozen cookie dough,
   above, slightly thawed

Cut four 14" x 12" pieces of waxed paper or plastic wrap; set aside. Cream shortening, granulated sugar, brown sugar and peanut butter in a large bowl. Beat in vanilla and eggs until light and fluffy. In a large bowl, combine flour and baking soda. Gradually stir flour mixture into egg mixture until blended.

Divide dough into 4 equal pieces. Shape each piece into an 8- to 10-inch roll. Wrap each roll in 1 piece of waxed paper or plastic wrap. Place wrapped rolls in a plastic freezer container with a tight-fitting lid, or wrap airtight in a 14" x 12" piece of heavy-duty foil. Label with date and contents. Store in freezer. Use within 6 months. Makes 4 rolls of dough or about 12-dozen cookies.

PEANUT-BUTTER COOKIES
Preheat oven to 350F (175C). Cut dough into 1-inch-thick slices. Cut each slice into fourths. Roll each piece into a ball. Place balls on an ungreased baking sheet about 1-1/2 inches apart. Use fork tines to flatten cookies in a criss-cross design. Bake 8 to 10 minutes until lightly browned around edges. Remove cookies from baking sheet and cool on wire racks. Makes about 36 cookies.

SLICE & BAKE SUGAR COOKIES

Cookie rolls can be thawed, rolled out and cut into shapes.

2 cups butter or margarine, softened
2 cups granulated sugar
3 eggs
2 teaspoons vanilla extract
1 teaspoon lemon extract
6 cups all-purpose flour
1 teaspoon baking soda

SLICE & BAKE SUGAR COOKIES makes:

Cookie Crust Fruit Tart,
    page 306

SUGAR COOKIES
1 roll frozen cookie dough, above, slightly thawed
Granulated sugar, if desired

Cut four 14" x 12" pieces of waxed paper or plastic wrap; set aside. In a large bowl, cream butter or margarine and sugar. Beat in eggs, vanilla and lemon extract until light and fluffy. In a large bowl, combine flour and baking soda. Gradually stir flour mixture into egg mixture until blended.

Divide dough into 4 pieces. Shape each piece into an 8- to 10-inch roll. Wrap rolls in waxed paper or plastic wrap. Place in a plastic freezer container with a tight-fitting lid, or wrap airtight in a 14" x 12" piece of heavy-duty foil; label. Store in freezer. Use within 6 months. Makes 4 rolls of dough or about 12-dozen cookies.

SUGAR COOKIES
Preheat oven to 350F (175C). Lightly grease 2 large baking sheets. Cut dough into 1/4-inch slices. Place slices on prepared baking sheets about 1/2 inch apart. Sprinkle slices lightly with granulated sugar, if desired. Bake 8 to 10 minutes until edges start to brown. Remove cookies from baking sheets and cool on wire racks. Makes about 36 cookies.

BEEF GRAVY MIX

Not quite as good as "Grandma" used to make, but so very convenient!

1-1/3 cups instant nonfat milk powder
3/4 cup instant flour
3 tablespoons instant beef bouillon granules
1/8 teaspoon ground thyme
1/4 teaspoon onion powder
1/8 teaspoon ground sage
1/2 cup butter or margarine
3 teaspoons brown sauce for gravy

BEEF GRAVY MIX makes:

Tasty Beef Birds, page 129
Smothered Hamburger Patties, page 131
Stuffed Pork Chops, page 201

BEEF GRAVY
1 cup cold water
1/2 cup BEEF GRAVY MIX, above

Combine milk powder, flour, bouillon granules, thyme, onion powder and sage. Stir with a wire whisk to blend. Use a pastry blender or 2 knives to cut in butter or margarine until evenly distributed. Drizzle brown sauce for gravy over mixture. Stir with wire whisk until blended. Spoon into a 3-cup container with a tight-fitting lid. Label with date and contents. Store in refrigerator. Use within 4 to 6 weeks. Makes about 2-2/3 cups BEEF GRAVY MIX.

BEEF GRAVY
Pour water into a small saucepan. Use a whisk to stir BEEF GRAVY MIX into water. Stir constantly over medium heat until gravy is smooth and slightly thickened, 2 to 3 minutes. Makes about 1 cup.

CHICKEN GRAVY MIX

Enhance any chicken dish with this lightly seasoned gravy.

1-1/3 cups instant nonfat milk powder
3/4 cup instant flour
3 tablespoons instant chicken bouillon granules
1/4 teaspoon ground sage
1/8 teaspoon ground thyme
1/8 teaspoon ground pepper
1/2 cup butter or margarine

Combine milk powder, flour, bouillon granules, sage, thyme and pepper. Stir with a wire whisk until blended. Use a pastry blender or 2 knives to cut in butter or margarine until evenly distributed. Spoon into a 3-cup container with a tight-fitting lid. Label with date and contents. Store in refrigerator. Use within 4 to 6 weeks. Makes about 2-2/3 cups CHICKEN GRAVY MIX.

CHICKEN GRAVY MIX makes:

Chicken Breasts en Croûte, page 150
Chicken in Mushroom Sauce, page 167
Turkey Dinner Pie, page 165
Chicken & Ham Foldovers, page 156
Zucchini Casserole, page 120

Potatoes au Gratin, page 118
Dinner in a Pumpkin, page 138
Chicken Continental, page 153
Hawaiian Haystack, page 158
Mexican Chicken Bake, page 168

CHICKEN GRAVY
1 cup cold water
1/2 cup CHICKEN GRAVY MIX, above

CHICKEN GRAVY
Pour water into a saucepan. Use a whisk to stir CHICKEN GRAVY MIX into water. Stir constantly over medium heat until gravy is smooth and slightly thickened, 2 to 3 minutes. Makes about 1 cup.

WHITE SAUCE MIX

White Sauce makes meats and vegetables into meals fit for a king. Make it even easier with this mix in your refrigerator.

2 cups instant nonfat dry milk,
or 1-1/2 cups regular
nonfat dry milk
1 cup all-purpose flour
2 teaspoons salt
I cup butter or margarine

Combine dry milk, flour and salt. Mix well. With a pastry blender, cut in butter or margarine until mixture resembles fine crumbs. Put in a large airtight container. Label with date and contents. Store in refrigerator. Use within 2 months. Makes 1 quart WHITE SAUCE MIX.

WHITE SAUCE MIX makes:

Basic White Sauce, page 101
Cream-of-Chicken Soup,
     page100
Eastern Corn Chowder,
     page 95
Hearty New England Clam
     Chowder, page 98
Potatoes Au Gratin, page 118
Broccoli Cheese Soup in Bread
     Bowls, page 99
Broccoli & Ham Rolls, page 199
Sunday Chicken, page 162
Swedish Meatballs, page 196

CHOCOLATE SYRUP MIX

For a quick treat, stir 2 table-spoons Chocolate Syrup Mix into a glass of cold milk.

1-1/3 cups unsweetened cocoa powder

2-1/4 cups granulated sugar

1/4 teaspoon salt, if desired

1-1/3 cups boiling water

1-1/2 teaspoons vanilla extract

In a heavy saucepan, combine cocoa powder, sugar and salt, if desired. Gradually stir in boiling water. Stir frequently over medium heat until smooth and slightly thickened, about 10 minutes. Remove from heat. Stir in vanilla.

Pour mixture into a 3-cup container with a tight-fitting lid. Label with date and contents. Store in refrigerator. Use within 10 to 12 weeks. Makes about 2-2/3 cups CHOCOLATE SYRUP MIX.

CHOCOLATE SYRUP MIX makes:

Quick Fudge Sauce, page 322

ORIENTAL STIR-FRY MIX

Peel fresh ginger before using, and shred in a fine-hole grater. Store ginger in freezer in plastic bags.

6 tablespoons cornstarch

3/4 teaspoon garlic powder

2-1/4 teaspoons instant beef boullion granules

3/4 teaspoon onion powder

6 tablespoons wine vinegar

6 tablespoons water

1-1/2 teaspoons grated fresh ginger

3/4 cup soy sauce

3/4 cup dark corn syrup

2-2/3 cups water

Combine cornstarch, garlic powder, bouillon granules and onion powder. Use a whisk to stir in vinegar, 6 tablespoons water and ginger until cornstarch is dissolved. Stir in soy sauce, corn syrup and 2-2/3 cups water.

Pour into a 5-cup container with a tight-fitting lid. Label with date and contents. Store in refrigerator. Use within 4 weeks. Stir well before using. Makes about 5 cups ORIENTAL STIR-FRY MIX.

ORIENTAL STIR-FRY MIX makes:

Teriyaki Beef & Vegetables, page 140
Shrimp & Vegetable Stir-Fry, page 195
Stir-Fry Cashew Chicken, page 161

Use small side of grater to grate ginger. Wrap and freeze remaining ginger to use later.

CAESAR SALAD DRESSING MIX

A traditional favorite. Don't forget the HERBED STUFFING MIX croutons, page 33.

1-1/2 teaspoons grated lemon peel

1 teaspoon ground oregano

1/8 teaspoon instant minced garlic

2 tablespoons grated Parmesan cheese

1/2 teaspoon pepper

Combine all ingredients in a small bowl until evenly distributed. Put mixture in foil packet or 1-pint glass jar. Label with date and contents. Store in a cool, dry place. Use within 3 to 4 months. Makes about 3 tablespoons CAESAR SALAD DRESSING MIX.

CAESAR SALAD DRESSING

1 pkg. CAESAR SALAD DRESSING MIX, above

1/2 cup vegetable oil

1/4 cup lemon juice

3 to 4 anchovy filets, chopped, if desired

CAESAR SALAD DRESSING
Combine all ingredients in a glass jar. Shake until well-blended. Chill before serving. Makes about 3/4 cup of Caesar Salad Dressing.

CHILI SEASONING MIX

For a special treat, sprinkle Chili Seasoning Mix over hot popcorn.

1 tablespoon all-purpose flour
2 tablespoons minced dried onion
1-1/2 teaspoons chili powder
1 teaspoon seasoned salt
1/2 teaspoon crushed dried red pepper
1/2 teaspoon instant minced garlic
1/2 teaspoon sugar
1/2 teaspoon ground cumin

Combine all ingredients in a small bowl until evenly distributed. Spoon mixture onto a 6-inch square of aluminum foil and fold to make airtight. Label with date and contents. Store in a cool, dry place. Use within 6 months. Makes 1 package or about 1/4 cup CHILI SEASONING MIX.

CHILI
1 lb. lean ground beef
2 (15.5-oz.) cans kidney beans, drained
2 (16-oz.) cans tomatoes
1 pkg. CHILI SEASONING MIX, above

CHILI
In a skillet, over medium heat, brown meat. Drain excess fat. Add beans, tomatoes and CHILI SEASONING MIX. Cover, reduce heat and simmer 10 minutes. Makes 4 to 6 servings.

CREAMY CRUDITÉ DIP MIX

Blanch your fresh vegetables (crudités) in hot water for about 2 minutes to intensify their color.

1 tablespoon dried chives
1/2 teaspoon dill weed
1 teaspoon garlic salt
1/2 teaspoon paprika

Combine all ingredients in a small bowl until evenly distributed. Spoon mixture onto a 6-inch square of aluminum foil and fold to make airtight. Label with date and contents. Store in a cool, dry place. Use within 6 months. Makes 1 package or about 2 tablespoons CREAMY CRUDITÉ DIP MIX.

CREAMY CRUDITÉ DIP
1 tablespoon lemon juice
1 cup mayonnaise
1 cup dairy sour cream or
  lowfat yogurt
1 pkg. CREAMY CRUDITÉ DIP
  MIX, above

CREAMY CRUDITÉ DIP
In a medium bowl combine all ingredients. Stir until well blended. Chill at least 1 hour before serving. Makes about 2 cups.

FRENCH DRESSING MIX

All-time favorite. For more variety use herb-flavored vinegar.

1/4 cup sugar
1-1/2 teaspoons paprika
1 teaspoon dry mustard
1-1/2 teaspoons salt
1/8 teaspoon onion powder

Combine all ingredients in a small bowl until evenly distributed. Put mixture in foil packet or 1-pint glass jar. Label with date and contents. Store in a cool, dry place. Use within 6 months. Makes about 5 tablespoons FRENCH DRESSING MIX.

FRENCH DRESSING
1 pkg. FRENCH DRESSING MIX, above
3/4 cup vegetable oil
1/4 cup vinegar

Variation

Sweet Italian Dressing—Increase sugar to 1/2 cup. Substitute 1 tablespoon celery seeds for paprika.

FRENCH DRESSING
Combine ingredients in a glass jar. Shake until well-blended. Chill before serving. Makes about 1-1/4 cups.

HOME-STYLE DRESSING MIX

Create your own famous dressing by adding herbs.

2 teaspoons instant minced onion
1/2 teaspoon salt
1/8 teaspoon garlic powder
1/2 teaspoon monosodium glutamate, if desired
1 tablespoon dried parsley flakes

Combine all ingredients in a small bowl until evenly distributed. Put mixture in foil packet or 1-pint glass jar. Label with date and contents. Store in a cool, dry place. Use within 6 months. Makes about 2 tablespoons HOME-STYLE DRESSING MIX.

HOME-STYLE DRESSING
1 recipe HOME-STYLE DRESSING MIX, above
1 cup mayonnaise
1 cup buttermilk

Variation

Substitute 1 cup sour cream or plain yogurt for buttermilk and use as a dip for fresh vegetables.

HOME-STYLE DRESSING
Combine ingredients in a glass jar. Shake until well blended. Chill before serving. Makes about 2 cups.

LOW-CALORIE DRESSING MIX

Add tomato juice for a welcome change. For weight-watchers, this fills the bill.

2 teaspoons dried minced onion
2 teaspoons dried parsley flakes
2 teaspoons dried green-pepper flakes

Combine all ingredients in a small bowl until evenly distributed. Put mixture in a foil packet or 1-pint glass jar. Label. Store in a cool, dry place. Use within 6 months. Makes about 2 tablespoons LOW-CALORIE DRESSING MIX.

LOW-CALORIE DRESSING
1 pkg. LOW-CALORIE DRESSING MIX, above
3/4 cup tomato juice
2 tablespoons lemon juice
1/4 teaspoon horseradish

LOW CALORIE DRESSING
Combine ingredients in a glass jar. Shake until well-blended. Chill before serving. Makes about 3/4 cup.

PRISCILLA'S SALAD DRESSING MIX

Serve this dressing over a spinach salad topped with crumbled bacon.

1/2 cup granulated sugar
1 teaspoon salt
1 teaspoon dry mustard
1 tablespoon poppy seeds
1 tablespoon dried minced
  onion

Combine all ingredients in a small bowl, stirring until evenly distributed. Pour into a 1/2-cup container with a tight-fitting lid or wrap airtight in heavy-duty foil. Seal container. Label with date and contents. Store in a cool, dry place. Use within 3 months. Makes 1 package or about 1/3 cup PRISCILLA'S SALAD DRESSING MIX.

PRISCILLA'S SALAD DRESSING
1-1/2 cups (12 oz.) small-curd
  cottage cheese
1 pkg. PRISCILLA'S SALAD
  DRESSING MIX, above
1/2 cup vegetable oil
1/2 cup vinegar

PRISCILLA'S SALAD DRESSING
Turn cottage cheese into a medium bowl; set aside. In a blender, combine PRISCILLA'S SALAD DRESSING MIX, oil and vinegar. Blend 5 to 8 seconds. Pour over cottage cheese. Fold oil mixture into cottage cheese until blended. Cover; refrigerate 30 minutes before serving. Makes about 3 cups.

Special Mixes, Clockwise from top: Fruit Slush, page 53, Marie's Fruit Cocktail, page 54, Hot Chocolate, page 78, Russian Refresher, page 81

SLOPPY JOE SEASONING MIX

So easy and so good!

Combine all ingredients in a small bowl until evenly distributed. Spoon mixture onto a 6-inch square of aluminum foil and fold to make airtight. Label with date and contents. Store in a cool, dry place. Use within 6 months. Makes 1 package or about 3 tablespoons SLOPPY JOE SEASONING MIX.

- **1 tablespoon instant minced onion**
- **1 teaspoon dried green-pepper flakes**
- **1 teaspoon salt**
- **1 teaspoon cornstarch**
- **1/2 teaspoon instant minced garlic**
- **1/4 teaspoon dry mustard**
- **1/4 teaspoon celery seeds**
- **1/4 teaspoon chili powder**

SLOPPY JOES
- **1 lb. lean ground beef**
- **1 pkg. SLOPPY JOE SEASONING MIX, above**
- **1/2 cup water**
- **1 (8-oz.) can tomato sauce**
- **6 hamburger buns, toasted**

SLOPPY JOES
Brown ground beef in a skillet over medium-high heat. Drain excess grease. Add SLOPPY JOE SEASONING MIX, water and tomato sauce. Bring to a boil. Reduce heat and simmer 10 minutes, stirring occasionally. Serve over toasted hamburger buns. Makes 6 servings.

SPAGHETTI SEASONING MIX

It makes great lasagna and pizza sauce, too!

1 tablespoon dried minced onion

1 tablespoon dried parsley flakes

1 tablespoon cornstarch

2 teaspoons dried green-pepper flakes

1-1/2 teaspoons salt

1/4 teaspoon instant minced garlic

1 teaspoon sugar

3/4 teaspoon Italian seasoning or combination of oregano, basil, rosemary, thyme, sage, marjoram

Combine all ingredients in a small bowl until evenly distributed. Spoon mixture onto a 6-inch square of aluminum foil and fold to make airtight. Label with date and contents. Store in a cool, dry place. Use within 6 months. Makes 1 package or about 1/3 cup SPAGHETTI SEASONING MIX.

SPAGHETTI SAUCE

1 lb. lean ground beef

2 (8-oz.) cans tomato sauce

1 (6-oz.) can tomato paste

2-3/4 cups tomato juice or water

1 pkg. SPAGHETTI SEASONING MIX, above

SPAGHETTI SAUCE
Brown ground beef in a medium skillet over medium-high heat. Drain excess grease. Add tomato sauce, tomato paste and tomato juice or water. Stir in SPAGHETTI SEASONING MIX. Reduce heat and simmer 30 minutes, stirring occasionally. Makes 4 to 6 servings.

CHICKEN CONTINENTAL RICE SEASONING MIX

If you have never tried brown rice, substitute it for the white rice in this recipe.

2 tablespoons instant chicken-bouillon granules

1 tablespoon dried parsley leaves, crushed

2 teaspoons minced dried onions

1/4 teaspoon dried basil leaves

1/4 teaspoon thyme

1/8 teaspoon white pepper

1/8 teaspoon garlic powder

Combine all ingredients in a large bowl. Stir until evenly distributed. Put mixture in foil packet or plastic bag. Label with date and contents. Store in a cool, dry place. Use within 6 to 8 months. Makes 1 package CHICKEN CONTINENTAL RICE SEASONING MIX.

CHICKEN CONTINENTAL RICE

1 pkg. CHICKEN CONTINENTAL RICE SEASONING MIX, above

2 cups cold water

1 cup long-grain white rice

1 tablespoon butter or margarine, if desired

CHICKEN CONTINENTAL RICE
Combine ingredients in a medium saucepan. Bring to a boil over high heat. Cover, reduce heat and cook 20 minutes or until liquid is absorbed. Makes 4 to 6 servings.

SPANISH RICE SEASONING MIX

For additional "zip" in your rice, add more crushed red peppers.

1 tablespoon minced dried onions
2 tablespoons dried green-pepper flakes
1 tablespoon dried celery flakes
1 teaspoon instant chicken-bouillon granules
1/2 teaspoon salt
1/8 teaspoon garlic powder
Dash of crushed red pepper

Combine all ingredients in a large bowl. Stir until evenly distributed. Put mixture in foil packet or plastic bag Label with date and contents. Store in a cool, dry place. Use within 6 to 8 months. Makes 1 pkg. SPANISH RICE SEASONING MIX.

SPANISH RICE
1 cup long grain rice
1 (16-oz.) can stewed sliced tomatoes
1 cup water
1 pkg. SPANISH RICE SEASONING MIX, above

SPANISH RICE
Spray a large skillet with vegetable cooking spray. Add uncooked rice. Cook over moderate heat, stirring constantly, until rice is lightly browned. Add tomatoes, water and SPANISH RICE SEASONING MIX. Stir to combine. Bring to a boil. Cover and reduce heat. Simmer 20 minutes. Makes 4 servings.

HOT CHOCOLATE MIX

For a nostalgic treat top each cup with a marshmallow. This is a camper's favorite.

1 (25.6-oz.) pkg. instant nonfat dry milk (10-2/3 cups)
1 (6-oz.) jar powdered nondairy creamer
2 cups powdered sugar
1 (6-oz.) can instant chocolate-drink mix

Combine all ingredients in a large bowl. Mix well. Put in a large airtight container. Label with date and contents. Store in a cool, dry place. Use within 6 months. Makes about 17 cups HOT CHOCOLATE MIX.

Variation

Substitute 2 cups unsweetened cocoa powder for chocolate drink mix. Increase powdered sugar to 4 cups.

HOT CHOCOLATE
Add HOT CHOCOLATE MIX to hot water. Stir to dissolve. Makes 1 serving.

HOT CHOCOLATE
3 tablespoons HOT CHOCOLATE MIX, above
1 cup hot water

One bundle will flavor 1 quart of apple cider, cranberry or pineapple juice. Simmer beverage with bundle for 20 minutes.

SPICE BUNDLES

Can be used to make hot or cold spice-flavored drinks.

10 sticks cinnamon, broken into pieces and crushed
2 whole nutmegs, crushed
1/3 cup whole cloves
1/3 cup orange peel, minced and dried
1/4 cup whole allspice berries

Combine all ingredients in a bowl. Mix well. Cut and lay out 10 double-thickness 5-inch squares of cheesecloth. Spoon approximately 1 tablespoon of mixture onto each cheesecloth square. Tie into a bundle with a thread or string. Store in airtight container. Makes 10 bundles.

SWEET SALAD DRESSING MIX

*Toss this dressing with crisp
greens or serve with fresh fruit.*

1/3 cup sugar
1 teaspoon dried minced onion
1 teaspoon salt
1 teaspoon dry mustard
1 teaspoon paprika
1 teaspoon celery seeds

Combine all ingredients in a small bowl until evenly distributed. Put mixture in a foil packet or 1-pint glass jar. Label. Store in a cool, dry place. Use within 6 months. Makes about 1/2 cup of SWEET SALAD DRESSING MIX.

SWEET SALAD DRESSING
1 pkg. SWEET SALAD
    DRESSING MIX, above
3/4 cup vegetable oil
1/4 cup vinegar

SWEET SALAD DRESSING
Combine ingredients in a glass jar. Stir until well-blended. Chill before serving. Makes about 1-1/4 cups.

RUSSIAN REFRESHER MIX

Your favorite citrus flavors combined in a flavorful drink.

**2 cups powdered orange-drink
   mix**
**1 (3-oz.) pkg. presweetened
   powdered-lemonade mix**
1-1/3 cups sugar
1 teaspoon ground cinnamon
1/2 teaspoon ground cloves

Combine all ingredients in a medium bowl. Mix well. Put in a 1-quart air-tight container. Label with date and contents. Store in a cool, dry place. Use within 6 months. Makes about 3-1/2 cups RUSSIAN REFRESHER MIX.

RUSSIAN REFRESHER
**2 to 3 teaspoons of RUSSIAN
   REFRESHER MIX, above**
1 cup hot water

RUSSIAN REFRESHER
Place RUSSIAN REFRESHER MIX in a cup, add hot water. Stir to dissolve. Makes 1 serving.

APPETIZERS & SNACKS

Don't be stuck in the kitchen preparing appetizers when you'd rather visit with your guests. Get out the mixes! Among our favorites are the seasoning mixes for dips. Be sure to try Quick Taco Dip.

Fried appetizers should be served hot. Won Tons and Mini-Chimis can be served as the first course of a meal or as finger foods for a buffet table. Both can be prepared ahead and frozen. They can be crisped and reheated for 10 minutes at 400F (205C) right before serving. Microwaving is not recommended for these because they lose their crispness.

Serve appetizers attractively, arranging tasty tidbits on small platters which can be easily replaced or replenished. Large trays soon lose their neat appearance. Simple, colorful garnishes on the trays will add to their eye appeal. Vary the appetizers served at a buffet table. Offer meat, cheese and seafood, combining one or two hot ones with several cold dishes. Include an assortment of crisp vegetables along with containers of Creamy Crudité Dip and Home Style Dip.

CURRIED SHRIMP ROUNDS

*Here's a unique seafood
combination you can't resist.*

3 cups QUICK MIX, page 21
2/3 cup milk or water
**2 (4.5-oz.) cans shrimp,
    drained and rinsed**
**4-oz. (1 cup) shredded Swiss
    cheese**
1/2 cup mayonnaise
**2 tablespoons finely chopped
    green onion**
1 tablespoon lemon juice
1/4 teaspoon curry powder
**1/2 cup thinly sliced water
    chestnuts**
Parsley flakes, for garnish

Preheat oven to 400F (205C). Grease 2 baking sheets. In a medium bowl, combine QUICK MIX and milk or water. Stir until blended. Let dough stand 5 minutes. On a lightly floured board, knead dough about 15 times. Roll out dough to 1/8 inch thickness. Cut with a small, floured cookie cutter and place biscuits on prepared baking sheets.

In a bowl, combine shrimp, Swiss cheese, mayonnaise, onion, lemon juice and curry powder. Spoon shrimp mixture onto biscuits. Top with water chestnuts and sprinkle with parsley. Bake 10 to 12 minutes. Makes about 40 appetizers.

Clockwise from the top: Melt-In-Your-Mouth Muffins, page 250, Curried Shrimp Rounds, page 83, Tuna-Cheese Swirls, page 197

QUICK TACO DIP

If you don't have a chafing dish, use a casserole dish and cover until cheese melts.

**2 cups ALL-PURPOSE
GROUND-MEAT MIX,
page 38, thawed**
1/2 cup ketchup
1 tablespoon chili powder
2 (15-oz.) cans kidney beans
**1/4 to 1/2 teaspoon hot
pepper sauce**
**4 oz. (1 cup) shredded Cheddar
cheese**
**1/2 cup sliced green olives with
pimientos, for garnish**

In a large saucepan, combine ALL-PUR-POSE GROUND-MEAT MIX, ketchup and chili powder. Mash kidney beans and add with bean juice to meat mixture. Add hot pepper sauce. Heat until hot, about 10 minutes.

Put in a chafing dish and top with shredded Cheddar cheese. Garnish with green olives. Makes about 6 cups dip, enough for 15 to 20 servings. Reheat in microwave if needed.

CHEESE FONDUE

You'll be tempted to serve this easy-to-make fondue often.

3 cups **FREEZER CHEESE-SAUCE MIX, page 54, thawed**
1/4 teaspoon dry mustard
Pinch of garlic powder
1 (1-lb.) loaf French bread, cut in 1-inch cubes
2 red Delicious apples, sliced

In a medium saucepan, combine FREEZER CHEESE-SAUCE MIX, dry mustard and garlic powder. Stir over medium heat until heated through. Pour into a warm fondue pot. Serve with French bread cubes and apple slices. Makes 8 to 10 servings.

Karine-
For fast nachos heat Freezer Cheese-Sauce Mix and pour over tortilla chips. Add hot peppers if you want a little more heat.

SPEEDY PIZZA

Great for a quick lunch or light supper. Our teenagers eat these by the dozen.

2 cups MEAT SAUCE MIX, page 45, thawed
6 English muffins, split
1 teaspoon dried oregano leaves
4 oz. (1 cup) shredded mozzarella cheese
Pepperoni, mushrooms, green peppers and olives, as desired

Preheat broiler. In a small saucepan, simmer MEAT SAUCE MIX about 5 minutes, until heated through. Toast English muffin halves. Spoon meat mixture over English muffins. Sprinkle with oregano and top with shredded mozzarella cheese. Add toppings as desired. Broil about 3 to 5 minutes, until cheese is bubbly. Makes 12 individual pizzas.

COCKTAIL MEATBALLS

A savory buffet item whether it's for the summer patio or winter holidays.

2 tablespoons butter or margarine
1/3 cup chopped green pepper
1/3 cup chopped onion
1 (10.75-oz.) can condensed tomato soup
2 tablespoons brown sugar, firmly packed
4 teaspoons Worcestershire sauce
1 tablespoon prepared mustard
1 tablespoon vinegar
1 container MEATBALL MIX, page 44, thawed (about 20 meatballs)

Preheat oven to 350F (175C). Melt butter or margarine in a small saucepan. Sauté green pepper and onion in butter or margarine until tender. In a 2-quart casserole, combine tomato soup, brown sugar, Worcestershire sauce, mustard and vinegar. Add sautéed green pepper and onion. Stir in MEATBALL MIX.

Bake about 20 minutes, until heated through. This appetizer can also be heated in the microwave oven for 5 minutes on high power. Keep warm. Serve meatballs on toothpicks. Makes about 20 appetizers.

MINI-CHIMIS

A guaranteed hit for your next Mexican party buffet.

Vegetable oil for frying
4 cups MEXICAN MEAT MIX, page 46, thawed
2 (16-oz.) pkgs. won-ton skins
Guacamole, page 174
Chile salsa

In a large skillet, heat 2 inches of oil to 375F (190C). Place 1 heaping teaspoonful of the meat mixture in lower corner of each won-ton skin. Fold point of won-ton skin up over filling, then fold corners in. Moisten top corner with water and roll skin into a cylinder. Repeat with remaining meat filling.

Lower several rolls at a time into hot oil. Fry 3 to 4 minutes or until golden brown, turning if necessary to brown evenly. Drain on paper towels. Serve with guacamole and salsa. Makes 120 mini-chimis.

If preparing ahead, cool and place in freezer containers. Cover and freeze up to 3 months. To serve, thaw and place in a single layer on baking sheets. Preheat oven to 375F (290C); bake rolls 10 to 15 minutes.

WON TONS

An Oriental snack that will get rave reviews at your party.

Sweet & Sour Sauce, below
2 cups CUBED PORK MIX, page 47, thawed, shredded
1/4 teaspoon grated fresh ginger
2 tablespoons finely sliced green onion
2 teaspoons soy sauce
1 (16-oz.) pkg. won-ton skins
Oil for deep-frying

Sweet & Sour Sauce
2 tablespoons cornstarch
1-1/4 cups pineapple juice
2 tablespoons white vinegar
1/3 cup brown sugar, packed
1/4 cup ketchup
1 tablespoon soy sauce

Prepare Sweet & Sour Sauce; keep warm. Combine PORK MIX, ginger, onion and soy sauce. Place 1 teaspoon of mixture in center of each won-ton skin. Moisten edges with water. Fold diagonally. Press edges to seal.

Pour oil 2 inches deep in a deep fryer or medium saucepan. Heat oil to 375F (290C). Carefully lower won tons into hot oil. Cook 30 seconds on each side until crisp and golden brown. Drain on paper towels. Serve with Sweet & Sour Sauce. Makes 60 won tons.

Sweet & Sour Sauce
In saucepan, combine cornstarch and 1/4 cup pineapple juice until smooth. Stir in remaining juice and remaining ingredients. Cook and stir until smooth and slightly thickened.

1. Remove meat cubes from mix. Shred meat by pulling apart with 2 forks.

2. Spoon filling onto skins. Moisten edges. Fold diagonally. Pinch to seal.

MEXICAN DELIGHT

Begin your next fiesta with this winning Southwest combination.

1 (30-oz.) can refried beans
2 cups **ALL-PURPOSE GROUND MEAT MIX**, page 38, thawed
1 (4-oz.) can diced or chopped green chiles
3 cups shredded Monterey Jack cheese (12 oz.)
1 (7-oz.) can green-chile salsa
1 avocado, peeled, pitted, mashed, or 1 (7.5-oz.) pkg. frozen avocado dip, thawed
1 cup dairy sour cream
1 cup pitted ripe olives, for garnish
1 (10-oz.) pkg. corn chips

Preheat oven to 400F (205C). Lightly butter a 13" x 9" baking dish. Spread refried beans in bottom of dish. Spread ALL-PURPOSE GROUND MEAT MIX evenly over beans. Sprinkle chiles over meat mixture. Sprinkle with cheese. Drizzle green-chile salsa over cheese.

Bake about 30 minutes in preheated oven until hot and bubbly. Remove from oven.

Spoon avocado or avocado dip onto center of casserole. Spoon sour cream in a circle around avocado. Arrange olives on sour cream and avocado. Tuck about 1/3 of the corn chips around edge of dish with points up. Serve with remaining corn chips. Makes 10 to 12 appetizer servings.

BIG SOFT PRETZELS

*For a great snack try these with a
cool drink.*

**1 tablespoon active dry yeast
  or 1 (1/4-oz.) package**
**1-1/2 cups lukewarm water
  110F (45C)**
2 eggs, beaten
**1/4 cup vegetable oil or melted
  margarine**
**5 to 6 cups HOT ROLL MIX,
  page 17**
1 egg, beaten
About 2 tablespoons coarse salt

Preheat oven to 425F (220C). Lightly grease 2 large baking sheets. In a bowl, dissolve yeast in lukewarm water. Blend in 2 eggs and oil or margarine. Add 5 cups HOT ROLL MIX. Stir well. Add more HOT ROLL MIX to make a soft dough. Knead about 5 minutes, until dough is smooth. Roll dough into ropes about 1/2 inch in diameter and 18 to 24 inches long. Form into pretzels. For sticks, cut dough into 5- to 6-inch lengths. Place on prepared baking sheets. Brush with beaten egg and sprinkle with salt. Bake immediately 12 to 15 minutes, until brown and crisp. Makes 12 to 15 large pretzels.

1. Place ropes of dough on cookie sheets to form a circle and twist the ends twice.

2. Lay the twisted ends of the dough across the circle and press to seal.

SOUPS & SALADS

A new addition to our soup line is Pasta e Fagioli. A salad and hot French bread add the finishing touches to this "down-home" meal. Also try our hearty Calico Bean Soup—it's a meal in a bowl. Our soups are great "tummy warmers" for the winter months, but don't reserve them for only one season. Enjoy soup any time of the year. Most can be prepared ahead and reheated in a jiffy. Best-Ever Minestrone Soup and New England Clam Chowder make frequent appearances at the table.

Master basic white sauce and all its variations with WHITE SAUCE MIX. Be creative in preparing your own homemade soups and sauces with it. WHITE SAUCE MIX is one of the few mixes that requires refrigeration for storage.

Gayle's Chicken Salad is a beautiful main dish for lunch or supper. To make a special presentation serve in a scooped-out melon, as pictured, or pineapple shell.

You must try Oriental Chicken Noodle Salad, an interesting blend of textures and flavors. Even though the combination of ingredients sounds unusual, this recipe will become a favorite for you as it is for us.

Be sure to look at the variety of recipes for delicious salad dressings.

CORN-TORTILLA CHICKEN SOUP

This recipe is quite spicy. If you prefer, reduce the chili powder.

1 medium onion, chopped
2 or 3 garlic cloves
1 tablespoon chili powder
2 teaspoons ground cumin
1/2 teaspoon dried oregano
   leaves
1 bay leaf
10 cups regular-strength
   chicken broth
1 (8-oz.) can tomato sauce
1-1/2 teaspoons salt
1/4 teaspoon pepper
2 cups CHICKEN MIX,
   page 39, thawed
2 cups fresh corn kernels or
   frozen corn, thawed
Fresh cilantro, chopped,
   garnish, if desired
Sour cream, garnish
Unsalted tortilla chips, garnish

Heat large kettle or Dutch oven to medium high heat. Lightly spray with vegetable cooking spray. Add onion, garlic, chili powder, cumin, oregano and bay leaf. Sauté until onion is cooked. Add chicken broth, tomato sauce, salt and pepper. Bring to a boil. Add CHICKEN MIX and corn.

Reduce heat and simmer 15 minutes. Serve steaming hot. Garnish with cilantro, sour cream and tortilla chips. Makes about 6 to 8 servings.

For lower fat, use baked tortilla chips or follow instructions with the Mexican Haystack, page 142, for making lowfat tortilla strips.

EASTERN CORN CHOWDER

A crisp salad with crackers completes this meal.

5 slices bacon
1 medium onion, thinly sliced
2 medium potatoes, pared
  and diced
Water
2 cups milk
1 cup WHITE SAUCE MIX,
  page 63
1 (17-oz.) can cream-style corn
1 teaspoon salt
Dash of pepper
1 tablespoon butter or
  margarine, for garnish

Cook bacon until crisp. Crumble and set aside. Reserve 1 tablespoon bacon drippings in pan. Add onion and cook until light brown. Add potatoes and water to cover. Cook 10 to 15 minutes, until potatoes are cooked.

Combine milk and WHITE SAUCE MIX, in a saucepan. Stirring constantly, cook over low heat until thick and smooth. Stir in corn, salt and pepper. Add to potato mixture and heat through 10 minutes. Top each serving with crumbled bacon and butter or margarine. Makes 6 servings.

1. Add white sauce and corn mixture to potatoes and heat through.

2. Serve in soup bowls. Top each serving with crumbled bacon.

FRENCH ONION SOUP GRATINÉ

You'll enjoy this quick version of a robust international favorite.

2 pkgs. ONION SEASONING MIX, page 35

4 cups water or beef broth

1/4 cup butter or margarine, softened

6 slices French bread, 1 inch thick

8 oz. (2 cups) shredded Swiss cheese

2 tablespoons grated Parmesan cheese

In a large saucepan, combine ONION SEASONING MIX and water or broth. Bring to a boil over medium-high heat. Simmer about 10 minutes. Preheat oven to 375F (190C). Spread butter or margarine evenly on 1 side of each bread slice. Arrange buttered bread slices on an ungreased baking sheet. Toast bread in oven until browned and quite dry, about 10 minutes.

Remove from oven. Sprinkle about 2 tablespoons Swiss cheese on each toasted bread slice. Return bread to oven until cheese melts. Divide remaining Swiss cheese in 6 soup bowls. Pour soup into bowls. Float bread slice on top of each. Sprinkle with Parmesan cheese. Makes 6 servings.

PASTA E FAGIOLI

A favorite Italian soup made with beans and pasta.

1 large onion, chopped
4 stalks celery, chopped
3 large carrots, chopped
2 garlic cloves, minced, or
   1 teaspoon garlic powder
3 (14.25-oz.) cans regular-
   strength chicken broth
3 cups NAVY BEAN MIX,
   page 48, thawed
1 (14.5-oz.) can diced peeled
   tomatoes, undrained
1 (8-oz.) can tomato sauce
1 teaspoon dried oregano
   leaves
1 teaspoon dried basil leaves
1/2 teaspoon pepper
2 bay leaves
1 tablespoon dried parsley
   flakes
Salt to taste
1 cup shell macaroni
Fresh grated Parmesan cheese,
   garnish

Variation

Substitute 1/2 small head of
   cabbage, chopped, for the
   shell macaroni.

Spray large pot or Dutch oven with non-stick vegetable cooking spray. Add onions, celery, carrots and garlic. Cook about 4 or 5 minutes until partially tender, stirring occasionally. Add chicken broth, NAVY BEAN MIX, tomatoes, tomato sauce, oregano, basil, pepper, bay leaves, parsley flakes and salt. Bring to a boil.

Add macaroni. Reduce heat to medium and cook 10 to 15 minutes until macaroni and vegetables are tender. Remove bay leaves. Sprinkle with Parmesan cheese. Makes about 8 servings.

This makes a great lowfat supper with tossed salad and French bread. For a thicker soup, add more macaroni.

HEARTY NEW ENGLAND CLAM CHOWDER

A tantalizing aroma says,
"Welcome home."

2 (6.5-oz.) cans minced clams
1 cup finely chopped onions
1 cup finely chopped celery
2 cups pared and diced
   potatoes
Water
1-1/2 cups WHITE SAUCE MIX,
   page 63
1 quart milk
1/2 teaspoon sugar
Salt and pepper to taste

Drain clams, reserving juice. In a large saucepan, combine clam juice, onions, celery and potatoes. Add enough water to cover vegetables. Cook about 15 minutes until tender.

While vegetables are cooking, combine WHITE SAUCE MIX and milk in a large pot or Dutch oven. Cook over low heat until thick and smooth, stirring constantly. Add clams, undrained vegetables and sugar. Heat about 15 minutes. Add salt and pepper to taste. Makes 6 servings.

BROCCOLI CHEESE SOUP IN BREAD BOWLS

Bakery hard rolls become a bowl for your soup.

1-1/2 lb. fresh broccoli, chopped (about 3 cups)
2 potatoes, peeled and diced
1 carrot, peeled and diced
1 onion, chopped
4 cups chicken broth
1-1/2 cups WHITE SAUCE MIX, page 63
1-1/2 cups milk
4 oz. (1 cup) shredded Muenster cheese
1/4 teaspoon ground nutmeg, if desired
Salt and pepper to taste
6 large (3-oz.) round hard rolls

In a 4-quart saucepan, put broccoli, potatoes, carrot and onion. Add chicken broth to cover vegetables. If more liquid is needed to cover vegetables, add water. Cook over medium heat 15 to 20 minutes until vegetables are tender.

In medium bowl, combine WHITE SAUCE MIX and milk. Add mixture to cooked vegetables, stirring constantly 2 to 3 minutes until thickened. Stir in cheese until melted. Add nutmeg, salt and pepper to taste.

Slice tops off of rolls. Scoop out soft bread from inside of roll leaving crusty shell. Spoon soup into bread bowls. Replace top of bread or serve to the side of soup. Makes about 2 quarts soup or 6 large servings.

Scooped-out bread bowls can be lightly toasted in oven.

Did you know that watercress is a wonderful source of vitamins A and C?

CREAM-OF-CHICKEN SOUP

Perfect on a cold winter day!

2 chicken-bouillon cubes
2 cups hot water
**1-1/2 cups WHITE SAUCE MIX,
    page 63**
**1 cup CHICKEN MIX, minced
    page 39**
1/2 cup finely chopped celery
1/2 cup finely chopped onion
1/2 teaspoon salt
1 teaspoon garlic salt
4 cups milk
1 egg yolk, beaten
**Chopped chives, watercress, or
    pimiento for garnish**

Dissolve bouillon cubes in hot water. Combine WHITE SAUCE MIX and bouillon mixture in a large pot or Dutch oven. Cook over low heat about 5 minutes, stirring constantly, until thick and smooth. Add CHICKEN MIX, celery, onion, salt and garlic salt.

Simmer 15 minutes, stirring constantly. Blend in milk and egg yolk. Simmer 5 more minutes. Remove from heat. Garnish with chopped chives, watercress or pimiento. Makes 6 servings.

BASIC WHITE SAUCE

Add 1 cup coooked vegetables and create your own cream soups.

1/2 cup WHITE SAUCE MIX, page 63
1 cup cool water
Pepper, herbs and spices, if desired

Variations

Substitute milk, tomato juice or chicken or beef stock for all or part of water.

Stir constantly until smooth and thickened. Stir in chopped mushrooms for Creamy Mushroom Sauce.

In a small saucepan, combine WHITE SAUCE MIX and water. For thinner sauce, decrease WHITE SAUCE MIX to 1/4 cup. For thick sauce, increase WHITE SAUCE MIX to 3/4 cup. Cook over low heat until smooth, stirring constantly. Season with pepper, herbs and spices, if desired. Makes about 1-1/2 cups sauce

Cheese Sauce
Add 1/2 to 1 cup shredded Cheddar cheese after mixture thickens. Stir until cheese is melted.

Curry Sauce
Add 1 teaspoon curry powder to thickened mixture.

Celery Sauce
In a skillet sauté 1/4 cup chopped onion and 3/4 cup chopped celery; add to sauce.

Creamy Mushroom Sauce
Add 1/2 cup chopped fresh mushrooms and 1 teaspoon Worcestershire sauce.

ORIENTAL NOODLE SOUP

This is one of the Westovers' favorite recipes. Linguine is also known as flat spaghetti.

1-1/2 cups water

1-1/2 teaspoons instant chicken-bouillon granules

2 cups CUBED PORK MIX, page 47, thawed

1-1/2 teaspoons soy sauce

1 (8-oz.) pkg. linguine

3 hard-cooked eggs, sliced, for garnish

3 chopped green onions, for garnish

In a medium saucepan, bring water to a boil. Add bouillon granules; stir until dissolved. Stir in CUBED PORK MIX and soy sauce. Bring to a boil. Simmer about 5 minutes over low heat, stirring occasionally. Cook linguine according to package directions.

Spoon cooked linguine evenly into 4 soup bowls. Pour pork mixture evenly over top of each. Garnish each with hard-cooked egg slices and chopped green onions. Makes 4 servings.

BEST-EVER MINESTRONE SOUP

Our favorite Italian soup!

1 (28-oz.) can tomatoes
2 cups **ALL-PURPOSE
  GROUND-MEAT MIX,**
  page 38, thawed
1 quart water
2 large carrots, peeled, sliced
2 (8-oz.) cans tomato sauce
2 cups beef broth
1 tablespoon dried parsley
  leaves
1/2 teaspoon dried basil leaves
1 teaspoon dried oregano
  leaves
1/4 teaspoon pepper
1/2 teaspoon garlic salt
1 (15-oz.) can garbanzo beans,
  drained
1 (16-oz.) can green beans,
  drained
1 (15-oz.) can kidney beans,
  drained
1-1/4 cups mostaccioli or other
  macaroni
Parmesan cheese, for garnish

Purée tomatoes in blender. In a large pot or Dutch oven combine ALL-PURPOSE GROUND-MEAT MIX, puréed tomatoes, water, carrots, tomato sauce, broth, parsley, basil, oregano, pepper and garlic salt. Bring to a boil. Cover, simmer over low heat about 20 minutes.

Add garbanzo beans, green beans and kidney beans. Return to a boil; add macaroni. Cook 10 minutes or until macaroni is tender. Garnish with Parmesan cheese. Makes 8 to 10 servings.

Gayle's Chicken Salad

GAYLE'S CHICKEN SALAD

An appealing combination of contrasting textures.

**2 cups CHICKEN MIX,
     page 39, thawed**
2 cups chopped celery
3 medium sweet pickles, diced
3 green onions, chopped
**1-1/2 cups fresh pineapple or
     1 (15.25-oz.) can pineapple
     tidbits, drained**
**1 (2-oz.) pkg. sliced almonds,
     toasted**
**1-1/2 cups seedless red flame
     or green grapes**
1 apple, chopped, if desired
**1 (8-oz.) can water chestnuts,
     drained**
1 cup mayonnaise
2 teaspoons sugar
Salt and pepper to taste
Lettuce leaves

In a large bowl, combine CHICKEN MIX, celery, pickles, green onions, pineapple, toasted almonds, grapes, apple and water chestnuts. Set aside. In a small bowl, stir together mayonnaise and sugar. Stir into chicken mixture; add salt and pepper. Cover; refrigerate several hours or up to 24 hours. Serve on lettuce leaves. Makes 6 to 8 servings.

For an especially attractive presentation, serve this salad in scooped-out melon or pineapple half and garnish with a cluster of grapes. We make this with fat-free mayonnaise for a lowfat dish.

HOT CHICKEN SALAD

Our Pan Rolls are the perfect accompaniment.

2 cups CHICKEN MIX,
   page 39, thawed
2 cups chopped celery
1 cup sliced almonds
1 tablespoon minced onion
2 tablespoons lemon juice
1 teaspoon salt
1-1/4 cups mayonnaise
4 hard-cooked eggs, chopped
4 oz. (1 cup) shredded Swiss
   cheese

Preheat oven to 400F (205C). Lightly butter a 2-quart casserole. In a medium bowl, combine CHICKEN MIX, celery, almonds, onion, lemon juice, salt and mayonnaise. Mix well. Add chopped eggs and toss lightly.

Put mixture into prepared casserole dish or individual soufflé dishes. Top with shredded cheese. Bake, uncovered, 20 to 25 minutes. Makes 6 servings.

Versatile as an appetizer in cream-puff shells or as a luncheon or main-dish salad. For a change of pace try this hot salad rather than the expected cold salad.

ORIENTAL CHICKEN NOODLE SALAD

An enticing blend of textures and flavors that are enhanced with chilling. Serve with your prettiest chop sticks.

1 (3-oz.) pkg. ramen noodles, without seasoning packet
1 (8-oz.) pkg. fresh coleslaw mix or 1/2 small head cabbage, finely chopped
2 green onions, chopped
2 cups CHICKEN MIX, page 39, thawed
2 tablespoons sugar
1/2 teaspoon pepper
1 teaspoon salt
3 tablespoons rice vinegar
1/3 cup vegetable oil
4 tablespoons sesame seeds, toasted
1 (2.25-oz.) pkg. slivered almonds, toasted
Chinese pea pods, for garnish
Mandarin oranges, for garnish

In a medium bowl, crumble dry ramen noodles into small pieces. Add cole slaw mix or shredded cabbage, green onions and CHICKEN MIX. Toss together to mix. In a small bowl, combine sugar, pepper, salt, rice vinegar and oil. Pour over chicken mixture. Toss to coat.

Chill at least 8 hours or up to 48 hours. Before serving, toss in toasted sesame seeds and toasted almonds.

If desired, garnish with Chinese pea pods and mandarin oranges alternated in spoke fashion around salad. Makes 4 to 6 servings.

STRAWBERRY-SPINACH SALAD

An eye-appealing, colorful combination accented with beautiful fresh strawberries.

Orange Dressing, below
**1/2 lb. fresh spinach leaves,
washed and patted dry**
**1 (10.5-oz.) can mandarin
oranges, well-drained**
**2 cups CHICKEN MIX,
page 39, thawed**
**2 cups fresh strawberries,
washed, hulled and halved**

Orange Dressing
1/4 cup vegetable oil
1/4 cup red-wine vinegar
3 tablespoons sugar
1/4 cup orange juice
1/4 teaspoon dry mustard
2 tablespoons poppy seeds
**1/2 teaspoon grated
orange peel**

Prepare Orange Dressing. In a large salad bowl, combine spinach leaves, mandarin oranges, CHICKEN MIX and strawberries. Toss to mix. Toss with Orange Dressing or pass dressing separately. Makes 4 to 6 servings.

Orange Dressing
Combine ingredients. Blend well. Chill for at least 2 hours before serving. Blend again right before serving. Makes about 3/4 cup.

GRANDMA'S HAMBURGER SOUP

The aroma creates memories of old-fashioned goodness as it simmers.

1 pkg. FIVE-WAY BEEF MIX, made with ground beef, page 40, thawed
1/4 cup chopped green bell pepper or 1 tablespoon dried green-pepper flakes
4 cups tomato juice
1/4 cup rice or barley, uncooked
1 bay leaf, crushed
1 teaspoon sugar
1 teaspoon Worcestershire sauce
Parmesan cheese, for garnish

Variation

Substitute 2 cups water for 2 cups tomato juice. Substitute 1 cup vermicelli for 1/4 cup rice or barley.

In a large saucepan or Dutch oven, combine all ingredients except cheese. Bring to a boil. Cover; simmer 20 to 30 minutes. Ladle into 6 to 8 soup bowls. Garnish each with Parmesan cheese. Makes 6 to 8 servings.

1.
Combine mix and rice or barley with other ingredients. Simmer to blend flavors.

2.
Serve piping hot, garnished with Parmesan cheese.

Taco Salad

TACO SALAD

Olé! Perfect to serve outside on a hot summer night.

2 cups **ALL-PURPOSE GROUND-MEAT MIX,** page 38, or 2 cups **CHICKEN MIX, page 39,** or 2 cups **MEXICAN MEAT MIX, page 46, thawed**
1 (7-oz.) can green-chile salsa
1 head of lettuce, torn into bite-size pieces
3 large tomatoes, chopped
1 large avocado, chopped
4 to 5 green onions, chopped
8 oz. (2 cups) shredded Monterey Jack or Cheddar cheese
1 (15-oz.) can kidney beans, drained or 1 (15-oz.) can ranch-style beans
1 (10-oz.) pkg. tortilla chips
Salsa or salad dressing of your choice

In a medium skillet, combine your choice of MIX with salsa. Heat. In a large salad bowl, combine lettuce, tomatoes, avocado, green onions, shredded cheese and beans. Add meat mixture. Toss gently. Add tortilla chips and top with salsa or salad dressing of your choice. Makes 8 servings.

For a party look, omit tortilla chips and serve in large taco shell. Layer ingredients instead of tossing. Guacamole, sour cream and olives may be added.

HEARTY CHOWDER

Thaw all frozen mixtures 24 to 48 hours in the refrigerator or more quickly in a microwave oven.

2 cups ALL-PURPOSE GROUND-MEAT MIX, page 38, thawed

4 cups tomato juice

1 cup water

2 (10.25-oz.) cans cream of celery soup

2-1/2 cups peeled, grated carrots

1 teaspoon sugar

1/4 teaspoon garlic salt

1/4 teaspoon pepper

1/8 teaspoon ground marjoram

6 thin slices Swiss cheese

Reduce heat and simmer In a large saucepan, combine ALL-PURPOSE GROUND-MEAT MIX, tomato juice, water and soup. Stir with a wire whisk to blend. Stir in carrots, sugar, garlic salt, pepper and marjoram. Bring mixture to a boil over medium-high heat. Reduce heat and simmer 30 minutes.

To serve, place Swiss-cheese slices in bottoms of 6 shallow soup bowls. Pour hot soup over cheese. Reduce heat and serve immediately. Makes 6 servings.

This is a real quickie on a chilly day. You'll speed things up even more by using grated carrots from the produce department.

112

SWISS HAMBURGER SOUP

Gruyère cheese, a smooth-textured cousin of Swiss cheese, melts in the hot soup.

1 pkg. **FIVE-WAY BEEF MIX**
   made with ground beef,
   page 40, thawed
1 **(16-oz.) can tomatoes**
2 **cups water**
8 **oz. (2 cups) Gruyére cheese,**
   cut into small cubes

In a large saucepan, combine FIVE-WAY BEEF MIX, tomatoes and water. Simmer 20 to 30 minutes over low heat. Before serving, stir in cheese cubes. Makes 6 to 8 servings.

CALICO BEAN SOUP

You'll find robust flavors in our new hearty soup.

**2 cups DRIED CALICO BEAN
    SOUP MIX, page 37**
Soaking water
8 cups water
**1-1/2 lb. ham hocks or ham
    bone**
1 onion, chopped
**1 garlic clove, minced, or
    1/2 teaspoon garlic powder**
**1 pod dried red chili pepper or
    1 teaspoon chili powder**
**1 (28-oz.) can tomatoes,
    undrained, cut up**
2 tablespoons lemon juice
1/2 teaspoon salt
1/4 teaspoon pepper

In a large colander, wash and sort beans. In a large pot or Dutch oven, combine beans and water to cover. Bring to a boil. Boil 2 minutes. Remove from heat, cover and let stand 1 hour.

Drain and discard soaking water from beans. Rinse beans and return to cooking pot. Add 8 cups water, ham hocks or ham bone, onion, garlic, chili pepper or chili powder and tomatoes. Simmer 45 minutes or until tender. Add lemon juice, salt and pepper and simmer 30 minutes. longer. Makes 6 to 8 servings.

VEGETABLES & SIDE DISHES

Nutritionists urge us to eat more vegetables and grains to obtain needed vitamins and minerals. For variety in taste, texture and color, vegetables can be added to most dishes. Serve contrasting varieties, for example red cabbage and baby carrots, or broccoli spears and sliced tomatoes.

Vegetables are at their best when freshly picked. Use your home-grown vegetables if possible or purchase them close to the time of preparation. Buy perishable fresh vegetables in season when prices are reasonable. Damaged vegetables are not a bargain. Buy those that are free from bruises, skin punctures and decay.

Old-Fashioned Vegetable Platter can be served as a side or main dish. FREEZER CHEESE-SAUCE MIX adds the necessary protein to make it a complete meal. Most vegetables are enhanced by adding a cheese sauce.

Those who like Italian cooking will enjoy Eggplant Parmesan and Green Peppers Mediterranean-Style, both made with ITALIAN-STYLE MEAT MIX. Zucchini Casserole complements roast chicken, steak or chops. For a change, serve this instead of potatoes.

MOLASSES-BAKED BEANS

Wonderful as a main dish or as an accompaniment for ribs, steak or hamburgers.

1/2 lb. bacon, diced
1 cup chopped onions
1 cup chopped celery
4 cups NAVY BEAN MIX,
  page 48, thawed
1/2 cup molasses
1/4 cup brown sugar, packed
1 tablespoon Worcestershire
  sauce
2 tablespoons ketchup
1 tablespoon prepared mustard
2 tablespoons apple-cider
  vinegar

Preheat oven to 300F (150C). In a large skillet, fry bacon until almost crisp. Drain and discard all but 1 tablespoon of drippings from skillet. Put bacon in a 2-quart casserole dish with a lid. Set aside. Sauté the onions and celery in the remaining bacon drippings until lightly browned.

In casserole dish combine bacon, sautéed vegetables, NAVY BEAN MIX, molasses, brown sugar, Worcestershire sauce, ketchup, mustard and vinegar. Stir together well. Cover and cook in preheated oven for about 2 hours, until moisture is absorbed. Makes 6 to 8 servings.

CAULIFLOWER FRITTERS IN CHEESE SAUCE

Fresh green beans, zucchini slices and spinach are also excellent dipped in this batter and fried.

1 medium cauliflower
1/2 teaspoon salt
**1-1/2 cups FREEZER CHEESE-
    SAUCE MIX, page 54,
    thawed**
3 eggs, separated
1/4 teaspoon salt
Vegetable oil for frying

Break cauliflower into flowerets. In a saucepan, cover flowerets with water. Add 1/2 teaspoon salt. Cook uncovered until crisp-tender, about 10 minutes. Remove from heat; drain well. In a saucepan, heat FREEZER CHEESE-SAUCE MIX over low heat. Do not boil. Keep warm.

In a large bowl, beat egg whites until stiff; set aside. In a another bowl, beat egg yolks until thickened. Beat in 1/4 teaspoon salt. Fold beaten egg yolks into egg whites; set aside. Pour oil about 3/4-inch deep in a skillet. Heat to 375F (190C).

Dip slightly cooled cauliflowerets into egg mixture, turning with a fork to coat all sides. Using a slotted spoon or 2 forks, carefully lower flowerets into hot oil. Cook 4 or 5 pieces at a time, turning until browned, about 1 minute. Drain on paper towels. Arrange on a platter. Drizzle with warmed FREEZER CHEESE-SAUCE MIX. Serve immediately. Makes 6 servings.

Dip flowerets in egg batter. Fry in hot oil. Drain on paper towels

We've made this into a dinner casserole by adding 1 cup cooked chicken and 1/2 cup frozen peas before baking.

POTATOES AU GRATIN

This week-day favorite disappears quickly at our homes.

1/2 cup WHITE SAUCE MIX, page 63

1 cup cool water

1-2/3 cup Chicken Gravy, page 62, or 1 (10.75-oz.) can condensed cream of chicken soup

1 cup shredded Cheddar cheese (4 oz.)

4 cups cooked, pared and cubed potatoes

3 tablespoons chopped fresh parsley or 1 tablespoon parsley flakes

Preheat oven to 350F (175C). Butter a 2-quart casserole. Combine WHITE SAUCE MIX and cool water in a small saucepan. Cook over low heat 3 to 5 minutes, stirring constantly, until thick and smooth. In a medium bowl, combine white sauce, Chicken Gravy or cream of chicken soup and cheese.

Put cooked potatoes in casserole dish. Pour cheese mixture over. Stir gently to coat potatoes. Sprinkle parsley on top. Bake 20 to 30 minutes, until sides are bubbly and cheese is melted. Makes 6 servings.

FAT-FREE REFRIED BEANS

Once you have tasted the flavor of your own refried beans, you'll never want to use the canned variety again.

**4 cups PINTO BEAN MIX,
    page 49, thawed
1/4 cup green-chile salsa**

Spray a medium skillet with non-stick vegetable cooking spray. Drain any excess liquid from the PINTO BEAN MIX and mash with fork or in a food processor until partially smooth.

Pour mashed-bean mixture into heated skillet and stir until heated through. Top with green-chile salsa. Makes 4 to 6 servings.

If you aren't concerned about additional fat, these are great topped with shredded Cheddar or Monterey Jack cheese.

ZUCCHINI CASSEROLE

*Another way to use the bounty
from your garden. A combination
that's sure to please.*

**4 medium zucchini, sliced
   1/2-inch thick**
**3/4 cup pared and sliced
   carrots**
Water, salted
1/2 cup chopped onion
**6 tablespoons butter or
   margarine**
**2-1/4 cups HERBED STUFFING
   MIX, page 33**
**1-2/3 cups Chicken Gravy,
   page 62, or 1 (10.75-oz.) can
   condensed cream of chicken
   soup**
1/2 cup dairy sour cream

Variation

Chicken-Zucchini Casserole—
   Add 1 package CHICKEN
   MIX, page 39, or 2 cups
   cooked, diced chicken.

In a saucepan, put zucchini and carrots in boiling, salted water to cover. Cover pan and simmer 15 minutes, until vegetables are tender. Drain.

In a saucepan, sauté onion in 4 tablespoons of the butter or margarine until tender. Stir in 1-1/2 cups of the HERBED STUFFING MIX, Chicken Gravy and sour cream. Gently stir in vegetables. Preheat oven to 350F (175C). Lightly butter a 1-1/2-quart casserole. Put mixture into casserole. Melt remaining butter or margarine in a saucepan. Add remaining HERBED STUFFING MIX to butter or margarine. Toss gently and sprinkle over casserole. Bake 30 to 40 minutes. Makes 6 to 8 servings.

*During the zucchini
season we all serve
this frequently.*

Zucchini Casserole

OLD-FASHIONED VEGETABLE PLATTER

*Ready for a meatless meal?
Zucchini, cocozelle, pattypan,
crookneck and straightneck are
all types of summer squash.*

1 lb. broccoli
1 medium cauliflower
1/4 lb. Brussels sprouts, if
    desired
4 large carrots
1/2 lb. summer squash
1/2 lb. fresh mushrooms
2 ears of corn, husked
Salt and pepper to taste
1-1/2 cups FREEZER CHEESE-
    SAUCE MIX, page 54,
    thawed

Cut broccoli and cauliflower into flowerets; set aside. Trim Brussels sprouts. Rinse; set aside. Peel carrots and cut in 1/4-inch slices; set aside. Rinse summer squash; trim ends and cut in 1/2-inch slices; set aside. Rinse mushrooms. Peel, if desired; set aside. Rinse corn. Break ears of corn in half or thirds; set aside.

Pour water about 1-1/2 inches deep in a large pot or Dutch oven. Insert steamer basket. Place broccoli, cauliflower, Brussels sprouts and carrots in steamer basket. Cover; bring water to a boil. Steam 15 minutes. Add squash, mushrooms and corn. Steam 10 minutes longer until vegetables are crisp-tender.

In a saucepan, warm FREEZER CHEESE-SAUCE MIX over low heat; do not boil. Arrange cooked vegetables on a large platter. Season to taste with salt and pepper. Top with warmed cheese sauce. Makes 3 to 4 main-dish or 6 side-dish servings.

GREEN PEPPERS MEDITERRANEAN-STYLE

An exceptional side dish, serve this with broiled fish.

2 tablespoons vegetable oil

4 large green peppers, cut in thin strips

1/2 teaspoon onion salt

1/4 teaspoon pepper

2 cups sliced fresh mushrooms

1/2 cup ITALIAN-STYLE MEAT MIX, page 42, thawed

Heat oil in a large skillet. Add green pepper strips, onion salt and pepper. Stirring occasionally, sauté over medium-high heat until peppers are crisp-tender, about 3 minutes. Stir in mushrooms and ITALIAN-STYLE MEAT MIX. Simmer over low heat until heated through, 10 to 15 minutes. Makes 6 to 8 servings.

Whip 4 eggs together and pour over cooked mixture. Slide skillet under the broiler until eggs are set, and you've created a frittata. That's Italian for fritter.

ITALIAN-STYLE ZUCCHINI

Impress your guests with this new side dish.

2 tablespoons vegetable oil
4 or 5 medium zucchini, cut into 1/4-inch slices
1 medium onion, sliced, separated in rings
1/4 teaspoon salt
1/8 teaspoon pepper
1-1/2 cups ITALIAN-STYLE MEAT MIX, page 42, thawed

Heat oil in a large saucepan. Add zucchini, onion rings, salt and pepper. Stirring occasionally, simmer until lightly browned, 3 to 4 minutes. Add ITALIAN-STYLE MEAT MIX. Cover and simmer over low heat until zucchini are crisp-tender, 5 minutes. Serve immediately. Makes 4 servings.

Many members of our families prefer this as a side dish. It's a nice change from potatoes or rice.

SUPPER STUFFING

Stuff your favorite poultry, roast or pork chops or use as a side dish to any meat.

1 teaspoon instant chicken bouillon
3/4 cup boiling water
6 tablespoons butter or margarine
1 onion, finely chopped
4 large stalks celery, finely chopped
7 cups HERBED STUFFING MIX, page 33
Turkey or roasting chicken, if desired

Dissolve bouillon in boiling water. Melt butter or margarine in a medium skillet. Sauté onion and celery until crisp-tender. In a large bowl, combine HERBED STUFFING MIX, bouillon-water mixture and vegetables. Toss lightly.

Use for stuffing turkey or chicken, if desired. Or preheat oven to 350F (175C) and put mixture in a lightly buttered casserole. Bake 30 minutes, until heated through.

MAIN DISHES - BEEF

Do you hate that last-minute frenzy when you are trying to put a meal together and everyone is hungry and in a hurry? Be ready by having these skip-a-step mixes on hand to trim your preparation time to minutes.

ALL-PURPOSE GROUND MEAT MIX can be made with ground beef, ground turkey or ground chicken and can be used in any recipe calling for hamburger. Use this mix for Enchilada Casserole or Saturday Stroganoff. Or surprise everyone with Dinner in a Pumpkin, which is especially nice for Halloween.

We have combined FIVE-WAY BEEF MIX with HOT ROLL MIX to produce Bread Basket Stew. Serve a hearty meal in the bread basket, then enjoy the tasty basket itself. Wintry-Day Chili couldn't be easier, thanks to one of our new mixes, the PINTO BEAN MIX.

We suggest serving Hurry-Up Curry for your next buffet. Place rice, meat, chutney and peanuts in separate bowls. Have an extra shaker with curry powder for those who like a little more spice. Then guests can serve themselves.

BAKED BEEF BRISKET

Begin baking the brisket in the morning so it will be ready for your evening meal.

1 (5-lb.) beef brisket

1 pkg. ONION SEASONING MIX, page 35

2 tablespoons water

1 teaspoon salt

1/4 teaspoon pepper

10 small boiling onions, peeled

1/4 lb. small fresh mushrooms

Variation

To cook a 3- or 4-pound brisket, bake 30 minutes at 350F (175C), then 5 or 6 hours longer at 250F (120C).

Preheat oven to 350F (175C). Cut two 18" x 12" pieces of heavy-duty foil. Place on a large baking sheet with raised sides. Place brisket in center of foil. Sprinkle with ONION SEASONING MIX, water, salt and pepper. Place onions and mushrooms on top of meat. Bring 2 short ends of top piece of foil together over meat. Fold tight against meat; fold sides to make a tight seal. Repeat with second piece of foil, making a double covering of foil.

Bake 1 hour. Reduce heat to 250F (120C). Bake 9 hours longer or until tender when pierced with a fork. Unwrap meat. Remove onions, mushrooms and any meat juice and place in bowl. Slice meat, arranging slices on a platter. To serve, pour onion mixture over sliced brisket. Makes 18 to 20 servings.

ONION POT ROAST

Slow cooking allows flavor to develop.

1/2 teaspoon salt
Pinch of pepper
3 to 4 lb. beef arm roast or
　7-blade pot roast
3 tablespoons all-purpose flour
3 tablespoons vegetable
　shortening
1 pkg. ONION SEASONING
　MIX, page 35
1 cup water
4 medium carrots, peeled,
　quartered
3 celery stalks, cut in sticks
3 medium potatoes, cut in half
1 bay leaf

Preheat oven to 325F (165C). Sprinkle salt and pepper over roast. Dredge in flour, turning to coat all sides. In a Dutch oven, melt shortening. Add roast, turning to brown all sides.

In a small bowl, combine ONION SEASONING MIX and water. Pour over roast. Add carrots, celery, potatoes and bay leaf; cover. Bake 3 hours or until meat is tender. On a platter, arrange cooked vegetables around roast. Serve immediately. Makes 6 to 8 servings.

For the best-tasting gravy, thicken the pan juices with corn-starch. Stir until smooth and thickened to desired consistency.

TASTY BEEF BIRDS

Serve with noodles, green beans and a salad.

1 cup dry breadcrumbs
1 oz. (1/4 cup) shredded
   Cheddar cheese
1/4 cup butter or margarine,
   melted
2 tablespoons chopped green
   onion
6 thin cubed steaks
3 tablespoons vegetable oil
1 cup BEEF GRAVY MIX,
   page 61
2 cups cold water

In a medium bowl, combine breadcrumbs, cheese, melted butter or margarine and green onions.

Arrange steaks on a flat surface. Spread evenly with breadcrumb mixture. Roll up jelly-roll fashion. Fasten with a wooden pick or skewer. Heat oil in a medium skillet. Add rolled steaks. Cook over medium heat until browned.

In a small saucepan, blend BEEF GRAVY MIX and water. Stir over medium heat with a wire whisk until smooth and slightly thickened. Pour gravy over steaks. Cover and simmer 25 to 30 minutes until steaks are tender. Makes 6 servings.

BREAD BASKET STEW

Believe it or not, the Bread Basket Bowls hold their shape when filled with stew.

Bread Basket Bowls, page 244
1 pkg. FIVE-WAY BEEF MIX made with cubed beef, page 40, thawed
2 (8-oz.) cans tomato sauce
1 (17-oz.) can whole-kernel corn, undrained
2 cups sliced fresh mushrooms or 1 (8-oz.) can mushroom pieces, drained
1 tablespoon Worcestershire sauce
1 bay leaf, if desired

Prepare Bread Basket Bowls; set aside. In a medium saucepan, combine FIVE-WAY BEEF MIX, tomato sauce, corn, mushrooms, Worcestershire sauce and bay leaf, if desired. Bring to a boil over medium-high heat. Cover and simmer over low heat 25 minutes. Remove bay leaf. Place each Bread Basket Bowl on a plate. Ladle stew into bowls. Makes 6 to 8 servings.

SMOTHERED HAMBURGER PATTIES

Tender patties topped with a creamy gravy.

2 lb. lean ground beef
2 tablespoons vegetable
** shortening**
1/3 cup all-purpose flour
1-1/4 cups Creamy Mushroom
** Sauce, page 101,**
** or 1 (10.75-oz.) can**
** condensed cream of**
** mushroom soup**
1-1/3 cups water
1/2 cup BEEF GRAVY MIX,
** page 61**

Preheat oven to 350F (175C). Form ground beef into 8 to 10 patties. In a large skillet, melt shortening. Dip each patty in flour, coating both sides. Sear in hot shortening, turning once. Arrange seared patties in a 13" x 9" baking dish.

In a medium saucepan, combine sauce or soup, water and BEEF GRAVY MIX. Stir with a wire whisk over medium heat until slightly thickened. Pour evenly over meat. Cover and bake 1 hour in pre-heated oven. Makes 6 to 8 servings.

Searing means to cook for a short time at a high temperature to form a brown crust. We think it helps to retain the juices as well.

SATURDAY STROGANOFF

Stroganoff-lovers will like the convenience of this dish.

2 cups ALL-PURPOSE GROUND-MEAT MIX, page 38, thawed
1-1/2 cups Celery Sauce, page 101, or 1 (10.75-oz.) can condensed cream of celery soup
1-1/2 cups Creamy Mushroom Sauce, page 101, or 1 (10.75-oz.) can condensed cream of mushroom soup
3/4 cup milk
2 cups dairy sour cream
Cooked noodles
Poppy seeds, for garnish

In a large saucepan, combine ALL-PURPOSE GROUND-MEAT MIX, Celery Sauce or soup, and Creamy Mushroom Sauce or soup and milk. Stir until well-blended. Simmer about 10 minutes.

Just before serving, add sour cream. Simmer 2 minutes. Serve over cooked noodles, garnish with poppy seeds. Makes 4 to 6 servings.

SKILLET ENCHILADAS

Olives and cheese nestle inside the rolled tortillas.

2 cups ALL-PURPOSE GROUND-MEAT MIX, page 38, thawed
1-2/3 cups Creamy Mushroom Sauce, page 101,
or 1 (10.75-oz.) can condensed cream of mushroom soup
1 (14-oz.) can enchilada sauce
1/4 cup milk
1 (4-oz.) can diced roasted green chiles
12 corn tortillas
12 oz. (3 cups) shredded Cheddar cheese
1 (2.25-oz.) can sliced olives

In a large skillet over medium heat, place ALL-PURPOSE GROUND-MEAT MIX, Creamy Mushroom Sauce or cream of mushroom soup, enchilada sauce, milk and green chiles. Stir occasionally until heated through.

Heat tortillas in microwave oven until softened. Place about 1/4 cup cheese and 1 teaspoon sliced olives in center of each tortilla. Roll and place, seam side down, on top of heated meat mixture. Cover and reduce heat. Simmer about 3 minutes until cheese melts. Spoon onto serving plates. Makes 6 servings.

Stove-top enchiladas!
Emily loves these
because she can eat
the rolled enchiladas
and leave the meat
for others who enjoy a
heartier meal.

NO-FUSS SWISS-STEAK STEW

Slow simmering tenderizes the meat and blends the flavors. Put everything but the noodles in a Dutch oven.

2 lb. lean beef, cut in 1-inch cubes
3 tablespoons all-purpose flour
1 (4-oz.) can diced or chopped green chiles
1 pkg. **ONION SEASONING MIX, page 35**
1/2 lb. fresh mushrooms or 1 (8-oz.) can mushrooms, drained
1 (28-oz.) can tomatoes, crushed
2 cups water
3 cups hot cooked noodles, buttered

Dredge beef cubes in flour; place in Dutch oven. Add green chiles, ONION SEASONING MIX, mushrooms, tomatoes and water. Stir to blend. Cover; place in cold oven.

Turn oven to 300F (150C). Bake 3 to 4 hours until tender. After 2 hours, add more water if needed to keep mixture moist. Serve immediately over hot buttered noodles. Makes 6 to 8 servings.

If you have a vegetarian in the family, omit beef and flour. Reduce water to 1 cup. Bake at 350F (175C) about 30 minutes.

VEGETABLE-CHEESE CASSEROLE

Hot biscuits are the perfect accompaniment to this colorful meal.

2 tablespoons butter or margarine
1 cup dry bread crumbs
1 pkg. FIVE-WAY BEEF MIX made with ground beef, page 40, thawed
4 oz. (1 cup) shredded Cheddar cheese or Monterey Jack cheese
1-1/2 cups Celery Sauce, page 101, or 1 (10.75-oz.) can condensed cream of celery soup

Preheat oven to 350F (175C). Butter a 2-1/2-quart casserole dish. In a small skillet, melt butter or margarine over medium-low heat. Stir in bread crumbs. Cook and stir until crumbs are crisp and golden brown. In buttered casserole dish, combine FIVE-WAY BEEF MIX, cheese and Celery Sauce or soup. Top with browned crumbs. Bake 30 minutes. Makes 4 to 6 servings.

Monterey Jack cheese is a good substitute for Cheddar. Plain nonfat yogurt makes a good substitute for sour cream.

ENCHILADA CASSEROLE

A simple introduction to Mexican cookery.

1 (6-oz.) pkg. corn chips
2 cups **ALL-PURPOSE GROUND-MEAT MIX,** page 38, thawed
1-1/2 cups **PINTO BEAN MIX,** page 49, or 1 (15-oz.) can chili with beans
1 (10-oz.) can enchilada sauce
1 (8-oz.) can tomato sauce
1 cup dairy sour cream
2 oz. (1/2 cup) shredded Cheddar cheese

Preheat oven to 375F (190C). Lightly butter a 2-quart casserole. Crush 1/2 cup of the corn chips and reserve for top. In a medium bowl, combine remaining corn chips, ALL-PURPOSE GROUND-MEAT MIX, PINTO BEAN MIX or chili, enchilada sauce and tomato sauce. Pour into prepared casserole. Bake about 20 minutes, until heated through.

Remove from oven. Spread sour cream on top. Sprinkle with shredded cheese and reserved crushed corn chips. Bake 5 more minutes until cheese is melted. Makes 6 servings.

COUNTRY CASSEROLE

Instead of flat noodles, introduce variety by using mostaccioli, rotini spirals or wheels.

2 cups ALL-PURPOSE GROUND-MEAT MIX, page 38, thawed

1 tablespoon sugar

1/2 teaspoon garlic salt

2 (8-oz.) cans tomato sauce

2 to 3 tablespoons water, if needed

1 (3-oz.) pkg. cream cheese, softened

1/4 to 1/2 cup milk

1 cup dairy sour cream

6 green onions, finely sliced

1 (8-oz.) pkg. noodles, cooked, drained

8 oz. (2 cups) shredded Cheddar cheese

Preheat oven to 350F (175C). Lightly butter a 2-quart casserole dish; set aside. In a medium saucepan, combine ALL-PURPOSE GROUND-MEAT MIX, sugar, garlic salt and tomato sauce. Simmer over medum heat about 10 minutes. Add water if needed to keep mixture moist.

In a small bowl, combine cream cheese, 1/4 cup milk and sour cream, stirring until smooth. Stir in additional milk if needed to make a medium-thick sauce. Stir in green onions.

In prepared casserole dish, layer 1/2 of noodles, 1/2 of meat mixture and 1/2 of sour cream mixture. Repeat layers. Top with shredded cheese. Bake 30 minutes until heated through and cheese melts. Makes 6 to 8 servings.

Sometimes we add a 10-oz. pkg. of frozen peas to the cooked noodles before layering. Sprinkle top with 1/4 cup chopped walnuts. Bake as directed.

DINNER IN A PUMPKIN

For a Halloween treat, paint a face on the pumpkin with acrylic paints before it is baked.

1 medium pumpkin
4 cups ALL-PURPOSE GROUND-MEAT MIX, page 38, thawed
1/4 cup soy sauce
2 tablespoons brown sugar, firmly packed
4 oz. fresh mushrooms, sliced, or 1 (4-oz.) can sliced mushrooms, drained
1-1/2 cups CHICKEN GRAVY MIX, page 39, or 1 (10.75-oz.) can condensed cream of chicken soup
2 cups hot cooked rice

Preheat oven to 375F (190C). Lightly grease a 10-inch circle in center of a baking sheet; set aside. Place pumpkin on a firm surface. Using a sharp knife, cut out stem end and about 3 inches around stem. Cut on a diagonal by slanting knife from outer edge of pumpkin in toward center. Reserve top. Remove seeds and pulp; discard.

In a medium bowl, combine ALL-PURPOSE GROUND-MEAT MIX, soy sauce, brown sugar, mushrooms, CHICKEN GRAVY MIX or soup and rice. Spoon mixture into pumpkin. Replace top. Place pumpkin on greased baking sheet. Bake about 1 hour in preheated oven until pumpkin is tender. Serve cooked pumpkin along with meat filling. Makes 6 to 8 servings.

HURRY-UP CURRY

Curry is an East Indian blend of spices, ranging from mild to extremely hot in flavor.

2 cups ALL-PURPOSE GROUND-MEAT MIX, page 38, or 2 cups CUBED PORK MIX, page 47, thawed
1/3 cup ketchup
3/4 cup water
1 cup sliced fresh mushrooms
1 teaspoon curry powder
2 teaspoons steak sauce
2 teaspoons Worcestershire sauce
4 cups hot cooked rice
3/4 cup chutney
1/2 cup chopped peanuts

In a large skillet, combine ALL-PURPOSE GROUND-MEAT MIX or CUBED PORK MIX, ketchup, water, mushrooms, curry powder, steak sauce and Worcestershire sauce. Stirring occasionally, cook over medium heat until heated through, about 10 minutes. Serve curry mixture over hot cooked rice. Top with a spoonful of chutney and a sprinkle of peanuts. Makes 4 to 6 servings.

TERIYAKI BEEF & VEGETABLES

A Japanese dish embellished with a delicious sauce.

1 lb. top sirloin
4 medium carrots
3 medium zucchini
About 1/4 cup vegetable oil
2 tablespoons brown sugar
1-1/2 cups ORIENTAL STIR-FRY
   MIX, page 65
4 cups hot cooked rice
5 green onions, thinly sliced,
   for garnish

On a cutting board, cut meat, carrots and zucchini in thin diagonal slices. Place 3 to 5 paper towels in a medium bowl; set aside. Heat 2 tablespoons oil in a large skillet or wok. Add meat slices; stir-fry over medium heat until meat is no longer red, 3 to 4 minutes.

Use a slotted spoon to remove cooked meat to prepared bowl. Cover; keep warm. Add remaining oil to skillet or wok. Add carrot slices. Cook and stir 2 to 3 minutes. Add zucchini slices. Cook and stir 2 to 3 minutes longer.

Stir in cooked meat, brown sugar and ORIENTAL STIR-FRY MIX. Cook and stir until mixture thickens slightly. Serve over hot rice. Garnish with sliced green onions. Makes 4 to 6 servings.

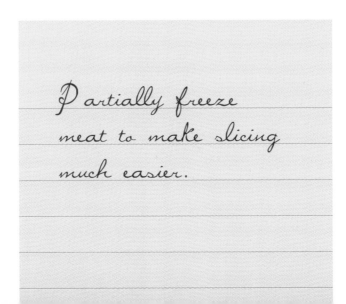

Partially freeze meat to make slicing much easier.

MEAT & POTATO PIE

Try this family favorite topped with fresh-tomato salsa.

Double Freezer Pie Crust, unbaked, page 309
1 lb. lean ground beef
1/2 cup milk
1 pkg. ONION SEASONING MIX, page 35
1/8 teaspoon pepper
4 cups grated cooked potatoes or 1 (12-oz.) pkg. hash brown potatoes, thawed

Prepare bottom crust in a 9-inch pie plate; set aside. Preheat oven to 350F (175C). In a medium bowl, combine ground beef, milk, ONION SEASONING MIX and pepper. Press into pastry-lined pie plate. Top with potatoes. Cover with top crust. Trim and flute edges. Cut slits in top crust to let steam escape. Bake 1 hour until crust is golden brown. Makes 6 servings.

MEXICAN HAYSTACK

Baked tortilla strips are amazingly crisp and so much better for you than fried.

8 (8-inch) flour tortillas
2 cups ALL-PURPOSE
   GROUND-MEAT MIX,
   page 38, OR CHICKEN MIX,
   page 39, thawed
1/2 teaspoon ground cumin
Shredded lettuce
4 cups PINTO BEAN MIX,
   page 49, thawed,
   or 2 (16-oz.) cans kidney
   beans, drained
3 medium tomatoes, diced
1 cup Guacamole, page 174,
   or 2 avocados, diced
8 oz. (2 cups) shredded
   Longhorn cheese
1/2 cup chopped green onion
1 cup dairy sour cream
1 (7-oz.) can green-chile salsa

Preheat oven to 375F (190C). Lightly spray baking sheet with vegetable cooking spray. Cut flour tortillas into 1/4-inch strips; place on prepared baking sheet. Lightly spray tortilla strips. Bake 5 to 8 minutes, until strips are lightly browned. Carefully remove from oven and cool.

In a skillet heat ALL-PURPOSE GROUND-MEAT MIX or CHICKEN MIX. Add cumin and simmer until heated through, about 10 minutes. On individual serving plates layer all ingredients. First stack tortilla strips and meat mixture. Then layer shredded lettuce, beans, tomatoes, Guacamole or avocados, cheese, onion, sour cream and salsa as desired. Makes 6 servings.

Our Hawaiian Haystack has been a favorite for years. We adapted the idea and took it South of the Border.

ORIENTAL-STYLE SKILLET DINNER

This one-pan meal is quick, with minimum clean-up. For added texture, serve with Chinese-style noodles.

**2 cups ALL-PURPOSE
  GROUND-MEAT MIX,
    page 38, thawed**
3-1/2 cups water
2-1/4 cups instant rice
1/4 cup soy sauce
**1/2 cup chopped canned
    bamboo shoots or
    water chestnuts**
1 teaspoon grated fresh ginger
Salt to taste

In a skillet, combine ALL-PURPOSE GROUND-MEAT MIX, water, rice, soy sauce, bamboo shoots or water chestnuts, and ginger.

Stirring occasionally, cook over medium heat until water is absorbed and rice is tender. Add salt to taste. Makes 4 to 6 servings.

Three-Layer Casserole

THREE-LAYER CASSEROLE

A hearty trio of flavors and colors, here's dinner for any family.

2 cups MEAT SAUCE MIX, page 45
1 (10-oz.) pkg. frozen green beans or 1 (16-oz.) can French-cut green beans, drained
2 cups mashed potatoes
4 oz. (1 cup) shredded mozzarella or Cheddar cheese

Preheat oven to 350F (175C). Lightly butter a 1-1/2-quart casserole. Layer casserole with MEAT SAUCE MIX, green beans and mashed potatoes. Sprinkle shredded cheese on top. Bake 25 to 30 minutes, until bubbly. Makes 4 servings.

If possible serve this in a clear-glass casserole and show off the distinctive three layers.

WINTRY-DAY CHILI

A favorite to take on camping trips or "snow picnics."

1 lb. lean ground beef
1 medium green bell pepper, chopped
1 (14.5-oz.) can tomatoes, crushed
1 (8-oz.) can tomato sauce
4 teaspoons chili powder
1 teaspoon ground cumin
2 teaspoons steak sauce
1 teaspoon Worcestershire sauce
1 teaspoon dried oregano leaves, crushed
1 teaspoon seasoning salt
4 cups **PINTO BEAN MIX**, page 49, thawed

In a large pot or Dutch oven, brown ground beef. Drain. Add green pepper, tomatoes with juice, tomato sauce, chili powder, cumin, steak sauce, Worcestershire sauce, oregano leaves, seasoning salt and PINTO BEAN MIX. Stir to combine thoroughly. Simmer over low heat to blend flavors, about 30 to 45 minutes. Makes 6 servings.

DEEP-DISH POT PIE

A hearty one-dish meal hides under a tender crust.

1 pkg. FIVE-WAY BEEF MIX made with ground beef, page 40, thawed
Single Freezer Pie Crust, unbaked, page 309
1 egg
1 tablespoon vegetable oil

Preheat oven to 425F (220C). Turn FIVE-WAY BEEF MIX into an 8- or 9-inch-square baking dish or a 2-1/2-quart casserole dish. Roll out pastry to a 10-inch square or to fit casserole dish. Place pastry over dish. Trim, letting dough extend 1/2 inch beyond edge of dish. Fold edge under; flute. Cut slits in crust to let steam escape. In a bowl, beat egg and oil with a fork or a whisk. Brush evenly on crust with a pastry brush, covering entire crust. Bake 45 to 60 minutes in preheated oven until deep golden brown. Makes 4 to 6 servings.

To freeze unbaked pie: Wrap airtight in heavy-duty freezer wrap or heavy-duty foil. Store in freezer. Use within 6 months. Thaw frozen pie in refrigerator 24 hours before baking.

SLUMGULLION

An old favorite. Serve this quick combination when time is short.

2 cups ALL-PURPOSE GROUND-MEAT MIX, page 38, thawed
1 (12-oz.) can whole-kernel corn, drained
2 (8-oz.) cans tomato sauce
1 tablespoon chopped fresh parsley
1 (6-oz.) pkg. noodles, cooked, drained

In a medium skillet, combine ALL-PURPOSE GROUND-MEAT MIX, corn and tomato sauce. Stirring occasionally, simmer over medium heat about 15 minutes.

Stir parsley into noodles. Spoon meat mixture over noodles or stir noodles into meat mixture. Makes 6 servings.

MAIN DISHES - CHICKEN

Chicken is enjoying an all-time high in popularity, and you can never have too many recipes.

The secret to make-a-mix cooking is planning ahead. Prepare several mixes when you have the time, then use them when you're in a hurry. Store CHICKEN MIX in 1-pint containers and you will have the basis for Sweet & Sour Chicken, Mexican Chicken Bake, Chicken Burgers and three other dishes. An additional benefit is that you will also have made 6 pints of broth for future use.

Save money by making your own HERBED STUFFING MIX, CRISPY COATING MIX and CHICKEN GRAVY MIX. Then impress your family with Chicken Strata, Chicken & Ham Foldovers, Crunchy-Crust Chicken or Chicken Breasts en Croûte. They'll think you slaved over that hot stove all day!

White Chili, one of our new recipes, reflects today's interest in a healthy diet. We combine cooked navy beans and chicken with the Southwestern flavors of cumin and oregano.

Give Chicken Cacciatore a different look by serving it over strands of spaghetti squash. The colors are great together.

CHICKEN BREASTS EN CROÛTE

Succulent chicken with a delicate filling.

2 tablespoons vegetable oil
6 chicken breast halves,
    skinned, boned
1 tablespoon fresh parsley or
    chervil leaves
Salt and pepper to taste
1 (3-oz.) pkg. cream cheese
    with chives
1 (6-pack) box frozen patty
    shells, slightly thawed
Chicken Gravy, page 62
Paprika, for garnish

Preheat oven to 400F (205C). Heat oil in a skillet. Add chicken. Sear over high heat 3 to 4 minutes, turning once. Stir in parsley or chervil, salt and pepper to taste. Remove chicken from pan; cool slightly. Cut cream cheese into 6 pieces. Insert 1 piece into underside indentation of each half chicken breast.

Between 2 sheets of waxed paper, roll out each patty shell to an 8-inch circle. Wrap each breast in 1 pastry circle. Pinch edges together to seal. Place wrapped breasts, seam-side down, on an ungreased baking sheet.

Bake 35 to 40 minutes until golden brown. Place baked chicken on a platter. Top with Chicken Gravy. Sprinkle with paprika, if desired. Makes 6 servings.

Save time by buying boneless, skinned chicken breasts.

CHICKEN BURGERS

One, two, three ingredients and lunch is ready.

**2 cups CHICKEN MIX,
   page 39, thawed**
1 cup barbecue sauce
8 hamburger buns

Combine CHICKEN MIX and barbecue sauce in a medium saucepan. Cook over medium heat about 10 minutes, until heated through. Serve over hamburger buns. Makes 8 burgers.

CHICKEN CACCIATORE

Guaranteed moist and tender.

Vegetable oil for frying
1/2 cup all-purpose flour
1 teaspoon salt
1/4 teaspoon pepper
1 (4-lb.) fryer chicken, cut up
**4 cups ITALIAN COOKING
   SAUCE MIX, page 41,
   thawed**

Preheat oven to 350F (175C). Heat oil in a skillet. Combine flour, salt and pepper in a plastic bag. Add chicken pieces and shake to coat with mixture. Brown chicken in hot oil until golden brown. Put chicken in a 13" x 9" baking dish. Pour ITALIAN COOKING SAUCE MIX over chicken. Cover with foil. Bake about 1 hour, until chicken is tender. Makes 4 to 6 servings.

We've served this over a mound of cooked spaghetti squash. The colors are great together.

CLUB CHICKEN CASSEROLE

You'll proudly serve this appetizing dish.

**2 cups CHICKEN BROTH,
    page 39, thawed**
1 cup uncooked long-grain rice
**3 tablespoons butter or
    margarine**
3 tablespoons all-purpose flour
1-1/2 teaspoons salt
1-2/3 cups evaporated milk
**2 cups CHICKEN MIX,
    page 39, thawed**
**1 (10-oz.) pkg. frozen chopped
    broccoli, cooked and drained**
4 oz. fresh mushrooms, sliced
**1/4 cup toasted slivered
    almonds**
Paprika, for garnish

Variation

Substitute a 10-oz. pkg. frozen
    peas for broccoli.

Lightly butter an 11" x 7" baking pan.
Combine CHICKEN BROTH and rice in
a saucepan. Cook about 25 minutes,
until rice is tender.

Preheat oven to 350F (175C). Melt butter or margarine in a large saucepan.
Gradually stir in flour and salt.
Gradually add evaporated milk. Cook
over medium heat about
5 minutes, stirring constantly, until mixture thickens. Add CHICKEN MIX,
cooked rice, broccoli and mushrooms.

Put in prepared baking pan. Top with
toasted almonds and paprika. Bake 30
to 35 minutes, until bubbly. Makes 8
servings.

You can't have too many good chicken recipes!

CHICKEN CONTINENTAL

Another great one-dish meal!

1-1/2 cups **CHICKEN GRAVY MIX, page 62, or 1 (10.75-oz.) can condensed cream of chicken soup**

2 tablespoons grated onion

1 teaspoon salt

Dash of pepper

3 tablespoons chopped fresh parsley or 1 tablespoon parsley flakes

1/4 teaspoon thyme

2 cups **CHICKEN BROTH, page 39, thawed**

2 cups **CHICKEN MIX, page 39, thawed**

2 cups instant rice

Preheat oven to 375F (190C). Lightly butter a 2-quart casserole. In a medium bowl, combine CHICKEN GRAVY MIX or soup, onion, salt, pepper, parsley, thyme and CHICKEN BROTH. Stir until well-blended. Add CHICKEN MIX and instant rice.

Put in prepared casserole. Cover and bake about 30 minutes, until rice is tender. Makes 6 servings.

CRUNCHY-CRUST CHICKEN

Old-fashioned goodness in a baked version.

1-1/2 cups CRISP COATING MIX, page 31
2 eggs
1 tablespoon milk
1 (2-1/2-lb.) broiler-fryer chicken, cut up

Preheat oven to 400F (205C). Lightly grease a baking sheet; set aside. Pour CRISP COATING MIX into a large plastic food storage bag; set aside.

In a shallow bowl, beat eggs and milk until blended. Rinse chicken; pat dry with paper towels. Dip each piece of chicken in egg mixture; drain briefly. Place chicken in plastic bag, shaking until coated.

Remove chicken from bag; arrange on prepared baking sheet. Cover with foil. Bake 40 minutes. Remove foil and bake 10 to 20 minutes longer until golden brown and crisp. Makes 4 to 6 servings.

CREAMY CHICKEN ENCHILADAS

Also known as enchiladas suizas, these feature a beautiful blend of flavors.

**2 cups CHICKEN MIX,
    page 39, thawed**
**1 (4-oz.) can diced roasted
    green chiles**
1 (7-oz.) can green-chile salsa
**10 oz. (2-1/2 cups) shredded
    Monterey Jack cheese**
Vegetable oil for frying
8 (6-inch) flour tortillas
2 cups whipping cream
1/2 teaspoon salt
**Chopped fresh cilantro, for
    garnish**
**Chopped green onions, for
    garnish**

Preheat oven to 350F (175C). In a medium bowl, combine CHICKEN MIX, green chiles, salsa and 1 cup of the cheese. Heat oil in medium skillet. To soften tortillas, quickly dip them in hot oil with tongs, one at a time. Drain on paper towel.

Put about 1/3 cup filling in center of each tortilla and roll up. Place close together in a shallow casserole dish or baking pan, seam-side down.

In a bowl, combine whipping cream and salt. Pour cream over pan of enchiladas and sprinkle with remaining cheese. Cover with foil. Bake 20 to 25 minutes until bubbly. Garnish with cilantro and green onions. Makes 4 to 6 servings.

If you prefer not to soften the tortillas in oil, you can quickly dip them in hot water instead.

CHICKEN & HAM FOLDOVERS

An impressive dish that belies how easy it is to prepare.

6 chicken breast halves, skinned, boned
3/4 cup CRISP COATING MIX, page 31, or 3/4 cup crushed cornflakes
6 thin slices ham
6 thin slices Muenster or Swiss cheese
3 tablespoons butter or margarine, melted
1 cup CHICKEN GRAVY MIX, page 62
2 cups water
Cherry tomatoes, for garnish
Fresh basil or parsley sprigs, for garnish

On flattened breast, layer ham and cheese. Fold in half and coat.

Preheat oven to 350F (175C). Lightly butter a 13" x 9" baking dish; set aside. Place each breast half between 2 layers of waxed paper or plastic wrap. Using a mallet or rolling pin, pound to 7" x 4".

Pour CRISP COATING MIX or cornflakes into a pie plate; set aside. Cut ham slices and cheese slices in half. On 1 side of each flattened chicken breast, layer 1 piece of ham and 1 piece of cheese. Repeat layers. Fold chicken breast over layered ham and cheese. Brush melted butter or margarine over folded chicken breasts. Press each breast into CRISP COATING MIX or cornflakes. Arrange in prepared baking dish. Bake 30 minutes.

In a saucepan, combine CHICKEN GRAVY MIX and water. Cook and stir until smooth and slightly thickened. Pour over partially cooked chicken breasts. Cover and bake about 30 minutes longer. To serve, arrange chicken on a platter. Garnish with cherry tomatoes and basil or parsley sprigs. Makes 6 servings.

CHICKEN À LA KING

A dish truly fit for a king!

1/2 cup butter or margarine
1 cup chopped celery
1/4 lb. fresh mushrooms or
**   1 (4-oz.) can mushrooms**
1/2 cup all-purpose flour
2 cups CHICKEN BROTH,
**   page 39, thawed**
2 cups CHICKEN MIX,
**   page 39, thawed**
1 cup milk
1/4 cup chopped pimiento
3 tablespoons chopped fresh
**   parsley or 1 tablespoon**
**   dried parsley flakes**
Hot cooked rice
Slivered almonds, for garnish

Variation

For a party luncheon, serve in
baked puff-pastry shells.

Melt butter or margarine in a skillet.
Add celery and mushrooms. Sauté until
tender. Blend in flour and simmer 1
minute. Slowly add CHICKEN BROTH.
Cook 3 to 5 minutes, stirring constantly
until thick.

Add CHICKEN MIX, milk, pimiento, and
parsley. Simmer 10 minutes. Serve over
hot, cooked rice. Garnish with slivered
almonds. Makes 6 servings.

1. Melt butter or margarine in a skillet, then add chopped celery and sliced mushrooms. Sauté until tender.

2. Simmer the ingredients in chicken broth 10 minutes. Serve in baked puff-pastry shells for a luncheon or over hot cooked rice for dinner.

HAWAIIAN HAYSTACK

This popular buffet recipe is one of our most requested. It can be elaborate enough for a ladies' luncheon or casual enough to satisfy kids at a family reunion.

2-1/2 cups Chicken Gravy, page 62, or 1 (10.75-oz.) can condensed cream of chicken soup

1 cup CHICKEN BROTH, page 39, thawed

2 cups CHICKEN MIX, page 39, thawed

4 cups hot cooked rice

1 (9.5-oz.) can chow-mein noodles

3 medium tomatoes, sliced

1 cup chopped celery

1/2 cup chopped green bell pepper

1/2 cup chopped green onion

1-1/2 cups fresh pineapple chunks

4 oz. (1 cup) shredded Cheddar cheese

1/2 cup slivered almonds

1/2 cup coconut

1 (2-oz.) jar pimiento, drained and diced, if desired

Combine Chicken Gravy or soup and CHICKEN BROTH in a medium saucepan. Stir to blend. Add CHICKEN MIX. Simmer 8 to 10 minutes, until heated through. On 8 individual serving plates layer all ingredients. First layer rice, chow-mein noodles and chicken and gravy. Add tomatoes, celery, bell pepper and green onion. Top with pineapple chunks, shredded Cheddar cheese and more chicken and gravy, if desired. Garnish with almonds, coconut and pimiento, if desired. Makes 8 servings.

To speed preparation, microwave Chicken Gravy and Broth together.

Hawaiian Haystack

CHICKEN OAHU

The sauce is the star of this blend of flavors from the Hawaiian Islands.

4 cups HERBED STUFFING MIX, page 33
1 cup fresh pineapple chunks or 1 (8-oz.) can crushed pineapple, undrained
1/4 cup water
1/2 cup all-purpose flour
1/2 teaspoon salt
1/2 teaspoon paprika
Dash of pepper
1 (2-1/2 to 3-lb.) fryer chicken, cut up
Creamy Sauce, see below

Creamy Sauce
1-1/2 cups chopped celery
1/2 cup chopped onion
2 tablespoons chopped green bell pepper
1/2 cup water
1-1/2 cups Creamy Mushroom Sauce, page 101, or 1 (10.75-oz.) can condensed cream of mushroom soup
1/2 cup dairy sour cream
1 tablespoon soy sauce

Preheat oven to 375F (190C). Lightly grease a 13" x 9" baking dish. In a bowl, combine HERBED STUFFING MIX, pineapple and water. Put into prepared baking dish.

In a plastic bag, combine flour, salt, paprika and pepper. Add chicken pieces 2 at a time and shake to coat. Place chicken on top of stuffing. Cover with foil. Bake 30 minutes. Remove foil and bake 30 minutes longer. Prepare Creamy Sauce and spoon over top of chicken. Makes 6 servings.

Creamy Sauce
In a medium skillet, combine celery, onion, green pepper and water. Cover and simmer 10 minutes. Drain off water. Add Creamy Mushroom Sauce or soup, sour cream and soy sauce. Heat through.

STIR-FRY CASHEW CHICKEN

Use colorful chopsticks when you entertain your guests with this Oriental dish.

4 chicken breast halves, skinned, boned

4 to 6 tablespoons vegetable oil

1 lb. fresh green beans, cut in 1-inch pieces

1 yam, peeled, cut in 1/4-inch slices

1 (8-oz.) can water chestnuts, drained, sliced

1-1/2 cups ORIENTAL STIR-FRY MIX, page 65

1 (3-oz.) pkg. cashew nuts

1 to 2 tablespoons water

4 cups hot cooked rice

Cut chicken into thin strips; set aside. In a skillet or wok, heat 2 to 3 tablespoons oil. Add chicken. Stir-fry until meat is tender, 4 to 5 minutes. Drain chicken on paper towels; cover and keep warm.

Add 2 to 3 tablespoons of the remaining oil to skillet or wok. Add green beans. Stir-fry about 3 minutes. Add yam slices. Stir-fry until beans are crisp-tender, 3 to 4 minutes. Add cooked chicken, water chestnuts and ORIENTAL STIR-FRY MIX. Cook until sauce is slightly thickened, about 10 minutes.

Stir in nuts. Add water if needed to make a thinner sauce. Simmer 2 minutes longer. Serve over hot cooked rice. Makes 4 to 6 servings.

No cashews? We've made this using walnuts and almonds with excellent results.

161

SUNDAY CHICKEN

*Your guests will rave about these
tender chicken pieces*

**1/2 cup WHITE SAUCE MIX,
  page 63**
1 cup cool water
**4 oz. (1 cup) shredded Cheddar
  cheese**
**1 cup sliced fresh mushrooms
  or 1 (4-oz.) can mushrooms,
  drained**
**6 whole chicken breasts,
  skinned and boned**
Flour
1 teaspoon salt
1 egg, slightly beaten
1 cup milk
2 cups dry breadcrumbs
Vegetable oil for frying

*Breaded chicken
can be covered and
refrigerated for a
day, then cooked
the next day.*

In a saucepan, combine WHITE SAUCE MIX with cool water. Cook over low heat until thick and smooth, stirring constantly. Add cheese and mushrooms. Stir until cheese is melted. Pour into an 8-inch-square pan. Chill until set.

Lay large pieces of chicken on a generously floured surface with sides just touching. Fill in gaps with small pieces of chicken. Sprinkle with flour. Cover with plastic wrap and pound together with a mallet. Roll lightly with a rolling pin to about 8" x 10". Remove plastic wrap. Sprinkle with salt.

Cut cheese mixture in 1/2- to 3/4-inch strips. Lay half of cheese strips along the long edge of chicken. Carefully wrap chicken around cheese and roll up lengthwise. With a knife, cut into 2- to 3-inch pieces. Combine egg and milk in a shallow dish. Dip chicken in egg mixture, then in breadcrumbs. Place on rack to dry, about 15 minutes.

Preheat oven to 350F (175C). Fry chicken in small amount of hot oil 2 to 3 minutes on each side, until golden. Place in a 13" x 9" baking pan. Cover and bake 45 minutes, until tender. Melt remaining cheese mixture and serve over chicken. Makes 8 to 10 servings.

CHICKEN STRATA

Give it a layered look!

1 (2-1/2- to 3-lb.) stewing
    chicken
1 carrot, pared and sliced
1 onion, sliced
2 teaspoons salt
2 qt. water
1/2 cup butter or margarine
1/2 cup all-purpose flour
1 teaspoon salt
1/2 cup milk
2 eggs, slightly beaten
3 cups **HERBED STUFFING MIX**,
    page 33
1 cup dry breadcrumbs
1/4 cup butter or margarine,
    melted

In a saucepan, combine chicken, carrot, onion, 2 teaspoons salt and water. Cover and cook until water boils. Reduce heat; simmer 1-1/2 to 2 hours, until chicken is tender.

Remove from heat. Strain broth and refrigerate; skim fat from top. Cool chicken. Remove meat; discard bones and skin.

Preheat oven to 375F (190C). Melt 1/2 cup butter or margarine in a saucepan. Stir in flour and 1 teaspoon salt. Cook 1 minute, stirring constantly. Slowly stir in 2 cups reserved broth and milk. Cook 3 to 5 minutes, stirring constantly, until mixture thickens.

Remove from heat and slowly add half of mixture to beaten eggs in a small bowl. Mix well. Blend egg mixture slowly into the hot mixture in saucepan. Cook 3 to 4 minutes. Remove from heat.

Butter a 2-1/2-quart casserole. Put HERBED STUFFING MIX in casserole. Pour half the sauce over stuffing. Add chicken. Add remaining sauce. In a bowl, mix breadcrumbs with 1/4 cup melted butter or margarine; sprinkle over casserole. Bake 20 to 30 minutes. Makes 8 servings.

SWEET & SOUR CHICKEN

It's time for a Hawaiian delight! This is an easy recipe to increase and serve to a crowd.

1/2 cup water
5 tablespoons cornstarch
3/4 cup brown sugar, packed
1 teaspoon salt
1-1/2 cups fresh pineapple
  chunks, drained, reserve
  juice
2 cups CHICKEN MIX,
  page 39, thawed
2 tablespoons soy sauce
1/4 cup white vinegar
2 cups CHICKEN BROTH,
  page 39, thawed
2 cups water
2 cups uncooked
  long-grain rice
1/2 cup thinly sliced onion
3/4 cup thinly sliced green bell
  peppers
2 large tomatoes, cut in
  wedges

In a saucepan, combine 1/2 cup water, cornstarch, brown sugar and salt. Stir until mixture is smooth. Add reserved pineapple juice. Cook over medium heat 5 to 7 minutes, until mixture starts to thicken. Add CHICKEN MIX, soy sauce and vinegar. Cover and simmer 15 minutes, stirring occasionally.

Put chicken broth and 2 cups water in a large saucepan. Add rice. Cover and cook about 25 minutes.

Spray skillet with vegetable cooking spray and sauté onion and green peppers until crisp-tender. Add pineapple chunks, onion and green peppers to the chicken mixture. Cook until heated. Before serving, stir in tomato wedges. Serve over the hot, cooked rice. Makes 6 to 8 servings.

TURKEY DINNER PIE

Simple, and special!

**Double Freezer Pie Crust,
  unbaked, page 309**
**1-1/2 cups cooked turkey or
  chicken, cut in 1/2-inch
  cubes**
**2 cups leftover turkey gravy
  or Chicken Gravy, page 62**
**1 (10-oz.) pkg. frozen carrots
  and peas, thawed**
**1 cup boiling onions, halved or
  1 (8-oz.) can onions, halved**
1 teaspoon salt
1/8 teaspoon pepper
1/8 teaspoon poultry seasoning
1/8 teaspoon ground thyme

Prepare bottom crust in a 9-inch pie plate. Preheat oven to 425F (220C). In a large bowl, combine turkey or chicken, gravy, carrots and peas, onions, salt, pepper, poultry seasoning and thyme. Stir to distribute. Pour into pastry shell. Cover with top crust. Trim and flute edges. Cut slits in top crust to let steam escape. Bake 35 to 40 minutes in preheated oven until golden brown. Makes 6 servings.

Sometimes we substitute mixed frozen vegetables for the onions. Stir in 1/4 cup cashews for added texture.

WHITE CHILI

This Southwestern favorite is just as appealing without the meat.

2 tablespoons olive oil
2 stalks celery, finely chopped
1 leek, white part only, finely chopped
1 container NAVY BEAN MIX, page 48, thawed
2 cups CHICKEN MIX, page 39, thawed, if desired
1 tablespoon chili powder
1 teaspoon ground cumin
1 teaspoon Mexican oregano
1/2 teaspoon white pepper
1/4 teaspoon cinnamon
Dairy sour cream, garnish
Chopped green onion, garnish
Salsa, garnish

In a large pot or Dutch oven heat oil. Sauté celery and leek until soft. Stir in NAVY BEAN MIX and CHICKEN MIX, if desired, chili powder, cumin, oregano, white pepper and cinnamon. Simmer over low heat to blend flavors, 30 to 45 minutes.

To serve, ladle into bowls and garnish with sour cream, green onion and salsa. Makes 4 to 6 servings.

CHICKEN IN MUSHROOM SAUCE

Little extra touches turn the ordinary into extraordinary.

1/4 cup butter or margarine
1 (3-lb.) chicken, cut up
1/2 cup CHICKEN GRAVY MIX, page 62
2 cups dairy sour cream
1 cup milk
1/2 lb. fresh mushrooms, sliced
1 tablespoon fresh parsley
1 tablespoon poppy seeds
1 tablespoon lemon juice
3/4 teaspoon grated lemon peel (1/2 lemon)
Cooked white and wild rice

Preheat oven to 325F (165C). In a large skillet, melt butter or margarine. Add chicken. Cook until browned. Remove chicken from skillet; arrange in a large casserole dish.

Stir CHICKEN GRAVY MIX into pan drippings. Blend in sour cream and milk. Stirring constantly, simmer 3 to 5 minutes. Do not boil. Pour sauce over chicken. Sprinkle with mushrooms, parsley and poppy seeds. Cover and bake 30 to 45 minutes until tender. Sprinkle lemon juice and lemon peel over casserole. Serve immediately with rice. Makes 6 servings.

Buy lemons when they're on sale.
Grate lemon peel before juicing lemons.
Freeze extra peel in small plastic
bags for future use.

MEXICAN CHICKEN BAKE

You'll need corn tortillas for this one. This is one of our all-time favorites.

1-1/2 cups Creamy Mushroom Sauce, page 101
1-1/2 cups Chicken Gravy, page 62, or 1 (10.75-oz.) can condensed cream of chicken soup
3/4 cup milk
2 cups CHICKEN MIX, page 39, thawed
1/2 teaspoon salt
1 large onion, finely chopped
1 (7-oz.) can green-chile salsa
10 oz. (2-1/2 cups) shredded Cheddar cheese
12 corn tortillas, each cut into 8 pieces

Variation

For added spice, add 1/4 cup chopped, roasted green chiles.

Preheat oven to 350F (175C). Lightly butter a 2-quart casserole. In a medium bowl, combine Creamy Mushroom Sauce, Chicken Gravy or soup, and milk. Stir to blend well.

Add CHICKEN MIX, salt, onion, green-chile salsa and 2 cups of the shredded cheese. Layer tortilla pieces and chicken mixture alternately in prepared casserole, ending with chicken mixture. Top with remaining shredded cheese. Bake 35 to 45 minutes, until bubbly. Makes 8 servings.

We often substitute pineapple tidbits and orange marmalade for apricot halves and apricot jam.

APRICOT CHICKEN

A bold-flavored sauce is created with just a few ingredients.

2 (3-lb.) frying chickens, cut up
1 cup French Dressing, page 69
**1 (16-oz.) can apricot halves,
   drained**
1 cup apricot jam
**1 pkg. ONION SEASONING
   MIX, page 35**
**Cilantro or parsley sprigs,
   for garnish**

Preheat oven to 350F (175C). Rinse chicken. Pat dry with paper towels; set aside. In a bowl, combine French Dressing, apricot halves, apricot jam and ONION SEASONING MIX.

Place chicken pieces on 2 large ungreased baking sheets with raised sides. Pour sauce evenly over chicken pieces. Bake uncovered 1-1/4 hours in preheated oven until chicken is lightly browned. Arrange chicken on a large platter. Spoon drippings over chicken pieces. Garnish with cilantro or parsley sprigs. Makes 8 servings.

MAIN DISHES - MEXICAN & ITALIAN

I TALIAN-STYLE MEAT MIX. MEXICAN MEAT MIX. ITALIAN COOKING SAUCE MIX—spend a morning or an evening putting these together, then store them in the freezer for delicious meals-in-minutes when you don't have time to cook. Clean-up will take less time too!

When your family is clamoring for Mexican take-out, you can treat them to Green-Chili Burros, Taco Supreme or our personal favorite—Chimichangas. Soft Chicken Tacos are the choice of those who prefer tortillas warm, but not fried.

Later in the week, go Italian with Cathy's Meatball Sandwiches or Eggplant Parmesan. Spaghetti Royale deserves freshly grated Parmesan or Romano cheese. Buy a small piece of either cheese at your local cheese shop or supermarket. Then grate the cheese yourself just before serving. Your family or guests will appreciate the fresh flavor.

CHALUPA

A simplified version of a classic Mexican dish.

6 cups PINTO BEAN MIX,
   page 49, thawed, or
   3 (15-oz.) cans pinto beans
3 cups MEXICAN MEAT MIX,
   page 46, thawed
1 teaspoon salt
1 tablespoon chili powder
1 (10-oz.) bag corn chips
4 oz. (1 cup) shredded
   Longhorn or Monterey Jack
   cheese
1/2 cup chopped onion
Shredded lettuce
2 tomatoes, chopped

Variation

Omit MEXICAN MEAT MIX and substitute shredded chicken or pork. Garnish with fresh tomato salsa.

In a Dutch oven combine PINTO BEAN MIX, MEXICAN MEAT MIX, salt and chili powder. Cook uncovered about 1 hour, stirring occasionally.

Serve in small bowls over crisp corn chips. Garnish with cheese, onion, lettuce and tomatoes. Makes 8 servings.

Chalupa means "small canoe." This is fashioned from tortilla dough, flattened and boat-shaped with a pinched rim. We are using corn chips.

171

CHIMICHANGAS

Chimis are great.

6 large flour tortillas
3 cups MEXICAN MEAT MIX,
   page 46, thawed
Vegetable oil for frying
Shredded lettuce
1 cup fresh salsa or 1 (7-oz.)
   can green-chile salsa
2 tomatoes, chopped
1 cup Guacamole, page 174
1 cup dairy sour cream
6 ripe olives, for garnish

Variation

Soft-Fry Method—To make
   ahead, dip flour tortillas in hot
   oil for about 3 seconds. Drain
   on paper towels and proceed
   as directed above.

Warm tortillas in microwave about 30 seconds. Heat MEXICAN MEAT MIX in a saucepan. Heat a small amount of oil in a large skillet. Spread 1/2 cup MEXICAN MEAT MIX over the lower third of each tortilla. Fold the bottom edge of tortilla up over filling. Fold both sides toward the center and roll into a cylinder. Secure with a wooden pick.

Fry 2 chimichangas at a time in hot oil 2 minutes until golden and crisp. Drain on paper towels. Serve hot over a layer of shredded lettuce. Top with salsa, tomatoes, Guacamole and sour cream. Garnish each with an olive. Makes 6 chimichangas.

1. Fill and roll each tortilla into a cylinder. Secure with a toothpick.

2. Top with green-chile salsa, tomatoes, Guacamole and sour cream.

SOUR-CREAM ENCHILADAS

MEXICAN MEAT MIX wins again!

1 (10-oz.) can enchilada sauce
2 cups chopped fresh tomatoes
  or 1 (16-oz.) can whole
  tomatoes, undrained and
  finely chopped
12 corn tortillas
3 cups MEXICAN MEAT MIX,
  page 46, thawed
6 oz. (1-1/2 cups) shredded
  Longhorn or Cheddar cheese
1-1/2 cups dairy sour cream or
  plain nonfat yogurt

Combine enchilada sauce and chopped tomatoes in a medium saucepan. Cook until mixture boils. Reduce heat and simmer.

Dip one tortilla at a time in hot enchilada-sauce mixture. Set aside. Heat MEXICAN MEAT MIX in a saucepan. Place about 1/4 cup MEXICAN MEAT MIX on each tortilla and sprinkle with 2 tablespoons shredded Cheddar cheese. Roll up and place close together in a shallow casserole dish, seam-side down.

Pour remaining sauce over enchiladas. Sprinkle with additional shredded cheese. Bake about 15 minutes, until bubbly. Spoon sour cream over enchiladas and serve hot. Makes about 6 servings.

GREEN-CHILE BURROS

That's Mexican!

3 cups MEXICAN MEAT MIX,
   page 46, thawed
6 large flour tortillas
Shredded lettuce
Green-chile salsa, garnish
Guacamole, below, garnish

Heat MEXICAN MEAT MIX in a small saucepan. Warm tortillas 1 at a time over low heat in a very large skillet until soft and pliable. Spread about 1/2 cup MEXICAN MEAT MIX over the lower 1/3 of each tortilla. Fold the bottom edge of tortilla up over filling. Fold both sides toward the center and roll into a cylinder. Place, seam-side down, on a bed of shredded lettuce and garnish with salsa and Guacamole. Serve warm. Makes 6 burros.

Guacamole
2 ripe avocados, peeled and
   mashed
1 teaspoon lemon juice
Salt and pepper to taste
Few drops of hot pepper sauce

Guacamole
Combine all ingredients in a small bowl.

TACO SUPREME

A super Mexican treat neatly wrapped in a tortilla!

Vegetable oil for frying
3 cups MEXICAN MEAT MIX,
    page 46, thawed
1 pkg. TACO SEASONING MIX,
    page 36
12 to 15 corn tortillas
8 oz. (2 cups) shredded
    Cheddar or Monterey Jack
    cheese
Shredded lettuce
2 fresh tomatoes, chopped
1/4 cup chopped green onion
1 cup fresh salsa or 1 (7-oz.)
    can green-chile salsa

Variation

For added convenience, use pre-cooked taco shells instead of forming your own. Or use flour tortillas warmed in the microwave for a soft-shell taco.

Heat 2 inches of oil to 375F (190C) in a large skillet. In a medium saucepan heat MEXICAN MEAT MIX and TACO SEASONING MIX; stir to combine.

Fry tortillas in hot oil. Using tongs, fold tortillas in half, then immediately open to 45-degree angle. Fry about 1 minute, until crisp. Drain on paper towels.

Place 2 tablespoons MEXICAN MEAT mixture in each cooked tortilla. Top with cheese, lettuce, tomatoes, green onion and salsa. Makes 12 to 15 tacos.

SOFT CHICKEN TACO

Soft tacos are the choice of many who want a tortilla that's not fried.

2 cups CHICKEN MIX,
    page 39
1/2 cup water
1 pkg. TACO SEASONING MIX,
    page 36
1/2 cup frozen peas
8 to 10 flour tortillas
6 oz. (1-1/2 cups) shredded
    Longhorn or Monterey Jack
    cheese
Shredded lettuce
1 cup fresh tomato salsa
6 to 8 radishes, sliced

In a medium skillet over medium-high heat combine CHICKEN MIX, water, TACO SEASONING MIX and peas. Reduce heat and simmer 10 minutes, stirring occasionally.

Warm tortillas in a microwave oven. Place about 1/4 cup chicken mixture in each tortilla. Fold in half. Top with cheese, lettuce, salsa and radishes. Makes 8 to 10 tacos.

Soft flour tortillas are available in various sizes. A few cooked peas added to the filling give color as well as authenticity.

CATHY'S MEATBALL SANDWICHES

This knife-and-fork sandwich is a big hit with our teenagers.

4 cups ITALIAN-STYLE MEAT MIX, page 42, thawed

2 tablespoons butter or margarine

1 cup fresh mushrooms, thinly sliced

1 small fresh zucchini, thinly sliced

6 to 8 French rolls or onion rolls, split

1/4 cup grated Romano cheese

In a medium saucepan, bring ITALIAN-STYLE MEAT MIX to a boil, about 10 minutes. In a small skillet, melt butter or margarine. Add mushrooms and zucchini; sauté until tender, about 2 minutes.

Spoon meat mixture evenly on bottom of rolls. Spoon sautéed vegetable mixture evenly over meat mixture. Sprinkle evenly with cheese. Cover with tops of rolls. Makes 6 to 8 servings.

EGGPLANT PARMESAN

Layers of goodness fill a tasty casserole. Fortunately, eggplant is available most of the year.

Oil for frying
1 medium eggplant, unpeeled
2 eggs, slightly beaten
2 tablespoons cold water
1-1/2 cups fine breadcrumbs
2-1/2 cups ITALIAN-STYLE
  MEAT MIX, page 42,
  thawed
1/2 cup grated Parmesan or
  Romano cheese
2 (6-oz.) pkgs. sliced
  mozzarella cheese

Preheat oven to 375F (190C). Pour small amount of oil in a large skillet. Cut eggplant into 15 slices about 1/4 inch thick; set aside. In a shallow dish or pie plate, beat eggs and water to combine; set aside. Pour breadcrumbs into another shallow dish or pie plate. Dip eggplant into egg mixture, then into breadcrumbs. Brown eggplant slices in hot oil, turning once, until tender when pierced with a fork. Add oil, if needed.

Butter a 2-quart casserole dish. Arrange 5 eggplant slices over bottom of dish, overlapping if necessary. Top with about 1/3 of the ITALIAN-STYLE MEAT MIX, 1/3 of the grated Parmesan or Romano cheese and 1/3 of the mozzarella cheese slices. Repeat, making 2 more layers. Bake uncovered 30 to 40 minutes. Makes 6 servings.

To prepare ahead, refrigerate the casserole overnight, then bake it about 45 minutes at 375F (190C).

SPAGHETTI CASSEROLE

Baked spaghetti is a favorite at the Harwards' house. They prepare 3 casseroles at a time and freeze the other 2 for later use.

1 (12-oz.) pkg. spaghetti
Water, lightly salted
1 tablespoon sugar
12 oz. (3 cups) shredded
    Cheddar cheese
2 cups ALL-PURPOSE
    GROUND-MEAT MIX,
    page 38, thawed
1/2 cup sliced fresh
    mushrooms
1 (10.5-oz.) can tomato soup
2 cups ITALIAN COOKING
    SAUCE MIX, page 41

Preheat oven to 300F (150C). Butter a 2-1/2- to 3-quart casserole. Cook spaghetti in lightly salted water according to package directions.

Put half of cooked spaghetti in bottom of prepared casserole. Sprinkle with half the sugar, half the cheese, half the GROUND-MEAT MIX, half the cheese, then half the mushrooms. Repeat layers. In a small bowl, combine tomato soup and ITALIAN COOKING SAUCE MIX. Pour over casserole. Cover. Bake 1-1/2 hours or until heated through. Makes about
6 servings.

SPAGHETTI ROYALE

Simply delicious. Add a tossed salad, Italian bread, a fantastic dessert and surprise unexpected company with this 30-minute dinner fit for a king.

4 cups ITALIAN-STYLE MEAT MIX, page 42, thawed
1 (12-oz.) pkg. spaghetti, cooked, drained
Grated Romano or Parmesan cheese
Chopped fresh basil or parsley

In a saucepan, simmer ITALIAN-STYLE MEAT MIX over low heat until hot, about 15 to 20 minutes. Pour cooked spaghetti onto a large platter. Spoon sauce over spaghetti. Sprinkle with cheese and basil or parsley. Makes 4 to 6 servings.

Spaghetti Royale

STUFFED MANICOTTI SHELLS

For special company or your special family.

12 manicotti shells
Water, salted slightly
2 cups ricotta cheese
1 egg, beaten
1/4 cup grated Romano cheese
3 tablespoons fresh chopped
    parsley or 1 tablespoon
    parsley flakes
4 cups ITALIAN COOKING
    SAUCE MIX, page 41,
    thawed
Romano and Parmesan cheese,
    for garnish

Cook manicotti shells in boiling salted water according to package directions. In a medium bowl, combine ricotta cheese, egg, Romano cheese and parsley. Blend well. Stuff into cooked manicotti shells.

Preheat oven to 350F (175C). Place 1 cup of the ITALIAN COOKING SAUCE MIX in bottom of a 13" x 9" baking dish. Place stuffed manicotti shells on top of sauce. Pour remaining sauce over top of shells. Sprinkle with Romano and Parmesan cheese, for garnish. Cover with foil and bake 30 minutes, until heated through. Makes 6 servings.

MEATBALL STEW

*Who said meatballs were only for
spaghetti? Enjoy a baked stew.*

1/4 cup water
2 tablespoons all-purpose flour
1 beef bouillon cube
1 (1-lb.) can tomatoes
**1 container MEATBALL MIX,
    page 44, thawed (about 20
    meatballs)**
2 cups pared and sliced carrots
2 onions, quartered
1 cup sliced celery
**1 cup peeled and cubed
    potatoes**

Preheat oven to 350F (175C). In a
medium saucepan, combine water, flour
and bouillon. Stir until well-blended.
Add tomatoes and cook about 5 minutes, until mixture thickens and boils,
stirring constantly.

Add MEATBALL MIX, carrots, onions,
celery and potatoes. Cover and simmer
15 minutes. Pour into a 3-quart casserole. Cover and bake 1-1/2 hours.
Makes 6 to 8 servings.

SWEET & SOUR MEATBALLS

A tangy sauce transforms meat-balls into a special dish!

1 tablespoon vegetable oil
1 cup fresh pineapple chunks
or 1 (10-oz.) can pineapple
chunks, drained, reserve
juice
2 tablespoons cornstarch
1 tablespoon soy sauce
3 tablespoons vinegar
6 tablespoons water
1/2 cup brown sugar, packed
1 container MEATBALL MIX,
page 44, thawed (about 20
meatballs)
1 large green pepper, sliced
About 4 cups cooked rice

In a large skillet, combine oil and reserved pineapple juice, adding water if necessary to make 1 cup. In a small bowl, combine cornstarch, soy sauce, vinegar, water and brown sugar. Stir into juice mixture. Cook over medium heat 5 to 7 minutes until thick, stirring constantly. Add MEATBALL MIX, pineapple chunks and green pepper. Simmer 20 minutes until heated through. Serve over hot cooked rice. Makes 6 servings.

MEAT LOAF WITH TANGY TOPPER SAUCE

You'll be amazed at the difference the sauce makes.

**1 pkg. MEAT LOAF MIX,
    page 43, thawed
Tangy Topper Sauce, below**

**Tangy Topper Sauce
1/4 cup ketchup
3 tablespoons brown sugar,
    firmly packed
1 tablespoon prepared mustard
1/2 teaspoon nutmeg**

Variation

Meat Loaf Tarts—Lightly grease
    muffin pan. Shape MEAT LOAF
    MIX into 12 equal portions.
    Place each in a muffin cup.
    Spread on Tangy Topper Sauce
    and bake at 350F (175C) for
    35 to 40 minutes until done.

Preheat oven to 350F (175C). Lightly
grease one 9" x 5" or one 7" x 3" loaf
pan. Put MEAT LOAF MIX in prepared
pan. Bake for 1 hour or until done.
Prepare Tangy Topper Sauce while meat
loaf is cooking. Spread Tangy Topper
Sauce over meat loaf during the last
5 to 7 minutes of baking. Makes about
6 servings.

Tangy Topper Sauce
In a small bowl, combine all ingredients.

Shape mixture into balls and place in
muffin cups.

185

STUFFED GREEN PEPPERS

Satisfy your appetite with an old favorite.

2 large green bell peppers
1 (8-oz.) can tomato sauce
1/4 cup water
1/4 teaspoon salt
1/8 teaspoon chili powder
1 pkg. MEAT LOAF MIX,
    page 43, thawed
1/2 cup instant rice, uncooked
Cherry tomatoes for garnish,
    if desired

In a saucepan, bring 2 quarts water to a rapid boil. Cut peppers in half lengthwise; remove membranes and seeds. With tongs place peppers in boiling water. Simmer 3 minutes. Remove peppers and discard water. Drain peppers, cut-side down on paper towels.

In a small bowl, combine tomato sauce, water, salt and chili powder; set aside. Preheat oven to 350F (175C).

Lightly grease a 9-inch-square baking dish. In a bowl combine MEAT LOAF MIX and rice. Fill peppers with rice mixture. Arrange peppers in prepared dish. Top with tomato mixture. Bake 40 minutes until rice is puffed and tender. Garnish with cherry tomatoes, if desired. Makes 4 peppers.

1. Cut in half lengthwise; remove membranes & seeds. Simmer 5 min.

2. Stuff peppers with meat mixture. Pour sauce over and bake.

RANCHER'S SLOPPY JOES

Feed a hungry crowd in minutes!

**2 cups MEAT SAUCE MIX,
    page 45, thawed**
1/4 cup brown sugar, packed
2 tablespoons vinegar
1/2 cup ketchup
1 tablespoon mustard
6 hamburger buns

In a medium saucepan, combine MEAT SAUCE MIX, brown sugar, vinegar, ketchup and mustard. Cover and cook over medium heat about 10 minutes, until heated through. Serve over hamburger buns. Makes 6 servings.

CHILI CON CARNE

Easy as one, two, three. Warms you from the inside out.

**2 cups MEAT SAUCE MIX,
    page 45, thawed, or
    MEXICAN MEAT MIX,
    page 46**
**2 cups cooked red kidney
    beans**
**1-1/2 teaspoons chili powder,
    more if desired**

Combine ingredients in a medium saucepan. Cover and cook over medium heat about 15 minutes, until heated through. Makes 6 servings.

HAMBURGER-NOODLE SKILLET

For variety buy whole wheat or vegetable-flavored noodles.

2 cups MEAT SAUCE MIX,
    page 45, thawed
2 cups cooked noodles
2 cups cooked mixed
    vegetables, with liquid
1 (8-oz.) can seasoned tomato
    sauce
2 oz. (1/2 cup) shredded
    Cheddar cheese
1 teaspoon chopped parsley

In a medium skillet, combine MEAT SAUCE MIX, cooked noodles, cooked mixed vegetables and tomato sauce. Cover and cook about 10 to 15 minutes, stirring occasionally, until heated through.

Sprinkle shredded cheese and parsley on top. Do not stir. Cover and heat long enough to melt cheese. Serve from skillet. Makes 5 to 6 servings.

HAMBURGER TRIO SKILLET

What could be easier?

2 cups MEAT SAUCE MIX,
    page 45, thawed
2 cups cooked rice
1 (17-oz.) can whole-kernel
    corn
1/4 teaspoon thyme
1/2 cup chopped green pepper

Combine all ingredients in a medium skillet. Cover and cook about 10 to 15 minutes, until heated through. Serve from skillet. Makes 4 to 6 servings.

MAIN DISHES - OTHER

This chapter contains a variety of main dishes for any occasion. Whether you're planning a dinner party for later in the week or just got home from work with no idea what to cook for supper, chances are you will be able to find inspiration among your supply of mixes.

If your freezer contains CUBED PORK MIX, you're on the way to Pork Chow Mein or Sweet & Sour Pork. For company fare, Stuffed Pork Chops are a cinch when you have HERBED STUFFING MIX and BEEF GRAVY MIX on hand.

Dry Mixes can be used in many ways—QUICK MIX in Self-Crust Cheese Tart, BUTTERMILK PANCAKE & WAFFLE MIX in Monte Cristo Sandwiches or CORN BREAD MIX to treat the kids to Corn Dogs.

You will also find seafood recipes in this chapter—Crunchy Fish Bake, Scallop Casserole and Shrimp & Vegetable Stir-Fry.

Convenience cooking with mixes would not be complete without stir-frying. It is quick and it is healthy. Keep a supply of ORIENTAL STIR-FRY MIX in your refrigerator to make it even easier. If you do not have a wok, use a heavy skillet. Prepare all of the ingredients before heating the oil because there won't be time once you begin cooking. The vegetables should be cooked just until crisp-tender, releasing their flavor while maintaining their bright color and texture.

Our new PINTO BEAN MIX was the inspiration for South of the Border Vegetarian Bake. You can substitute yogurt for the sour cream called for in the recipe. The combination of beans and rice make this a complete-protein dish.

MONTE CRISTO SANDWICHES

Make lunch memorable by giving special treatment to ham-and-cheese sandwiches.

12 slices white bread
Mayonnaise
12 thin slices natural Swiss cheese
6 thin slices baked ham
6 thin slices roast turkey
2 eggs, beaten
1 cup milk
1 cup BUTTERMILK PANCAKE & WAFFLE MIX, page 25
Butter for griddle
Powdered sugar, for garnish
Currant jelly, for garnish

Variations

Omit turkey slices and use 12 slices of ham.
Omit turkey and use chicken
Omit turkey and ham slices; use thinly sliced fresh mushrooms and zucchini.

Preheat griddle to 350F (175C). Spread mayonnaise on 1 side of each slice of bread. Assemble each sandwich, using 2 slices of Swiss cheese, 1 slice ham and 1 slice turkey. Trim crusts with knife, making the edges even. Cut sandwiches in half. Set aside.

Combine eggs and milk in a shallow dish. Add BUTTERMILK PANCAKE & WAFFLE MIX. Butter griddle. Dip each sandwich into the batter. Grill 3 to 4 minutes, until browned on both sides and cheese begins to melt. Lightly sprinkle with powdered sugar and currant jelly. Makes 6 sandwiches.

Monte Cristo Sandwiches

SOUTH OF THE BORDER VEGETARIAN BAKE

We like to include meatless meals every week and this one has a Mexican flair. In a hurry? Just pop it into the microwave to heat instead of baking.

4 cups cooked rice
3 cups PINTO BEAN MIX,
  page 49, thawed
1 cup mild green-chile salsa
2 cups Monterey Jack or Colby
  cheese
1/2 cup chopped onion
1 green pepper, diced
1 large tomato, diced
Sour cream, garnish
Guacamole, page 174, or
  sliced avocado, garnish

Preheat oven to 350F (175C). In a 2-quart casserole dish, layer cooked rice and PINTO BEAN MIX. Spread green-chile salsa over the top and sprinkle with cheese.

Bake in preheated oven 20 to 30 minutes or until heated through and cheese is melted. Sprinkle onion, green pepper and tomato on top.

Garnish with sour cream and Guacamole or avocado just before serving. Makes 6 to 8 servings.

You can tell if the filling is set by shaking the pie with a gentle back and forth motion.

SPANISH CHEESE PIE

A quiche with a Spanish flavor.

**Single Freezer Pie Crust,
   unbaked, page 309**
**6 oz. (1-1/2 cups) shredded
   Monterey Jack cheese**
**1 (4-oz.) can diced or chopped
   green chiles**
**4 oz. (1 cup) shredded Cheddar
   cheese**
4 eggs
1-1/2 cups half-and-half
**1/4 cup sliced pimiento-stuffed
   olives, if desired**
1/4 teaspoon salt
1/8 teaspoon ground cumin

Prepare pie crust in a 9-inch pie plate; set aside. Preheat oven to 350F (175C). Sprinkle Monterey Jack cheese in bottom of unbaked crust. Top with green chiles and 1/2 cup Cheddar cheese.

In a medium bowl, beat eggs thoroughly. Stir in half-and-half, olives, salt and cumin. Pour over cheese in pie crust. Top with remaining 1/2 cup Cheddar cheese. Bake 50 to 60 minutes until set. Makes 4 to 6 servings.

SCALLOP CASSEROLE

For a festive look, bake our delicacy in scallop shells.

1 cup chopped onion
1 tablespoon butter or
    margarine
1/2 cup water
1/2 teaspoon salt
1 lb. frozen scallops, thawed
4 eggs, slightly beaten
2 cups HERBED STUFFING MIX,
    page 33
4 slices Gouda or Colby cheese

Preheat oven to 350F (175C). In a medium saucepan, sauté onion in butter or margarine until tender. Add water and salt. Bring to a boil and add scallops. Cook 5 minutes over medium-high heat. Lightly butter a 2-quart casserole or baking dish.

Combine eggs and HERBED STUFFING MIX in casserole. Stir in scallop mixture. Bake 25 to 30 minutes. Remove from oven. Top with cheese slices. Return to oven just long enough to melt cheese. Makes 4 servings.

For a less-expensive dish substitute frozen cooked shrimp or imitation crab for the fresh shrimp.

SHRIMP & VEGETABLE STIR-FRY

A beautiful combination of colors and textures.

About 1-1/4 lb. broccoli
4 tablespoons vegetable oil
1 medium onion, thinly sliced
1/4 lb. fresh mushrooms, thinly
  sliced
2 tablespoons vegetable oil
3/4 lb. fresh shrimp, shelled,
  deveined
1-1/2 cups ORIENTAL STIR-FRY
  MIX, page 65
2 cups fresh bean sprouts
3 cups hot cooked rice

Cut broccoli stems into pieces. Cut flowerets into 3/4-inch pieces; set aside. In a large skillet or wok, heat 4 tablespoons oil over medium heat. Add cut broccoli stems, sliced onion and sliced mushrooms. Cook and stir until stems are crisp-tender, 5 to 7 minutes. Add 2 tablespoons oil.

When oil is hot, add shrimp and broccoli flowerets. Cook and stir 5 to 7 minutes longer. Add ORIENTAL STIR-FRY MIX. Stir gently until mixture thickens slightly. Gently stir in bean sprouts; cook 1 minute longer. To serve, spoon hot mixture over cooked rice. Makes 4 to 6 servings.

195

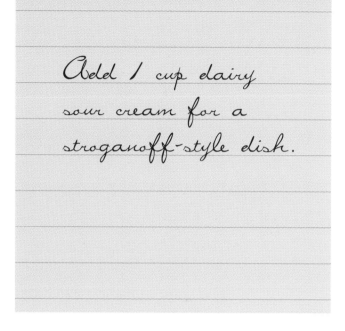

Add 1 cup dairy sour cream for a stroganoff-style dish.

SWEDISH MEATBALLS

Nevada serves these over one of the herb-flavored pastas, such as lemon-pepper or spinach.

1 cup WHITE SAUCE MIX, page 63
2 cups beef broth
1 cup finely chopped fresh mushrooms
1/8 teaspoon ground nutmeg
1 container MEATBALL MIX, page 44, thawed, about 20 meatballs
1 (12-oz.) pkg. extra-wide egg noodles

In a large saucepan combine WHITE SAUCE MIX and beef broth. Cook over medium heat, stirring constantly, until mixture thickens. Add mushrooms and nutmeg. Stir in MEATBALL MIX and continue cooking until heated through.

While mixture is cooking, prepare noodles according to package directions. Serve mixture over hot, drained noodles. Makes about 4 to 6 servings.

TUNA-CHEESE SWIRLS

A treat for your eyes as well as your mouth.

1 (12.5-oz.) can light tuna, drained
1 cup frozen peas
1-1/4 cups CHICKEN BROTH, page 39
1/2 cup cooked rice
1-1/2 cups QUICK MIX, page 21
1/3 cup milk or water
3 oz. (3/4 cup) shredded Cheddar or Fontina cheese

Preheat oven to 425F (220C). Butter a 1-1/2-quart casserole. Combine tuna, peas, broth and rice in a medium bowl. Pour into prepared casserole.

In a small bowl, combine QUICK MIX and milk or water. Stir until blended. On a lightly floured surface, knead dough gently 10 times. Roll out to 6" x 10", about 1/4 inch thick. Sprinkle with cheese and roll like a jelly roll. Seal edge. Cut into 1/2-inch slices. Place slices on top of casserole. Bake 15 to 20 minutes, until biscuits are golden brown. Makes 4 to 6 servings

With a little change this becomes a bean tostada. Omit flour tortilla. Fry a corn tortilla 'til crisp. Top with remaining ingredients.

WHOLE-BEAN VEGGIE BURROS

We developed this recipe after a visit to our favorite Mexican restaurant.

6 flour tortillas
3 cups PINTO BEAN MIX,
   page 49, thawed
6 strips roasted green chiles
1 avocado, cut into 12 wedges
Shredded Cheddar cheese
Shredded lettuce, garnish
Green-chile salsa, garnish

Heat flour tortillas in microwave until soft. In a medium saucepan heat PINTO BEAN MIX until heated through.

Using a slotted spoon, place about 1/2 cup of bean mix on top of heated tortilla. Top with a strip of green chile, 2 wedges of avocado and shredded cheese. Serve on bed of shredded lettuce. Top with salsa. Makes 6 servings.

BROCCOLI & HAM ROLLS

An easy, delicious dish that is great for entertaining

2 lb. fresh broccoli spears, or 2 (1-lb.) pkgs. frozen broccoli spears
1/2 cup WHITE SAUCE MIX, page 63
1 cup cool water
1-1/2 teaspoons fresh basil or 1/2 teaspoon dried basil leaves
Dash of pepper
2 tablespoons butter or margarine
2 medium onions, cut and separated into rings
6 slices Swiss cheese
6 (1/4-inch) slices of lean ham

Cook broccoli until crisp-tender or prepare frozen broccoli according to package directions; set aside. In a saucepan, combine WHITE SAUCE MIX, water, basil and pepper. Cook over low heat until smooth, stirring constantly.

In a saucepan, melt butter or margarine. Sauté onion rings until tender. Stir into WHITE SAUCE mixture. Set aside and keep warm.

Preheat oven to 350F (175C). Spray a 13" x 9" baking dish with vegetable cooking spray. Place a slice of cheese on top of each ham slice. Place two broccoli spears on cheese (flowerettes extending beyond side edges), roll up and secure with a wooden pick.

Place rolls in baking dish, seam-side down. Do not cover. Bake about 25 minutes until heated. Place rolls on serving plate and top with onion sauce. Serve immediately. Makes 6 servings.

A no-fuss treat. Make these early in the day and heat just before serving.

BAKED PORK CHOPS

*A crisp coating helps to keep
these chops tender and juicy.
Serve with broccoli, stewed
apricots and coleslaw.*

**2-1/2 tablespoons butter or
   margarine**
2-1/2 tablespoons vegetable oil
**1-1/2 cups CRISP COATING
   MIX, page 31**
2 eggs
1 tablespoon milk
**6 pork chops, shoulder cut,
   3/4-inch thick, trimmed**

Preheat oven to 400F (205C). Combine butter or margarine and oil on large baking sheet with raised edges. Place in preheating oven until mixture melts.

Pour CRISP COATING MIX into a large plastic food bag; set aside. In a shallow bowl, beat eggs and milk until blended. Rinse pork chops; pat dry with paper towels. Dip each chop in egg mixture; drain briefly.

Place 1 chop at a time in plastic bag, shaking until coated. Arrange on baking sheet, turning to coat with oil mixture. Bake 30 minutes in preheated oven until golden brown and crispy, turning once. Makes 4 to 6 servings.

STUFFED PORK CHOPS

Team these chops with Brussels sprouts and pickled beets.

**4 pork chops (double-thick),
    1 to 1-1/2 inches thick**
1/4 cup raisins
Supper Stuffing, page 125
**1/2 cup BEEF GRAVY MIX,
    page 61**

Preheat oven to 350F (175C). Butter a 9-inch-square baking dish; set aside. Cut pockets in sides of pork chops, 3 inches wide and 2-1/2 inches deep.

Stir raisins into Supper Stuffing. Spoon 3 to 4 tablespoons stuffing into each pocket. Spoon remaining stuffing into bottom of prepared baking dish. Spoon BEEF GRAVY MIX evenly over all sides of stuffed pork chops.

Place coated chops on stuffing. Cover with foil. Bake about 1-1/2 hours in preheated oven until well-browned. Makes 4 servings.

1. Using a sharp knife, cut large pockets inside of each pork chop.

2. Stuff pockets. Place on stuffing in baking pan.

PORK CHOW MEIN

Fried rice is a nice accompaniment to this recipe.

**2 cups CUBED PORK MIX,
    page 47, thawed**
1-1/2 cups water
3 tablespoons soy sauce
4 tablespoons oil or margarine
**4 to 5 celery stalks, sliced
    diagonally 1/4 inch thick**
**1 cup thinly sliced fresh
    mushrooms**
**1 (8-oz.) can water chestnuts,
    drained, thinly sliced**
2 cups fresh bean sprouts
4 green onions, thinly sliced
**1 (9.5-oz.) can chow-mein
    noodles**

In a saucepan, combine CUBED PORK MIX, water and soy sauce. Simmer over low heat about 5 minutes.

In a medium skillet, heat oil or margarine. Add celery, sauté until crisp-tender, about 10 minutes. Add fresh mushrooms and water chestnuts. Sauté 2 minutes, stirring occasionally. Stir into pork mixture. Stir occasionally over medium heat 5 minutes.

Gently stir in bean sprouts and green onion slices. Simmer 1 minute longer. Serve over chow-mein noodles. Makes about 6 servings.

SWEET & SOUR PORK

Serve this tangy sweet-and-sour sauce over rice, noodles or spaghetti squash.

2 cups fresh pineapple chunks or 1 (20-oz.) can pineapple chunks

2 cups CUBED PORK MIX, page 47, thawed

2 tablespoons white vinegar

1 tablespoon soy sauce

1/3 cup brown sugar, firmly packed

1/4 cup ketchup

1 medium green bell pepper, cut in julienne strips

4 cups hot cooked rice

Drain juice from pineapple into a large saucepan. Stir in CUBED PORK MIX, vinegar, soy sauce, brown sugar and ketchup. Stir occasionally over medium heat about 10 minutes.

Stir in drained pineapple chunks and pepper strips. Simmer about 2 minutes until heated through. Serve over hot cooked rice. Makes 4 to 6 servings.

Break out the chopsticks, buy some fortune cookies and have a party.

QUICK CHOW MEIN

Enjoy the fresh flavors of Oriental vegetables.

4 oz. fresh mushrooms, chopped

1 tablespoon grated fresh ginger or 1 teaspoon ground ginger

2 tablespoons soy sauce

2 cups beef broth

2 cups CUBED PORK MIX, page 47, or ALL-PURPOSE GROUND-MEAT MIX, page 38, thawed

2 cups shredded Chinese cabbage

2 cups chopped celery

1/2 lb. fresh bean sprouts

1 (8-oz.) can water chestnuts, drained, sliced

2 tablespoons cornstarch

1/4 cup cold water

4 cups hot cooked rice

2 tablespoons sliced blanched almonds, for garnish

In a large skillet or wok, combine mushrooms, ginger, soy sauce and beef broth. Cover and simmer over medium heat 5 minutes. Add CUBED PORK MIX or GROUND-MEAT MIX, cabbage, celery, bean sprouts and water chestnuts. Simmer until vegetables are hot, about 5 minutes.

Stir cornstarch into cold water to dissolve. Stir into meat mixture. Continue stirring until mixture boils. Cover; simmer over low heat 5 minutes longer. Serve over hot cooked rice. Garnish with sliced almonds. Makes 4 to 6 servings.

Serve over hot rice. Garnish with sliced almonds.

VEAL PARMIGIANA

Serve this for that special occasion. Your friends will love it.

6 thin veal cutlets
1 egg, slightly beaten
2 to 3 tablespoons milk
3/4 cup seasoned dry
   breadcrumbs
3/4 cup grated Parmesan
   cheese
Butter or olive oil for frying
2 cups ITALIAN COOKING
   SAUCE MIX, page 41,
   thawed
8 oz. mozzarella cheese, sliced

Pound veal cutlets with wooden mallet or other flat object, until thin. Combine egg and milk in a small bowl. In another small bowl, combine dry breadcrumbs and grated Parmesan cheese. Dip veal into egg mixture, then into breadcrumb mixture. Let veal stand at least 15 minutes before cooking.

Preheat oven to 400F (205C). Heat butter or olive oil in a large skillet. Sauté veal cutlets in butter or oil about 2 minutes on each side until crisp. Put veal into a 13" x 9" baking pan. Pour ITALIAN COOKING SAUCE MIX over top. Place a slice of mozzarella cheese on each cutlet. Bake 10 to 15 minutes, until veal is golden brown and cheese is melted. Makes 4 to 6 servings.

For a corn dog on a stick, insert a long wooden skewer about three-fourths of the length into a frank-furter. Do this before dipping into batter.

CORN DOGS

Select whichever type of frank-furters you wish—beef, pork, turkey or chicken.

Vegetable oil for frying
4 frankfurters
**1/4 cup CORN BREAD MIX,
    page 15**
2 tablespoons all-purpose flour
1/8 teaspoon dry mustard
Pinch of paprika
1 egg, slightly beaten
1 tablespoon water

Pour oil 2 to 3 inches deep in a deep-fryer or medium-size heavy saucepan. Heat. Dry frankfurters with paper towels; set aside. In a pie plate, combine CORN BREAD MIX, flour, dry mustard and paprika. Stir in egg and water until thoroughly combined. Batter will be stiff.

Roll frankfurters in batter, covering com-pletely. Use tongs to lower into hot oil. Turning once, fry until golden brown, 2 to 3 minutes. Drain on paper towels. Makes 4 corn dogs.

LAST-MINUTE LASAGNA

Simplicity at its best, the blend of flavors is superb.

**6 cups ITALIAN COOKING
  SAUCE MIX, page 41**
**1 (8-oz.) pkg. lasagna noodles,
  cooked**
1 lb. ricotta cheese
**12 oz. (3 cups) shredded
  mozzarella cheese**
**3 oz. (1 cup) grated Romano
  and Parmesan cheese**

Variation

Substitute 6 cups ITALIAN-STYLE
  MEAT MIX, page 42, for ITAL-
  IAN COOKING SAUCE MIX.

Preheat oven to 350F (175C). Lightly butter a 13" x 9" baking pan. Spread 1/3 ITALIAN COOKING SAUCE MIX in bottom of pan. Cover with 1/3 lasagna noodles. Add 1/3 ricotta cheese, thinned with water for easier spreading, if necessary. Add 1/3 mozzarella cheese and 1/3 Romano and Parmesan cheese.

Repeat layers twice, topping with Romano and Parmesan cheese. Cover with foil. Bake 30 to 35 minutes, until heated. Let stand 10 minutes before serving. Makes 8 to 10 servings.

When you can find them, use spinach lasagna noodles. They add great color and delicate flavor.

Make this an impressive vegetarian dish by substituting fresh sliced tomatoes for the bacon and adding 2 to 3 teaspoons of dried basil or tarragon leaves.

SELF-CRUST CHEESE TART

Ideal for a light supper. Serve with a crisp red-and-green coleslaw.

Paprika
4 oz. (1 cup) shredded Swiss cheese
4 strips bacon, cooked and crumbled
3 eggs
1/4 teaspoon salt
1/4 teaspoon ground nutmeg, if desired
1-1/2 cups milk
1 teaspoon dried minced onion
1/3 cup QUICK MIX, page 21

Preheat oven to 325F (165C). Generously butter a 9-inch pie plate. Sprinkle bottom and sides of prepared pie plate with paprika. Layer cheese and bacon on bottom of pie plate.

Combine eggs, salt, nutmeg, milk, onion and QUICK MIX in a blender. Blend at medium speed about 1 minute, until thoroughly mixed. Pour over cheese and bacon in pie plate. Bake 30 to 40 minutes, until wooden pick inserted in center comes out clean. Serve hot. Makes 6 servings.

CRUNCHY FISH BAKE

Crisp on the outside—moist on the inside.

2-1/2 tablespoons butter or margarine
2-1/2 tablespoons vegetable oil
1-1/2 cups CRISP COATING MIX, page 31
2 eggs
1 tablespoon milk
1-1/2 lb. boneless red snapper, sole, halibut or turbot fillets

Preheat oven to 500F (260C). Combine butter or margarine and oil on a large baking sheet with raised sides. Place in preheating oven until mixture melts.

Pour CRISP COATING MIX into a large plastic food-storage bag; set aside. In a shallow bowl, beat eggs and milk until blended. Rinse fish; pat dry with paper towels. Dip each fish fillet in egg mixture; drain briefly. Place 1 fillet at a time in plastic bag, shaking until coated.

Arrange on baking sheet, turning to coat with oil mixture. Bake 7 to 10 minutes in preheated oven until fish flakes when tested with a fork, turning once. Makes 4 to 6 servings.

BREAKFAST & BRUNCH

The aroma of freshly baked rolls coming from your kitchen is the best way to wake up your family. Is it too hard for you to get up early enough to do that? With Master Mixes on your pantry shelf, you have a whole collection of Breakfast and Brunch delights to serve your family or guests in minutes. You already know that a well-balanced breakfast contributes to your family's well-being throughout the day. A mix you've made is a great way to begin those easy, nutritious meals.

Look closely at the rolls and breads in this chapter, in Yeast Breads & Quick Breads and in Muffins & Rolls. By starting with the basic dough from HOT ROLL MIX, you can make a variety of baked goods, such as Cinnamon Rolls, Butterscotch Butter Balls and Swedish Cinnamon Twists.

Pancakes and waffles made from our WHOLE-GRAIN PANCAKE MIX, are a great choice for breakfast. Serve these light, tender pancakes and waffles with a variety of toppings. Puff Pancakes create a brunch spectacular right before your eyes. Try them for a late-evening supper, too. For best results, let pancake batters stand about five minutes before cooking.

For weekends with company, the Sausage-Cheese Breakfast Strata is wonderfully different. It is quickly prepared the night before and just popped in the oven to bake in the morning. Let mixes help you entertain with ease.

Prepare extra waffles or French toast. Cool on racks to prevent sogginess. Place on baking sheets in a single layer; cover. Freeze until solid, then store in plastic freezer bags or containers. To serve, thaw them in microwave or at room temperature for a few minutes, then pop in toaster to crisp.

ALMOND KRINGLE

The filling puffs up and makes a soft, flaky layer.

1 pkg. CREAM-CHEESE PASTRY MIX, page 50, thawed
1/2 cup water
1/4 cup butter or margarine
1/2 cup all-purpose flour
2 eggs
1/4 teaspoon almond extract
Kringle Icing, below
1/4 cup sliced almonds

Kringle Icing
1/2 cup powdered sugar
1-1/2 teaspoons cream or milk
2 teaspoons butter or margarine
1/2 teaspoon almond extract

Preheat oven to 350F (175C). Roll out CREAM-CHEESE PASTRY MIX to 14" x 4". Place rolled-out dough on a large baking sheet. Crimp and shape sides of dough. In a saucepan, combine water and butter or margarine. Bring to a boil. Add flour all at once, stir vigorously until mixture forms a ball and leaves side of pan. Remove from heat. Add eggs 1 at a time, beating well after each addition. Beat in almond extract. Spread mixture over pastry. Bake 40 to 45 minutes in preheated oven until golden brown. Cool 5 minutes. Prepare Kringle Icing. Spread over filling. Sprinkle with almonds. Cut into 1-1/2-inch slices. Makes about 6 servings.

Kringle Icing
Combine all ingredients, beating until smooth.

1 Roll dough on a large baking sheet. Crimp and shape edges.

2. Spread frosting over baked filling. Cut Kringle diagonally.

211

BUTTERSCOTCH BUTTER BALLS

Finger-lickin' good!

**1 tablespoon active dry yeast
 or 1 (1/4-oz.) package**
**1-1/2 cups lukewarm water
 110F (45C)**
2 eggs, beaten
**1/4 cup vegetable oil or melted
 margarine**
**5 to 6 cups HOT ROLL MIX,
 page 17**
**1 (3-oz.) pkg. regular butter-
 scotch pudding**
**1 cup butter or margarine,
 melted**
1 cup brown sugar, packed
**1 (1-1/2-oz.) pkg. pecans,
 chopped**
2 teaspoons ground cinnamon

In a large bowl, dissolve yeast in water. Blend in eggs and oil or margarine. Add 5 cups HOT ROLL MIX. Stir well. Add more HOT ROLL MIX to make a soft dough. Knead about 5 minutes, until dough is smooth. Lightly butter bowl. Put dough in bowl and turn to butter top. Cover dough with a damp towel and let rise in a warm place until doubled, about 1 hour.

Punch down dough. Divide into 48 balls. Place balls on a baking sheet. Cover with plastic wrap and freeze. When frozen, transfer to bags for storage in freezer. Use within 1 to 2 months.

About 8 hours before serving, or the night before, place 24 frozen balls in each of 2 unbuttered Bundt pans. Sprinkle half of butterscotch pudding on each pan of frozen rolls. Combine melted butter or margarine and brown sugar in a small bowl. Pour half of mixture over each pan of rolls. Sprinkle pecans and cinnamon over each pan.

Cover with towels and let rise about 8 hours or overnight. Preheat oven to 350F (175C). Bake about 30 minutes, until golden brown. Makes 2 butterscotch rings.

Sprinkle on butterscotch pudding, pour mixture over rolls.

CINNAMON ROLLS

The family's breakfast favorite.
Watch them disappear!

1 tablespoon active dry yeast
   or 1 (1/4-oz.) package
1-1/2 cup lukewarm water
   110F (45C)
2 eggs, beaten
1/4 cup vegetable oil or melted
   margarine
5 to 6 cups HOT ROLL MIX,
   page 17
2 tablespoons butter or
   margarine, melted
1/2 cup brown sugar, packed
2 teaspoons ground cinnamon
1/2 cup raisins, if desired
1/4 cup chopped nuts,
   if desired
Sweet Glaze, below

Sweet Glaze
2 cups sifted powdered sugar
1/2 teaspoon vanilla extract
About 4 tablespoons milk

In a large bowl, dissolve yeast in water. Blend in eggs and oil or margarine. Add 5 cups HOT ROLL MIX. Stir well. Add more HOT ROLL MIX to make a soft dough. Knead about 5 minutes, until dough is smooth. Lightly butter bowl. Put dough in bowl and turn to butter top. Cover dough with a damp towel and let rise in a warm place until doubled, about 1 hour.

Grease 2 baking sheets. Punch down dough. Let stand 10 minutes. On a lightly floured surface, roll out dough to 12" x 24" about 1/4 inch thick. Brush surface with butter or margarine. Sprinkle on brown sugar, cinnamon and raisins and nuts, if desired. Roll dough like a jelly roll and cut into 24 1-inch slices. Place on prepared baking sheets. Cover with a damp towel and let rise in a warm place until doubled, 30 to 60 minutes. Preheat oven to 375F (190C). Bake 20 to 25 minutes, until golden brown. Prepare Sweet Glaze, and brush on warm rolls.
Makes about 24 rolls.

Sweet Glaze
In a small bowl combine powdered sugar, vanilla and enough milk to make a thin mixture.

WHOLE-WHEAT CINNAMON ROLLS

Incredible flavor and texture.

**2 tablespoons active dry yeast
or 2 (1/4-oz.) packages**
**1-1/2 cups lukewarm water
110F (45C)**
2 eggs, beaten
**1/3 cup melted butter or
vegetable oil**
**5 to 6 cups WHOLE-WHEAT
HOT ROLL MIX, page 18**
Cinnamon Butter, below
Caramel Topping, below

Cinnamon Butter
**5 tablespoons butter or
margarine, melted**
1 teaspoon ground cinnamon
1/2 cup packed brown sugar
3/4 cup raisins
1/2 cup chopped nuts

Caramel Topping
1 cup whipping cream
1/2 cup packed brown sugar
1/2 cup chopped nuts

In a bowl, dissolve yeast in water. Blend in eggs and butter or oil. Add 5 cups WHOLE-WHEAT HOT ROLL MIX. Stir well; let rest 2 minutes. Add more HOT ROLL MIX to make a soft dough. Knead 7 to 10 minutes. Put dough in buttered bowl and turn to butter top. Cover with damp towel and let rise until doubled, about 1 hour.

Combine ingredients for Cinnamon Butter; set aside. Combine ingredients for Caramel Topping; spread in 15" x 10" baking sheet. Punch down dough. Let rest 10 minutes. On a floured surface, roll dough to 12" x 20" about 1 inch thick. Spread with Cinnamon Butter. Roll dough tightly. Cut into 20 slices. Place on prepared baking sheets. Cover. Let rise until doubled, 30 to 50 minutes. Preheat oven to 375F (190C). Bake 20 to 25 minutes. Cool. Invert rolls onto platter. Serve warm. Makes 20 rolls.

Cool rolls
5 minutes.
Invert onto
a platter.
Serve warm.

PLUCKIT

A fun pull-apart bread for snacking or mealtime.

**1 tablespoon active dry yeast
or 1 (1/4-oz.) package**
**1-1/2 cups lukewarm water
110F (45C)**
2 eggs, beaten
**1/4 cup vegetable oil or melted
margarine**
**5 to 6 cups HOT ROLL MIX,
page 17**
3 teaspoons ground cinnamon
3/4 cup sugar
**1/2 cup butter or margarine,
melted**

Variation

To make a coffee cake, roll the
balls of dough in cinnamon-
sugar mixture, then in 1/2 cup
chopped nuts.

In a large bowl, dissolve yeast in water.
Blend in eggs and oil or margarine. Add
5 cups of HOT ROLL MIX. Stir well. Add
more HOT ROLL MIX to make a soft
dough. Knead about 5 minutes, until
dough is smooth. Lightly butter bowl.
Put dough in bowl and turn to butter
top. Cover dough with a damp towel
and let rise in a warm place until
doubled, about 1 hour.

Punch down dough. Roll dough into
walnut-size balls. Combine cinnamon
and sugar in a bowl. Dip balls in melted
butter or margarine and roll in cinnamon-sugar mixture. Pile loosely in an
ungreased tube pan. Let rise until doubled, about 30 minutes.

Preheat oven to 400F (205C). Bake
about 10 minutes. Lower temperature to
350F (175C) and continue baking 30
minutes until golden. Loosen edges with
a knife and turn out onto a plate. Rolls
can be plucked off one at a time.
Makes 1 large pan of rolls.

SWEDISH CINNAMON TWISTS

Our beautiful cover photo.

**1 tablespoon active dry yeast
or 1 (1/4-oz.) package**
1 tablespoon sugar
**1/4 cup lukewarm water
110F (45C)**
1 cup buttermilk
1/4 teaspoon baking soda
**1/4 cup butter or margarine,
melted**
2 eggs, beaten
**4 to 5 cups HOT ROLL MIX,
page 17**
Cinnamon Filling, below
3 tablespoons butter, melted
Powdered-Sugar Glaze, below

Cinnamon Filling
1/2 cup brown sugar, packed
1/2 teaspoon ground cinnamon
1/2 cup chopped nuts

Powdered-Sugar Glaze
**1-1/2 cups sifted powdered
sugar**
**1/2 tablespoon butter or
margarine, melted**
2 tablespoons hot water

In a cup, dissolve yeast and sugar in water. Set aside. Bring buttermilk to a boil; it should curdle. Add baking soda and 1/4 cup melted butter or margarine. Add eggs. When mixture is lukewarm, add dissolved yeast. Stir in 4 cups HOT ROLL MIX until the soft dough forms a ball. On a floured surface, knead 5 minutes. Add more HOT ROLL MIX if necessary to make a soft dough. Lightly butter bowl. Put dough in bowl and turn to butter top. Cover and let rise until doubled, about 1 hour.

Grease 2 baking sheets. Combine ingredients for Cinnamon Filling. Punch down dough. Roll out to 12" x 10". Brush dough with 3 tablespoons melted butter. Sprinkle Cinnamon Filling lengthwise over half of dough to within 1/2 inch of long edge. Fold in half lengthwise to cover filling. Seal edges. Cut dough into 18 strips about 3/4 inch wide. Twist each strip twice and place 1 inch apart on prepared baking sheets.

Cover; let rise until doubled, 30 to 40 minutes. Preheat oven to 375F (190C). Bake 10 to 12 minutes. Combine ingredients for Powdered-Sugar Glaze; brush on warm rolls. Makes 18 twists.

Swedish Cinnamon Twists

SUNSHINE COFFEE CAKE

A moist muffin-textured cake with a limitless number of variations.

3 cups QUICK MIX, page 21
1/3 cup sugar
1 egg, slightly beaten
1 cup milk or water
1 teaspoon vanilla extract
Cinnamon Crumble Topping,
   below

Preheat oven to 350F (175C). Spray an 8-inch-square pan with vegetable cooking spray. In a medium bowl, combine QUICK MIX and sugar until evenly distributed. In a small bowl, combine egg, milk or water and vanilla. Stir until just blended. Add liquid ingredients all at once to the dry ingredients. Fold mixture together until blended. Prepare Cinnamon Crumble Topping. Spread half the batter in the prepared pan. Spread half of topping over the batter. Top with remaining batter and topping. Bake 40 to 50 minutes. Makes one 8-inch cake.

Cinnamon Crumble Topping
1/3 cup all-purpose flour
1/2 cup dry breadcrumbs or
   cookie or cake crumbs
1/2 cup brown sugar, packed
1 teaspoon ground cinnamon
1/4 cup butter or margarine

Cinnamon Crumble Topping
In a medium bowl combine flour, crumbs, brown sugar and cinnamon. With a pastry blender, cut in butter or margarine until mixture is crumbly.

Variations

Fruit Crumble Topping—Prepare 1-1/2 cups sweetened, sliced fresh or frozen fruit. Spread over first half of batter and top with Cinnamon Crumble Topping as in basic recipe.

Apple Crumble Topping—Add 1-1/2 cups peeled, chopped apples and 1/2 cup raisins to Cinnamon Crumble Topping. Spread mixture on top before baking for a crusty topping, or on bottom of pan for a moist coffeecake.

Date-Nut Topping—Omit Cinnamon Crumble Topping. In a bowl, combine 1 cup brown sugar and 1/4 cup all-purpose flour. Mix in 1/2 cup chopped nuts, 1/2 cup pitted dates and 1 teaspoon vanilla. Cut in 1/4 cup butter or margarine until mixture is crumbly.

Chocolate Swirl Topping—Omit Cinnamon Crumble Topping. Melt 1/3 cup semisweet chocolate chips in a small saucepan. In a bowl, combine 1/3 cup flaked coconut, 1/4 cup chopped nuts, 1/4 cup sugar and 1 tablespoon melted butter or margarine. Pour coffeecake batter into prepared pan. Spoon melted chocolate over batter. With a knife, cut through batter several times for a marbled effect. Sprinkle coconut mixture over the top, and bake as directed.

If you create your own toppings you will have a different treat for each day of the week.

BUTTERMILK WAFFLES

All waffles should be like these—light, crisp and golden outside, tender and moist inside.

**2-1/2 cups BUTTERMILK
    PANCAKE & WAFFLE MIX,
    page 25**
2 cups water
3 eggs, separated
1/4 cup vegetable oil

Variation

Nut or Berry Waffles—Add 1/2
    cup chopped pecans or dried
    blueberries to batter.

Preheat waffle baker. In a large bowl, combine BUTTERMILK PANCAKE & WAFFLE MIX, water, egg yolks and oil. Beat with a wire whisk until just blended. In medium bowl, beat egg whites until stiff. Fold into egg-yolk mixture. Bake according to waffle-baker instructions. Makes 3 or 4 large waffles.

WHOLE-GRAIN WAFFLES

Separating the eggs and folding in the egg whites guarantees a light, fluffy waffle.

**3 cups WHOLE-GRAIN
    PANCAKE MIX, page 26**
3 cups buttermilk
3 eggs, separated
**1/4 cup melted butter or
    vegetable oil**

Preheat waffle baker. In a large bowl, combine WHOLE-GRAIN PANCAKE MIX, buttermilk, egg yolks and melted butter or oil. Beat with a wire whisk until just blended. In medium bowl, beat egg whites until stiff. Fold into egg-yolk mixture. Bake according to waffle-baker instructions. Makes 3 or 4 large waffles.

QUICK PANCAKES

*Light, crisp and brown outside,
moist and tender inside.*

**2-1/4 cups QUICK MIX,
    page 21**
1 tablespoon sugar
1 egg, beaten
1-1/2 cups milk or water

Combine QUICK MIX and sugar in a
medium bowl. Mix well. Combine egg
and milk or water in a small bowl. Add
all at once to dry ingredients. Blend
well. Let stand 5 to 10 minutes. Cook
on hot, oiled griddle 3 to 4 minutes,
until browned on both sides. Makes ten
to twelve 4-inch pancakes.

WHOLE-GRAIN PANCAKES

*This nutritious pancake will be a
very pleasant way to get your
daily fiber.*

**1-1/2 cups WHOLE-GRAIN
    PANCAKE MIX, page 26**
1-1/2 cups buttermilk
1 egg
**2 tablespoons melted butter or
    vegetable oil**

Put WHOLE-GRAIN PANCAKE MIX in a
small bowl. Set aside. In a small bowl
combine buttermilk, egg and melted
butter or vegetable oil. Add all at once
to dry ingredients. Blend well. Let stand
5 to 10 minutes. Cook on hot, oiled
griddle 3 to 4 minutes, until browned on
both sides. Makes about twelve 4-inch
pancakes.

BUTTERMILK PANCAKES

Serve these at a pancake supper with a variety of syrups.

1 egg, beaten
2 tablespoons vegetable oil
1 cup water, more if desired
1-1/2 cups BUTTERMILK
    PANCAKE & WAFFLE MIX,
    page 25
Syrup

In a medium bowl, combine egg, oil and 1 cup water. With a wire whisk, stir in BUTTERMILK PANCAKE & WAFFLE MIX until blended. Let stand 5 minutes. Stir in additional water for a thinner batter. Preheat griddle according to manufacturer's instructions. Lightly oil griddle.

Pour about 1/3 cup batter onto hot griddle to make 1 pancake. Cook until edge is dry and bubbles form. Turn with a wide spatula. Cook 35 to 45 seconds longer until browned on both sides. Repeat with remaining batter. Serve with syrup. Makes ten 4-inch pancakes.

PUFF PANCAKES

Try stewed apples as a topping for this spectacular dish.

**4 tablespoons butter or
  margarine**
4 eggs
2/3 cup milk
**2/3 cup BUTTERMILK PANCAKE
  & WAFFLE MIX, page 25**
Fiesta Fruit Topping, below

Fiesta Fruit Topping
**1 (10-oz.) pkg. frozen
  raspberries or strawberries,
  thawed**
**1 cup pineapple chunks,
  drained**
1 banana, sliced
1/4 cup brown sugar, packed
**1/4 cup dairy sour cream
  or 1 cup frozen non-dairy
  whipped topping, thawed**

Variation

Tart Lemon Topping—Sprinkle
  1-1/2 teaspoons lemon juice
  over top of each warm pancake. Sprinkle powdered sugar
  over top. Cut into wedges and
  serve immediately.

Preheat oven to 450F (230C). Put 2 tablespoons butter or margarine in each of two 9-inch pie plates. Put in preheating oven to melt. In a blender, combine eggs, milk and BUTTERMILK PANCAKE & WAFFLE MIX. Pour batter into pie plates. Bake about 18 minutes, until pancakes are puffy and browned. DO NOT OPEN OVEN while pancakes are cooking. Top with Fiesta Fruit Topping. Makes 2 large pancakes for 4 servings.

Fiesta Fruit Topping
In a medium bowl combine raspberries or strawberries with pineapple and banana. Spoon over pancakes. Sprinkle with brown sugar. Top with teaspoonfuls of sour cream or nondairy topping. Cut into wedges and serve immediately

223

SAUSAGE-CHEESE BREAKFAST STRATA

A complete, attractive one-dish meal for morning.

5 cups **HERBED STUFFING MIX,**
   page 33
1 lb. **ground sausage, cooked**
   and drained
8 oz. **(2 cups) shredded**
   Cheddar cheese
5 **eggs, slightly beaten**
1 teaspoon **dry mustard**
2-1/4 cups **milk or**
   half-and-half
1 teaspoon **salt**
Dash of pepper

Lightly grease a 13" x 9" baking pan. Cover bottom of pan with HERBED STUFFING MIX. Add layer of cooked sausage, then layer of cheese. In a medium mixing bowl, combine eggs, mustard, milk or half-and-half, salt and pepper. Pour over cheese. Cover pan and refrigerate overnight. Preheat oven to 325F (165C). Bake covered for 1 hour. Makes 6 to 8 servings.

Prepare this dish the night before, then bake in the morning for a wonderful weekend breakfast or brunch. How convenient when you have overnight guests.

ENGLISH POACHED EGGS & HAM

A special breakfast treat!!

**1-1/2 cups FREEZER CHEESE-
  SAUCE MIX, page 54,
  thawed**
6 eggs
3 English muffins
6 slices ham
Cherry tomatoes, for garnish
Parsley sprigs, for garnish

Variation

Eggs Florentine—Omit ham,
  spoon 2 tablespoons cooked,
  chopped spinach on each
  muffin. Top with FREEZER
  CHEESE-SAUCE MIX and
  poached egg.

In a small saucepan, warm FREEZER
CHEESE-SAUCE MIX over low heat.

Pour water 1-1/2 inches deep in a
medium skillet. Bring to a simmer over
medium-high heat; do not boil. Break
1 egg into a small bowl or custard cup.
Carefully pour egg into simmering
water. Cover and cook until egg white is
set, 3 to 5 minutes. If desired, poach
several eggs at once, not letting eggs
touch one another. Lift poached eggs
from water with a slotted spoon or spatula. Drain on paper towels. Cut muffins
in half. In broiler or toaster, lightly toast
muffin halves. Place each half on a
separate plate.

Spoon 2 tablespoons of the warmed
FREEZER CHEESE-SAUCE MIX over
each muffin half. Top each with 1 slice
ham and 1 poached egg. Spoon
remaining sauce over eggs. Garnish
with tomatoes and parsley. Makes
6 servings.

PUFFY OMELET

The perfect brunch idea when everyone gets a late start.

1 tablespoon butter or
    margarine
1 cup thinly sliced fresh
    mushrooms
1/2 cup chopped green pepper
6 eggs, separated, room
    temperature
1/8 teaspoon cream of tartar
1/2 teaspoon salt
Pinch of pepper
1/3 cup milk
1 tablespoon butter or
    margarine
1 tablespoon vegetable oil
1-1/2 cups FREEZER CHEESE-
    SAUCE MIX, page 54,
    thawed
1/2 cup chopped tomatoes

Preheat oven to 350F (175C). In a small skillet, melt 1 tablespoon butter or margarine. Sauté mushrooms and green pepper until crisp-tender. Drain; set aside. In a large bowl, beat egg whites with cream of tartar until stiff peaks form. In a bowl, beat egg yolks until thick and pale. Gradually beat in salt, pepper and milk. Gently fold egg-yolk mixture into beaten egg whites.

In a large skillet or omelet pan with an oven-proof handle, heat 1 tablespoon butter or margarine and oil until hot, but not browned. Tilt pan to coat sides. Spread egg mixture evenly in pan. Without stirring, cook over low heat until lightly browned on bottom. Place in pre-heated oven. Bake 8 to 10 minutes until top feels somewhat firm.

In a small saucepan, heat FREEZER CHEESE-SAUCE MIX over low heat, stirring occasionally. Invert omelet onto a large platter. Spoon sauce over omelet. Sprinkle top evenly with tomatoes and sautéed mushrooms and green peppers. Cut in wedges. Makes 4 to 6 servings.

SIMPLIFIED QUICHE

Wonderful flavor in every bite.

Single Freezer Pie Crust, baked,
   page 309
1 egg, separated
3 eggs
1-3/4 cups milk or cream
1/2 teaspoon salt
1/4 teaspoon paprika
Dash of cayenne pepper
4 oz. (1 cup) shredded
   Swiss cheese, divided
4 strips bacon, cooked,
   crumbled
1/4 cup minced cooked onion
Chicken gravy, if desired
Pimiento, for garnish

Prepare pie crust in a 9-inch pie plate; set aside to cool. Beat egg white and brush on bottom of pie crust. Reserve egg yolk. Preheat oven to 375F (190C). In a small bowl combine reserved egg yolk with 3 eggs, milk or cream, salt, paprika and pepper. Beat until blended, but not frothy. Put half of cheese in crust. Top with bacon and onion. Pour egg mixture over top. Sprinkle with remaining cheese. Bake 40 to 50 minutes or until a knife inserted in center comes out clean. Let stand 10 minutes before serving. Serve with chicken gravy, if desired. Garnish with pimiento. Makes 1 quiche or 6 servings.

Oo-la-la! A French delicacy made easy! This is a main dish as well as a great way to use up leftover vegetables and meat.

SWISS PORRIDGE

*Try this different breakfast treat
for dessert.*

1 pt. fresh strawberries
1 (20-oz.) can crushed
   pineapple
1 cup MUESELI OATMEAL MIX,
   page 34
2 bananas, sliced
1/3 cup finely chopped nuts
1 tablespoon lemon juice
Grated peel of 1 lemon
   (about 1-1/2 teaspoons)
1 cup whipping cream
1 (8-oz.) carton plain yogurt

Reserve 8 whole strawberries. Slice remaining strawberries; set aside. Drain pineapple, reserving juice. In a bowl, combine MUESELI OATMEAL MIX and pineapple juice; set aside.

In a bowl, combine pineapple, sliced strawberries, bananas and nuts. Sprinkle with lemon juice and lemon peel. Toss lightly with 2 forks. In a bowl, whip cream until stiff peaks form. Reserve 1 cup whipped cream. Fold yogurt into remaining whipped cream. Fold fruit mixture into yogurt mixture. Gently stir in oatmeal mixture. Refrigerate at least 1 hour. Spoon porridge evenly into 8 parfait glasses or custard cups. Garnish each serving with 2 tablespoons reserved whipped cream and 1 whole strawberry. Makes 8 servings.

You can reduce the fat by substituting an 8-oz. container "light" frozen nondairy topping for the whipping cream.

YEAST BREADS & QUICK BREADS

People often think breads are difficult to make—quick breads are not quick enough and yeast breads are scary. They are all easy and delicious when you make them with your own mixes.

Let SWEET QUICK-BREAD MIX work wonders on those quick breads you don't have time to make the old way. Check Breakfast & Brunch for additional bread ideas. Our HOT ROLL MIX takes the fear out of working with yeast dough. This versatile mix is the basis for 22 recipes. We've added a savory Tomato-Rosemary Bread, which is great for sandwiches.

Quick breads are similar to muffins because they have the same proportion of liquid to dry ingredients. Be careful not to overbeat them. Stir the batter briskly about 30 seconds and let your oven complete the preparation process.

FRENCH BREAD

Make this "fat free" by using egg substitute or egg whites.

**1 tablespoon active dry yeast
or 1 (1/4-oz.) package**
**1-1/2 cups lukewarm water
110F (45C)**
2 eggs, beaten
**5 to 6 cups HOT ROLL MIX,
page 17**
1 tablespoon cornmeal
Sesame seeds, if desired

In a bowl, stir yeast into water until softened. Stir in eggs. Beat in 5 cups HOT ROLL MIX until blended. Let rest 2 minutes. Stir in enough of the remaining mix to make a soft dough. Knead until smooth, 7 to 10 minutes. Grease bowl. Place dough in bowl, turning to grease all sides. Cover with a damp towel. Let rise in a warm draft-free place until doubled in bulk, about 1 hour.

Generously grease 2 baking sheets. Sprinkle with cornmeal; set aside. Punch down dough. On a lightly oiled surface, divide dough into 2 balls. Roll out each ball to one 10" x 3" rectangle. Roll up firmly, jelly-roll fashion, starting with one long side. Pinch to seal edges. Place rolled loaves seam-side down on prepared baking sheets. Make 5 diagonal slashes across top of each loaf. Brush with water. Let rise until doubled in bulk.

Preheat oven to 375F (190C). Brush loaves again with water. Sprinkle with sesame seeds, if desired. Place a baking pan filled with water on lowest shelf of oven. Place loaves on a rack in center of oven. Bake 30 to 35 minutes in preheated oven until golden brown. Cool on a rack. Makes 2 loaves.

HOMEMADE WHITE BREAD

If you have a bread-making machine see our mix on page 13 for great variations.

**2 tablespoons active dry yeast
  or 1 (1/4-oz.) package**
**1 cup lukewarm water
  110F (45C)**
2 eggs, beaten
1 cup water
1/4 cup vegetable oil
**6-1/2 to 7 cups HOT ROLL MIX,
  page 17**
Butter or margarine, if desired

Variation

Raisin-Cinnamon Bread—
  Add 1 cup raisins and 1 to 2
  teaspoons ground cinnamon
  with HOT ROLL MIX.

In a large bowl, dissolve yeast in luke-warm water. When yeast starts to bubble, add eggs, water and oil. Blend well. Add HOT ROLL MIX 1 cup at a time until dough is stiff. On a lightly floured surface, knead dough 5 to 7 minutes, until smooth and satiny. Lightly butter bowl. Put dough in bowl and turn to butter top. Cover with damp towel and let rise in a draft-free place until doubled in bulk, 45 to 60 minutes. Punch down dough. Let stand 10 minutes. Shape into 2 loaves.

Grease two 9" x 5" loaf pans. Place 1 loaf of dough in each pan, seam-side down. Cover and let rise again until slightly rounded above top of pan, 30 to 40 minutes. Preheat oven to 350F (175C). Bake 30 to 40 minutes, until deep golden brown. Remove from oven and brush tops with butter or margarine, if desired. Remove from pans and cool. Makes 2 loaves.

SAVORY TOMATO-ROSEMARY BREAD

A wonderful sandwich bread.

**1 tablespoon active dry yeast
or 1 (1/4-oz.) package**
1/2 cup lukewarm water
1 egg, beaten
1/2 cup tomato juice
**2 tablespoons olive or
vegetable oil**
**3 tablespoons chopped fresh
rosemary or 1 tablespoon
dried**
**4 sun-dried tomatoes, drained,
chopped**
**3 to 4 cups HOT ROLL MIX,
page 17**
Butter or margarine, if desired

In a large bowl, dissolve yeast in luke-warm water. When yeast starts to bubble, add egg, tomato juice, oil, rosemary and dried tomatoes. Blend well. Add HOT ROLL MIX 1 cup at a time until dough is stiff. On a lightly floured surface, knead dough 5 to 7 minutes, until smooth. Lightly butter bowl. Put dough in bowl and turn to butter top. Cover with damp towel and let rise in a warm draft-free place until doubled in bulk, 45 to 60 minutes.

Punch down dough. Let stand 10 minutes. Shape into 1 loaf. Grease a 9" x 5" loaf pan. Place dough in pan, seam-side down. Cover and let rise again until slightly rounded above top of pan, 30 to 40 minutes. Preheat oven to 350F (175C). Bake 30 to 40 minutes, until deep golden brown. Remove from oven and brush top with butter or margarine, if desired. Remove from pan and cool on a wire rack. Makes 1 loaf.

SWEDISH RYE BREAD

Swedish limpa bread is dark,
dense and delicious.

2 tablespoons active dry yeast
or 2 (1/4-oz.) packages
1-1/4 cups lukewarm water
110F (45C)
1/4 cup melted butter or
margarine
1/4 cup dark molasses
2 to 3 tablespoons grated fresh
orange peel
1-1/2 cups rye flour
3 to 3-1/2 cups WHOLE-
WHEAT HOT ROLL MIX,
page 18
1 tablespoon butter or
margarine, melted

Variation

Add 1 teaspoon each crushed
anise and fennel seeds and
1/2 teaspoon ground
cardamom to rye flour.

In a large bowl, stir yeast into lukewarm water until softened. Stir in butter or margarine, molasses and orange peel. Beat in rye flour and 3 cups WHOLE-WHEAT HOT ROLL MIX. Let rest 2 minutes. Stir in more mix to make a soft dough. Knead 7 to 10 minutes until smooth. Grease bowl. Place dough in bowl, turning to grease all sides. Cover with a damp towel. Let rise in a warm draft-free area until doubled in bulk, about 1 hour. Punch down dough. Let rest 10 minutes.

Grease 1 large baking sheet. Divide dough in half. Shape each half into a slightly flattened ball. Place on baking sheet. With a sharp knife make 2 horizontal and 2 vertical slashes on top of loaves. Cover and let rise until doubled in bulk. Preheat oven to 375F (190C). Bake 25 to 30 minutes until browned. Brush tops with 1 tablespoon butter or margarine. Cool. Makes 2 loaves.

MARY'S HONEY-WALNUT SWIRL

The compliments will be as sweet as the bread!

**2 tablespoons active dry yeast
    or 2 (1/4-oz.) packages**
**1 cup lukewarm water
    110F (45C)**
2 eggs, beaten
1 cup water
1/4 cup vegetable oil
1 teaspoon grated orange peel
1 teaspoon grated lemon peel
**6-1/2 to 7 cups HOT ROLL MIX,
    page 17**
Honey-Nut Filling, below
**Powdered-Sugar Glaze,
    page 216**

Honey-Nut Filling
3/4 cup sugar
1/4 cup honey
1 egg, beaten
1/2 teaspoon vanilla extract
1 teaspoon ground cinnamon
1/4 teaspoon salt
1/2 cup chopped walnuts

In a bowl, dissolve yeast in 1 cup water. When yeast starts to bubble, add eggs, 1 cup water, oil, orange peel and lemon peel. Blend well. Add HOT ROLL MIX 1 cup at a time to make a soft dough. On a floured surface, knead dough 5 to 7 minutes, until smooth and satiny.

Butter bowl. Put dough in bowl and turn to butter top. Cover with a damp towel and let rise in a warm place until doubled, about 1 hour. Punch down dough. Prepare Honey-Nut Filling. Butter two 9" x 5" loaf pans. Divide dough in half. Roll out each half to 9" x 14", about 1/2 inch thick. Spread Honey Filling to within 1 inch of edges. Roll up from small end, lifting dough slightly and sealing edges as you roll. Seal ends and put into prepared pans, seam-side down. Cover and let rise in a warm place until dough is slightly rounded above top of pan.

Preheat oven to 375F (190C). Bake 45 to 50 minutes, until golden brown. Cool. Drizzle Powdered-Sugar Glaze on warm loaves. Makes 2 loaves.

Honey-Nut Filling
Combine all ingredients in a small bowl. Blend well.

HOW TO MAKE
MARY'S HONEY-WALNUT SWIRL

1. On a lightly floured surface, knead the yeast dough 5 to 7 minutes until smooth and satiny.

2. Spread filling to within 1 inch of dough edges, roll like a jelly roll.

3. While baked loaves are still warm, drizzle glaze over top of each.

BANANA-NUT BREAD

Overripe bananas make the best banana-nut bread. Freeze over-ripe bananas in peel. Thaw, peel and mash just before using.

3-1/2 cups SWEET QUICK-BREAD MIX, page 20
1/3 cup vegetable oil
2 eggs, beaten
1 tablespoon lemon juice
2 medium bananas, mashed (about 1 cup)
1/2 cup chopped nuts

Variation

Tropical Bread—Add 1/2 cup flaked coconut and 1/4 cup chopped dried pineapple.

Preheat oven to 325F (165C). Grease one 9" x 5" loaf pan or two 7" x 3" loaf pans; set aside. In a medium bowl, combine all ingredients, stirring to blend. Turn into prepared pan or pans. Bake 50 to 60 minutes in preheated oven until a wooden pick inserted in center comes out clean. Cool on a rack 5 minutes. Turn out of pan. Cool right-side up on rack. Makes 1 or 2 loaves.

CARROT-ORANGE LOAF

Make one to eat and one to share with a friend. When cool, serve with Cinnamon Whipped Topping, page 243.

3-1/2 cups SWEET QUICK-BREAD MIX, page 20
1/3 cup vegetable oil
2 eggs, beaten
1 cup grated carrots
1/2 cup orange juice
1 teaspoon grated orange peel
1 teaspoon ground nutmeg
1 teaspoon ground cinnamon
1/2 cup chopped nuts
1/2 cup raisins

Preheat oven to 325F (165C). Grease one 9" x 5" loaf pan or two 7" x 3" loaf pans; set aside. In a medium bowl, combine all ingredients, stirring to blend. Turn into prepared pan or pans.

Bake 60 to 70 minutes in preheated oven until a wooden pick inserted in center comes out clean. Cool on a rack 5 minutes. Turn out of pan. Cool right-side up on rack. Makes 1 or 2 loaves.

GOLDEN CORN BREAD

Wonderful with beans, chili, stew or any winter soup!

Honey Butter, below
2 cups QUICK MIX, page 21
6 tablespoons cornmeal
2/3 cup sugar
2 eggs
1 cup milk or water
1/4 cup melted butter or
    margarine

Honey Butter
1 cup butter, softened
1-1/4 cups honey
1 egg yolk

Variation

Mexican Corn Bread—
    Add 1 (4-oz.) can chopped
    roasted green chiles and
    1/2 cup shredded Cheddar
    cheese.

Prepare Honey Butter. Preheat oven to 350F (175C). Butter a 9-inch-square baking pan. Put QUICK MIX, cornmeal and sugar in a medium bowl and stir to blend. Combine eggs with milk or water in a small bowl. Add all at once to dry ingredients. Blend. Add melted butter or margarine and stir to blend. Fill prepared pan. Bake 35 to 40 minutes until golden brown. Cut into 2-1/2-inch squares. Serve hot with Honey Butter. Makes 8 to 10 servings.

Honey Butter
Combine butter, honey and egg yolk in a deep bowl. Beat with electric mixer 10 minutes. Store in refrigerator. Makes about 1-1/2 cups.

Corn Muffins: Butter muffin pans. Fill 3/4 full with cornbread batter. Bake 15 to 20 minutes, until golden brown. Makes 8 to 10 muffins.

Clockwise from top: Crispy Breadsticks, page 253, Orange Butterflake Rolls, page 261, Banana-Nut Bread, page 236, Homemade White Bread, page 231.

For a different shape, bake this bread in a Bundt pan at 325F (165C) for about 1 hour. Serve with cream cheese.

DATE-NUT BREAD

Dates provide a moist, rich, natural sweetness that contrasts with the chopped nuts.

1 cup boiling water
1 cup chopped dates
2 eggs, beaten
**3-1/2 cups SWEET QUICK-
    BREAD MIX, page 20**
1/3 cup vegetable oil
1 teaspoon vanilla extract
1/2 cup chopped nuts

Preheat oven to 350F (175C). Grease one 9" x 5" loaf pan or two 7" x 3" loaf pans; set aside. In a small bowl, pour boiling water over dates. Let stand 5 minutes. In a medium bowl, combine eggs, SWEET QUICK-BREAD MIX, vegetable oil, vanilla and nuts, stirring to blend. Stir in date mixture.

Pour into prepared pan or pans. Bake 60 to 65 minutes in preheated oven until a wooden pick inserted in center comes out clean. Cool 5 minutes. Turn out of pan or pans. Cool. Makes 1 or 2 loaves.

CRANBERRY BREAD

Freeze fresh cranberries when they are in season so you can make this bread all year.

3/4 cup orange juice
1 cup fresh or frozen cranberries
2 eggs, beaten
3-1/2 cups SWEET QUICK-BREAD MIX, page 20
1/3 cup vegetable oil
1 teaspoon grated orange peel

Preheat oven to 325F (165C). Grease one 9" x 5" loaf pan or two 7" x 3" loaf pans; set aside. Combine orange juice and cranberries in blender. Process on chop 4 or 5 seconds. In a bowl, combine eggs, SWEET QUICK-BREAD MIX, vegetable oil, orange peel and orange juice mixture, stirring to blend.

Pour into prepared pan or pans. Bake 60 to 70 minutes in preheated oven until a wooden pick inserted in center comes out clean. Cool on rack 5 minutes. Turn out of pan or pans. Cool. Makes 1 or 2 loaves.

POPPY SEED-LEMON BREAD

For an extra lemon "zing" add 1/2 teaspoon lemon zest to batter. Glaze with a lemon glaze for additional flavor and sweetness.

**3-3/4 cups SWEET QUICK-
 BREAD MIX, page 20**
**1/3 cup melted butter or
 vegetable oil**
2 eggs, beaten
3/4 cup lemon juice
3/4 cup milk
2 teaspoons lemon zest
**1 tablespoon poppy seeds,
 more if desired**
Lemon Glaze, below

Preheat oven to 325F (165C). Grease one 9" x 5" loaf pan or two 7" x 3" loaf pans; set aside. In a medium bowl, combine all ingredients except Lemon Glaze, stirring to blend. Pour into prepared pan or pans.

Bake 60 to 75 minutes in preheated oven until a wooden pick inserted in center comes out clean. Cool on a rack 5 minutes. Turn out of pan. Cool right-side up on rack. Spoon Lemon Glaze over bread. Makes 1 or 2 loaves.

Lemon Glaze
1 cup powdered sugar
1 tablespoon lemon juice

Lemon Glaze
In a small bowl, stir sugar and lemon juice until smooth.

PUMPKIN BREAD

Simply delicious. Serve the Cinnamon Whipped Topping with any sweet quick bread.

3-1/2 cups SWEET QUICK-BREAD MIX, page 20
1/3 cup vegetable oil
1 cup mashed cooked pumpkin
2 eggs, beaten
1/2 cup milk or orange juice, if desired
1/2 teaspoon ground cinnamon
1/2 teaspoon ground nutmeg
1/2 teaspoon ground cloves
1/2 cup chopped nuts
1/2 cup raisins
Cinnamon Whipped Topping, below

Cinnamon Whipped Topping
1 cup whipping cream
1 teaspoon ground cinnamon
3 tablespoons powdered sugar

Preheat oven to 350F (175C). Grease one 9" x 5" loaf pan or two 7" x 3" loaf pans; set aside. In a bowl, combine SWEET QUICK-BREAD MIX, vegetable oil, pumpkin, eggs, milk or juice, cinnamon, nutmeg and cloves until blended. Add nuts and raisins. Pour into prepared pan or pans.

Bake 55 to 60 minutes in preheated oven until a wooden pick inserted in center comes out clean. Cool 5 minutes. Turn out of pan. Cool right-side up on rack. Prepare topping To serve, cut into 1/2-inch slices; spread each with Cinnamon Whipped Topping. Makes 1 or 2 loaves.

Cinnamon Whipped Topping
In a medium bowl, whip cream until soft peaks form. Gently stir in cinnamon and powdered sugar. Refrigerate until served. Makes about 2 cups.

BREAD BASKET BOWLS

*Eat the contents and then
the bowl.*

**1 tablespoon active dry yeast
    or 1 (1/4-oz.) package
1-1/2 cups lukewarm water
    110F (45C)
1 egg, slightly beaten
2 tablespoons vegetable oil
About 5-1/2 cups HOT ROLL
    MIX, page 17
1 egg
1 tablespoon water**

In a bowl dissolve yeast in water. When yeast bubbles, stir in beaten egg and oil. Gradually stir in 3 cups HOT ROLL MIX until blended. Add additional HOT ROLL MIX to make a stiff dough. Turn out on a floured surface. Knead until smooth, about 10 minutes. Add more flour as needed. Grease bowl. Place dough in greased bowl, turning to grease all sides. Cover and let rise in a warm place until doubled, about 1 hour.

While dough is rising, grease the outsides and bottoms of eight 10-ounce custard cups; set aside. Punch down dough. Turn out on floured surface. Knead about 5 times. Divide dough into 8 pieces.

Shape into smooth balls. Roll 1 ball into a 6-inch circle. Lay over 1 inverted and greased custard cup. Mold dough to cover cup. Repeat with other balls of dough. Place dough-covered cups on 2 ungreased baking sheets, about 2 inches apart. Let stand uncovered 10 minutes.

Preheat oven to 375F (190C). Bake 20 minutes. Beat 1 egg with 1 tablespoon water. Remove custard cups from oven. Brush bread bowls with egg-water mixture. Bake 5 minutes longer. Remove from oven.

Turn right side up; remove custard cups. Brush inside of each bread bowl with egg-water mixture. Bake 10 to 15 minutes longer until lightly browned. Cool. Makes 8 bread baskets.

SPICY APPLESAUCE BREAD

*Cool, smooth cream cheese is
the perfect companion.*

**3-1/2 cups SWEET QUICK-
   BREAD MIX, page 20**
1/3 cup vegetable oil
**1-1/2 teaspoons ground
   cinnamon**
1/2 teaspoon ground allspice
1/2 teaspoon ground cloves
1 cup applesauce
1/2 cup chopped nuts
1/2 cup raisins
Whipped cream cheese

Preheat oven to 325F (165C). Grease
one 9" x 5" loaf pan or two 7" x 3" loaf
pans; set aside. In a medium bowl,
combine all ingredients except cream
cheese, stirring to blend. Pour into
prepared pan or pans.

Bake 60 to 70 minutes in preheated
oven until a wooden pick inserted in
center comes out clean. Cool on a rack
5 minutes. Turn out of pan or pans.
Cool right-side up on rack. Spread
cooled slices with cream cheese. Makes
1 or 2 loaves.

Variation—
Use pistachios and
1/4 cup chopped
dried pineapple or
crystallized ginger.

ZUCCHINI BREAD

Take advantage of the bountiful zucchini harvest. Freeze bags of grated zucchini to use in this bread and in Zucchini Muffins, page 253. To prevent tunnels in your bread, stir only until all the ingredients are moistened.

3-1/2 cups SWEET QUICK-BREAD MIX, page 20
1/3 cup vegetable oil
2 eggs, beaten
2 cups grated unpeeled zucchini
3 tablespoons orange juice
1 teaspoon grated orange peel
1/2 cup chopped nuts

Preheat oven to 325 F (165C). Grease one 9" x 5" loaf pan or two 7" x 3" loaf pans; set aside. In a medium bowl, combine all ingredients, stirring to blend. Pour into prepared pan or pans.

Bake 60 to 75 minutes in preheated oven until a wooden pick inserted in center comes out clean. Cool on a rack 5 minutes. Turn out of pan. Cool right-side up on rack. Makes 1 or 2 loaves.

COUNTRY FRENCH BREAD

*Some bakers make this bread
round, rather than the traditional
long loaf.*

**1 tablespoon active dry yeast
   or 1 (1/4-oz.) package**
**1-1/2 cups lukewarm water
   110F (45C)**
2 eggs, beaten
**5 to 6 cups WHOLE-WHEAT
   HOT ROLL MIX, page 18**
1 tablespoon cornmeal
**1 to 2 tablespoons butter or
   margarine, melted, if desired**

In a bowl, stir yeast into water until softened. Stir in eggs. Beat in 5 cups
WHOLE-WHEAT HOT ROLL MIX until
blended. Let rest 2 minutes. Stir in more
mix to make a soft dough. Knead 7 to
10 minutes until smooth. Grease bowl.
Place dough in bowl, turning to grease
all sides. Cover with a damp towel. Let
rise in a warm draft-free place until
doubled in bulk, about 1 hour. Punch
down dough. Let rest 10 minutes.

Grease 2 large baking sheets. Sprinkle
with cornmeal; set aside. On a lightly
oiled surface, divide dough in half.
Shape each into a ball. Roll each ball to
a 10" x 3" rectangle. Roll up firmly
starting with one long side. Pinch to seal
edges. Place loaves seam-side down on
prepared sheets. Make 5 diagonal
slashes across top of each loaf. Brush
with water. Let rise until almost doubled.

Preheat oven to 375F (190C). Brush
loaves with water again. Place a baking
pan on lower oven shelf. Pour 1 inch
warm water in pan. Place loaves in center of oven. Bake 30 to 35 minutes until
golden brown. Brush with butter, if
desired. Makes 2 loaves.

MUFFINS & ROLLS

Homebaked muffins or rolls are welcome at any time, especially morning. Can you think of a better way to awaken your family than with the aroma of biscuits or muffins just out of the oven? In just a few minutes you can prepare any of the Melt-In-Your-Mouth Mufffins for breakfast. For those who are running late, wrap a Gran Muffin in a napkin, to be enjoyed on the way to work or school.

Madeline is our "muffin lady" and she has come up with combinations sure to please even the most finicky person. We encourage you to personalize our recipes by adding fruit, herb and nut combinations that appeal to you.

To make biscuits lighter, knead the dough 10 to 15 times. Your biscuits will rise higher and you will wish you had always made them this way. Be sure to try our Orange Biscuits as well as the Cheese and Herb Biscuits.

Make your own Hamburger Buns and English Muffins and try our new Squash Roll that's sure to be a hit. Our best-ever Pan Rolls have been standbys for years. Our new English Griddle Scones are topped with a delicious Peach Devonshire Cream.

In every cookbook, there are recipes that are difficult to categorize. At the end of this chapter you will find "other" recipes including Bagels, Crispy Breadsticks, Pizza Crust and Super-Duper Doughnuts.

LEMON-POPPY SEED MUFFINS

Fragrant lemon paired with crunchy poppy seeds.

2-1/4 cups MUFFIN MIX, page 19
1 (3.4-oz.) package instant lemon-pudding mix
1 tablespoon poppy seeds
1/4 teaspoon grated lemon peel
1 cup milk
2 eggs, beaten
1/4 cup vegetable oil
Lemon Glaze, page 242

Preheat oven to 400F (205C). Spray muffin pans with vegetable cooking spray. In a medium bowl, combine MUFFIN MIX, lemon-pudding mix, poppy seeds and lemon peel.

Combine milk, eggs and oil in a medium bowl. Add all at once to dry ingredients. Stir until moistened; batter should be lumpy. Fill prepared muffin pans 3/4 full. Bake in preheated oven 12 to 15 minutes until golden brown. Prepare Lemon Glaze. Drizzle Glaze on warm muffins. Makes 10 large muffins.

Freeze-Ahead Muffins: Line muffin cup with paper liner. Fill with batter. Pop pan in the freezer. When frozen, remove muffins from pan and transfer to freezer container. When ready to bake, place frozen muffins into pan and place in preheated oven. Increase baking time 3 to 6 minutes.

MELT-IN-YOUR-MOUTH MUFFINS

A delicious addition to any meal. Serve for breakfast with bacon and eggs.

2-3/4 cups MUFFIN MIX, page 19

1 egg, beaten

1 cup milk

1/2 cup butter or margarine, melted, or 1/2 cup vegetable oil

Variations

Cornmeal Muffins—Decrease MUFFIN MIX to 2-1/4 cups. Add 1/2 cup cornmeal.

Butterscotch-Pecan Muffins—Melt 6 tablespoons butter in saucepan. Stir in 6 tablespoons brown sugar. Place 1 tablespoon of brown-sugar mixture and 2 to 3 pecans in bottom of each muffin cup. Fill cups 3/4 full with batter.

Dried Fruit Muffins—Add 1 cup chopped dried fruit (apricots, cherries, peaches, blueberries, pineapple, strawberries) to liquid ingredients.

Preheat oven to 400F (205C). Spray muffin pans with vegetable cooking spray. Put MUFFIN MIX in a medium bowl. Combine egg, milk and butter, margarine or oil in a small bowl. Add all at once to MUFFIN MIX. Stir until mix is just moistened; batter should be lumpy. Fill prepared muffin pans 3/4 full. Bake 18 to 20 minutes, until golden brown. Makes 10 large muffins.

Fresh Peach Muffins—Gently fold 1 cup diced fresh peaches into batter before filling muffin pans.

Banana Muffins—Mash 1 banana (1/2 cup) and add to liquid ingredients before adding liquid to MUFFIN MIX.

Blueberry Muffins—Gently fold 1 cup fresh, frozen or drained canned blueberries into basic muffin batter just before filling muffin pans.

Cranberry-Nut Muffins—Gently fold 1 cup chopped fresh or frozen cranberries, 1/2 cup chopped nuts and 3 tablespoons sugar into basic muffin batter just before filling muffin pans.

MOLASSES BRAN MUFFINS

These sweet-tasting, fiber-rich muffins were described as "too good to be breakfast muffins" by one of our children whose tastes are hard to please.

2 cups all-bran cereal
   or 1 cup all-bran plus
   1 cup bran flakes
1/4 cup melted butter or
   vegetable oil
1/4 cup molasses
1 cup milk
1 egg
1/2 cup raisins, optional
1-1/2 cups MUFFIN MIX,
   page 19

Variation

Chocolate Nut—Omit raisins and substitute 1/2 cup each mini-chocolate morsels and chopped nuts.

Preheat oven to 400F (205C). Spray muffin pans with vegetable cooking spray. In a medium bowl combine cereal, butter or oil, molasses, milk and egg. Let stand 5 minutes.

Add raisins, if desired, and MUFFIN MIX. Stir just until ingredients are moistened. Fill prepared muffin pans 3/4 full. Bake 15 to 20 minutes, until edges are brown. Makes 10 large muffins.

251

MORNING MUFFINS

Make these sweet and moist muffins a variety of ways. Our favorite is the fresh peach.

2-1/2 cups QUICK MIX, page 21
4 tablespoons sugar
1 egg, beaten
1 cup milk or water
Butter and honey, if desired

Preheat oven to 425F (220C). Generously butter muffin pans. Place QUICK MIX, in a medium bowl. Add sugar and mix well. In a bowl, combine egg and milk or water. Add all at once to dry ingredients. Stir until just blended. Fill prepared muffin pans 2/3 full. Bake 15 to 20 minutes, until golden brown. Serve hot with butter and honey, if desired. Makes 12 large muffins.

Variations

Dried Fruit or Nut Muffins—Add 1/2 cup chopped raisins, dates, dried berries or fruits, or nuts to dry ingredients. Before baking, sprinkle with mixture of cinnamon and sugar.

Blueberry Muffins—Gently fold 1 cup fresh, frozen or drained blueberries into batter before putting into muffin pans.

Oatmeal or Bran Muffins— Reduce QUICK MIX to 1-3/4 cups. Add 3/4 cup quick rolled oats or all-bran cereal to dry ingredients before adding liquid ingredients.

Apple Muffins—Fold 1 cup grated raw apple into muffin batter before putting into muffin pans and increase baking time to 20 to 25 minutes.

Fresh Peach Muffins—Fold 1 cup diced fresh peaches into batter before putting into muffin pans and increase baking time to 20 to 25 minutes.

Orange Muffins—Add 1 tablespoon fresh orange peel or 1-1/2 teaspoons dried orange peel to dry ingredients before adding liquid ingredients.

Cranberry Muffins—Gently fold 2/3 cup chopped cranberries into muffin batter before putting into muffin pans.

ZUCCHINI MUFFINS

These are similar to a favorite restaurant specialty. Scrumptious!!

2 cups MUFFIN MIX, page 19
1/2 cup sugar
1/2 cup chopped nuts
1 tablespoon ground cinnamon
1 cup grated zucchini
1 egg, beaten
1/2 cup butter, melted
2 teaspoons vanilla extract

Preheat oven to 400F (205C). Spray muffin pans with vegetable cooking spray. In a medium bowl, combine MUFFIN MIX, sugar, nuts and cinnamon. Combine zucchini, egg, butter and vanilla in a medium bowl.

Add all at once to dry ingredients. Stir until just moistened; batter should be lumpy. Fill prepared muffin pans 3/4 full. Bake 20 to 25 minutes until golden brown. Makes 10 medium muffins.

CRISPY BREADSTICKS

A nice accompaniment for your Italian dishes.

2 cups QUICK MIX, page 21
1/2 cup cornmeal or all-
**   purpose flour**
1/2 teaspoon salt
About 1/2 cup milk or water
Sesame, caraway or poppy
**   seeds, if desired**

Preheat oven to 400F (205C). Lightly grease baking sheet. In a medium bowl, combine QUICK MIX, cornmeal or flour and salt. Add milk or water to form dough. Knead about 12 times, until dough is smooth. Divide into 12 balls of dough. Shape into pencil-like strands 1/2 inch thick. Roll in sesame, caraway or poppy seeds, if desired. Bake about 20 minutes, until brown and crisp. For extra crispness, turn off oven and leave breadsticks in oven 5 to 10 more minutes. Makes 12 breadsticks.

Clockwise from top: Molasses-Bran Muffins, page 251, Melt-In-Your-Mouth Muffins with apricots, page 250

BISCUITS

*When time is short, try this
simplified biscuit recipe.*

**3 cups QUICK MIX, page 21
3/4 cup milk or water**

Preheat oven to 450F (230C). Grease a
baking sheet. Combine QUICK MIX and
milk or water in a medium bowl. Stir
until just blended. Drop dough by tablespoonfuls onto prepared baking sheet.
Bake 10 to 12 minutes, until golden
brown. Makes 12 large drop biscuits.

Variations

Cheese and Herb Biscuits—Add
1/3 cup grated Cheddar
cheese and chopped parsley,
chives or herbs to taste while
stirring dough.

Buttermilk Biscuits—Substitute
3/4 cup buttermilk for milk
or water.

Country Dumplings—Drop
dough by tablespoonfuls over
top of boiling beef or chicken
stew. Boil gently 10 minutes
uncovered. Cover and cook
over medium-high heat 10
more minutes, until completely
cooked. Makes 12 dumplings.

Orange Biscuits—Add 1 tablespoon
grated orange peel. If desired, substitute 2 tablespoons orange juice for
part of milk or water.

Fruit Cobbler—Spoon dough over top of
hot, sweetened fruit or berries and
bake in an 8-inch-square pan about
20 to 25 minutes until golden brown.

255

NEVER-FAIL ROLLED BISCUITS

These light biscuits separate into layers.

3 cups QUICK MIX, page 21
2/3 cup milk or water

Preheat oven to 450F (230C). Combine QUICK MIX and milk or water in a medium bowl. Blend. Let dough stand 5 minutes. On a lightly floured board, knead dough about 15 times. Roll out to 1/2-inch thickness. Cut with a floured biscuit cutter. Place about 2 inches apart on ungreased baking sheet. Bake 10 to 12 minutes, until golden brown. Makes 12 large biscuits.

Variations

Cinnamon Rolls—Preheat oven to 400F (205C). Roll out dough to a rectangle. Brush with melted butter. Sprinkle with brown sugar and cinnamon. Roll dough like a jelly roll and cut into 1/2-inch slices. Bake 10 to 15 minutes. Glaze with mixture of powdered sugar and a few drops of water.

Pizza—Use dough as crust for 12 individual pizzas or two 12-inch pizzas. Pat dough to 1/8-inch thickness. Top with tomato sauce, spices, cheese, meat and choice of toppings.

Meat Pinwheels—Preheat oven to 450F (230C). Roll out dough to a rectangle. Chop cooked meat and combine with gravy. Spread over dough. Roll dough like a jelly roll and cut into 12 1-inch slices. Bake 10 to 12 minutes. Serve with gravy, soup or cheese sauce.

Pot Pie—Use as the top crust of a chicken or meat pot pie.

CREAM CHEESE SWIRLS

Smooth and delicious.

**1 tablespoon active dry yeast
  or 1 (1/4-oz.) package**
**1-1/2 cups lukewarm water
  110F (45C)**
2 eggs, beaten
**1/4 cup vegetable oil or melted
  margarine**
**5 to 6 cups HOT ROLL MIX,
  page 17**
**2 tablespoons butter or
  margarine, melted**
1/2 cup brown sugar, packed
2 teaspoons ground cinnamon
Cream-Cheese Filling, below
Sweet Glaze, below

Cream-Cheese Filling
1 (8-oz.) pkg. cream cheese
6 tablespoons sugar
1 egg, slightly beaten
1/2 teaspoon lemon extract
Combine all ingredients.

Sweet Glaze
2 cups sifted powdered sugar
**1/2 teaspoon vanilla or lemon
  extract**
About 4 tablespoons milk
Combine all ingredients.

In a large bowl, dissolve yeast in water. Blend in eggs and oil or margarine. Add 5 cups HOT ROLL MIX. Stir well. Add HOT ROLL MIX to make a soft, but not too sticky, dough. Knead about 5 minutes, until dough is smooth. Lightly butter bowl. Put dough in bowl and turn to butter top. Cover dough with a damp towel and let rise in a warm place until doubled in bulk, about 1 hour. Generously grease 2 baking sheets.

Prepare Cream-Cheese Filling. Punch down dough. Let stand 10 minutes. On a floured surface, roll dough to 12" x 24", about 1/4 inch thick. Brush with melted butter or margarine. Sprinkle brown sugar and cinnamon over butter. Roll dough like a jelly roll. Cut into 1-inch slices. Place on prepared baking sheets. Cover with a damp towel and let rise in a warm place until doubled in bulk, 30 to 60 minutes.

Preheat oven to 375F (190C). With a tablespoon, press a deep indentation in the center of each bun. Fill each indentation with 3 tablespoons Cream-Cheese Filling. Bake 20 to 25 minutes, until golden brown. Prepare Sweet Glaze. Drizzle glaze on warm buns. Makes about 24 rolls.

CRESCENT ROLLS

Buttery, rich and golden.

**1 tablespoon active dry yeast
or 1 (1/4-oz.) package**
**1-1/2 cups lukewarm water
110F (45C)**
2 eggs, beaten
**1/4 cup vegetable oil or melted
margarine**
**5 to 6 cups HOT ROLL MIX,
page 17**
**2 tablespoons butter or
margarine, softened**

In a large bowl, dissolve yeast in luke-warm water. Blend in eggs and oil or margarine. Add 5 cups HOT ROLL MIX. Blend well. Add more HOT ROLL MIX to make a soft, but not too sticky, dough. Knead 5 minutes, until dough is smooth. Lightly butter bowl. Put dough in bowl and turn to butter top. Cover dough with a damp towel and let rise in a warm place until doubled in bulk, about 1 hour. Generously grease baking sheets. Punch down dough. Divide in half. Let stand 10 minutes.

On a lightly floured surface, roll out each half to a 12-inch circle. Brush each circle with 1 tablespoon soft butter or margarine. Cut each circle into 16 pie-shaped wedges. Roll up each wedge from the wide end. Place point-side down in a crescent shape on prepared baking sheets. Cover and let rise again until doubled in bulk, 45 to 60 minutes. Preheat oven to 400F (205C). Bake 15 to 20 minutes, until golden brown. Makes 32 rolls.

It's nice to brush orange marmalade on top of buttered wedges before rolling into crescents.

ENGLISH MUFFINS

Toast lightly and top with butter, honey or jam.

2 tablespoons active dry yeast
 or 2 (1/4-oz.) packages
1-1/2 cups lukewarm water
 110F (45C)
1/4 cup butter or margarine,
 melted
4 to 4-1/2 cups HOT ROLL MIX,
 page 17
3 tablespoons cornmeal
Butter or margarine

In a large bowl, dissolve yeast in water. When yeast bubbles, add butter or margarine and 3 cups HOT ROLL MIX. Blend well. Add more HOT ROLL MIX until dough is firm. On a lightly floured surface, knead dough 5 minutes, until smooth. Lightly butter bowl. Put dough in bowl and turn to butter top. Cover with a damp towel and let rise in a warm place until doubled in bulk, about 30 minutes.

Sprinkle 2 baking sheets lightly with cornmeal. DO NOT PUNCH DOWN DOUGH. On a lightly floured surface roll out dough to 1/2-inch thickness. Cut with 3- to 4-inch-round cookie cutters or muffin rings. Place cut dough on cornmeal. Turn and pat cornmeal into surface. Cover with waxed paper. Let rise until doubled, about 30 minutes.

Heat an electric skillet or griddle to 325F (165C). Butter skillet. With a spatula, place muffins on hot surface. Cook each side 8 to 10 minutes, until golden. Cool. Makes twelve 4-inch muffins.

Split muffins before toasting. With a fork pierce muffin from the side to the middle. Gently pry apart.

259

HAMBURGER BUNS

To make hot-dog buns, shape the dough into long ovals.

2 tablespoons active dry yeast or 2 (1/4-oz.) packages
1-1/2 cups lukewarm water 110F (45C)
2 eggs, beaten
1/4 cup vegetable oil
5 to 6 cups HOT ROLL MIX, page 17
2 tablespoons butter or margarine, melted

Variation

Seeded Buns—Beat 1 egg white with 1 tablespoon water, brush on risen buns. Sprinkle with sesame or poppy seeds.

In a large bowl, stir yeast into lukewarm water until softened. Stir in eggs and oil. Beat in 5 cups of the HOT ROLL MIX until blended. Let rest 2 minutes. Add enough of the remaining mix to make a soft dough. Knead until smooth, 7 to 10 minutes. Grease bowl. Place dough in bowl, turning to grease all sides. Cover with a damp towel. Let rise in a warm place, free from drafts, until doubled in bulk. Grease 2 baking sheets; set aside.

Punch down dough. Let rest 10 minutes. Use a rolling pin to roll out dough 1/2 inch thick. Cut buns with a large can or bun cutter, or divide dough into 12 equal pieces, shaping each into a 4-inch circle, 1/2 inch thick. Let rise 10 to 15 minutes. Preheat oven to 425F (220C). Bake 10 minutes until golden brown. Remove from baking sheets; cool. To keep the buns soft, brush with butter or margarine then cover with a dry cloth. Makes twelve 5-inch buns.

ORANGE BUTTERFLAKE ROLLS

Here's one of our most requested recipes. Rich, flaky rolls deserve the praise they receive.

**1 tablespoon active dry yeast
  or 1 (1/4-oz.) package**
**1-1/2 cups lukewarm water
  110F (45C)**
2 eggs, beaten
**1/4 cup vegetable oil or melted
  margarine**
**5 to 6 cups HOT ROLL MIX,
  page 17**
Orange Butter, below
Orange Glaze, below

Orange Butter
**4 tablespoons butter or
  margarine, melted**
3/4 cup sugar
**4 tablespoons grated
  orange peel**

Orange Glaze
2 cups sifted powdered sugar
**About 4 tablespoons
  orange juice**

In a bowl, dissolve yeast in water. Blend in eggs and oil or margarine. Add 5 cups HOT ROLL MIX. Blend well. Add more HOT ROLL MIX to make a soft dough. Knead 5 minutes, until dough is smooth. Lightly butter bowl. Put dough in bowl and turn to butter top. Cover dough with a damp towel and let rise in a warm place until doubled, about 1 hour. Grease muffin pans. Prepare Orange Butter. Punch down dough. Let stand 10 minutes.

On a lightly floured surface, roll out dough to a 10" x 20" rectangle. Brush with Orange Butter. Cut into 20 1" x 10" strips. Stack 5 strips together. Cut each stack into 6 equal pieces. Place each cut stack upright in prepared muffin pans. Twist slightly to fan out. Cover and let rise until doubled, about 30 minutes. Preheat oven to 375F (190C). Bake 12 to 15 minutes, until golden brown. Let stand 10 minutes before removing. Prepare Orange Glaze and drizzle on warm rolls. Makes 24 rolls.

Orange Butter
Combine butter, sugar and orange peel.

Orange Glaze
Blend powdered sugar and orange juice until smooth.

PAN ROLLS

One of our favorites. They have the most wonderful light texture.

1 tablespoon active dry yeast or 1 (1/4-oz.) package
1-1/2 cups lukewarm water 110F (45C)
2 eggs, beaten
1/2 cup vegetable oil or melted margarine
5 to 6 cups HOT ROLL MIX, page 17

In a large bowl, dissolve yeast in luke-warm water. Blend in eggs and oil or margarine. Add 5 cups HOT ROLL MIX. Blend well. Add additional HOT ROLL MIX to make a soft, but not too sticky, dough. Knead about 5 minutes, until dough is smooth. Lightly butter bowl. Put dough in bowl and turn to butter top. Cover dough with a damp towel and let rise in a warm place until doubled in bulk, about 1 hour.

Grease a 13" x 9" baking pan or two 9-inch round pans. Punch down dough. Let rest 10 minutes. Divide into 24 to 30 balls. Place in prepared pans. Cover and let rise until about doubled in bulk. Preheat oven to 375F (190C). Bake 20 to 25 minutes until browned. Brush tops with butter or margarine. Makes 24 to 30 rolls.

For cloverleaf rolls, roll dough into 1-inch balls. Grease muffin cups and place 3 balls in each. If desired sprinkle with poppy seeds before baking.

SQUASH ROLLS

Enjoy the lovely yellow color and mild squash taste. Serve them at your next dinner.

**1 tablespoon active dry yeast
or 1 (1/4-oz.) package**
**3/4 cup lukewarm water
110F (45C)**
2 eggs, beaten
2 tablespoons sugar
3 tablespoons oil
**1 (12-oz.) pkg. frozen winter
squash, cooked, or 1 cup
canned pumpkin**
**5 to 6 cups HOT ROLL MIX,
page 17**

Variation

Herbed squash—Add 2 to 3 tablespoons mixed dried herbs to HOT ROLL MIX.

In a large bowl, dissolve yeast in luke-warm water. Blend in eggs, sugar, oil and squash or pumpkin. Add 5 cups HOT ROLL MIX. Blend well. Add additional HOT ROLL MIX to make a soft, but not too sticky, dough. Knead about 5 minutes, until dough is smooth. Lightly butter bowl. Put dough in bowl and turn to butter top. Cover dough with a damp towel and let rise in a warm place until doubled in bulk, about 1 hour.

Grease a 13" x 9" baking pan or two 9-inch round pans. Punch down dough. Divide dough into 24 to 30 balls of equal size. Place balls in prepared pans. Cover and let rise again until doubled in bulk. Preheat oven to 375F (190C). Bake 15 to 20 minutes, until golden brown. Makes 24 to 30 rolls.

BAGELS

The bagel shop will have one less customer when you make your own at home.

**1 tablespoon active dry yeast
   or 1 (1/4-oz.) package**
**1-1/2 cups lukewarm water
   110F (45C)**
**5 cups HOT ROLL MIX,
   page 17**
Cornmeal
3 qt. water
1 tablespoon sugar
1 egg yolk, beaten
1 tablespoon water
**Poppy seeds, sesame seeds or
   coarse salt**

In a large bowl, dissolve yeast in 1-1/2 cups lukewarm water. Beat in 4-1/2 cups HOT ROLL MIX. Let rest 2 minutes. Add enough mix to make a very stiff dough. On a lightly floured surface knead dough until smooth, 5 to 10 minutes. Add more mix to surface as needed. Dough will be quite firm. Lightly butter bowl. Put dough in bowl and turn to butter top. Cover dough with a damp towel and let rise in a warm place until doubled in bulk, 30 to 45 minutes.

Punch down dough; knead 4 or 5 times. Divide in half. Divide each half into 8 pieces. Shape each piece into a smooth ball. Flatten each ball with palm of hand. Holding a ball with both hands, force one thumb through center. Place bagel on lightly floured surface. Repeat with remaining dough. Cover lightly; let rise in a warm place 20 to 30 minutes.

Lightly grease 2 baking sheets. Sprinkle with cornmeal; set aside. In a 5-quart pot, bring 3 quarts of water to a boil. Add sugar. Lower heat to keep water boiling gently.

Use slotted spoon to carefully lower bagels, one at a time, into boiling water. Turning often, cook until slightly puffed, about 5 minutes. Add more water if necessary. Drain bagels briefly on paper towels.

Preheat oven to 400F (205C). Arrange bagels, not touching, on prepared baking sheets. Combine egg yolk and 1 tablespoon water. Brush bagels with egg yolk mixture. Leave plain, or sprinkle with poppy seeds, sesame seeds or coarse salt. Bake 15 to 20 minutes in oven until browned. Cool on a rack. Makes 16 bagels.

Here's an opportunity to make your favorite variety of bagels. Add 1/2 teaspoon ground cinnamon and 3/4 cup raisins or dried blueberries to mix. For a savory touch, add 3 tablespoons of chopped chives. Have you tried bagels spread with ripe avocado?

TATONUTS

It's a tradition to serve these at the Eliasons' home every Halloween.

**1 tablespoon active dry yeast
   or 1 (1/4-oz.) package**
**1/2 cup lukewarm water
   110F (45C)**
2 eggs, beaten
**1/4 cup melted butter or
   margarine**
3 tablespoons sugar
1/2 cup instant potato flakes
1 cup milk, scalded
**4-1/2 to 5 cups HOT ROLL MIX,
   page 17**
Vegetable oil for frying
Vanilla Glaze, page 269

Potatoes are the secret ingredient in this family favorite. Use leftover mashed potatoes.

Lightly grease 2 baking sheets. In a large bowl, dissolve yeast in lukewarm water. Stir in eggs and butter or margarine. Add sugar, potato flakes and milk. Blend well. Mix in 4-1/2 cups HOT ROLL MIX. Add additional MIX to make soft, but not too sticky, dough. Turn out on a lightly floured surface. Knead about 5 minutes, until dough is smooth and satiny. Lightly butter bowl. Put dough in bowl and turn to butter top. Cover dough with a damp towel and let rise in a warm place until doubled in bulk, about 1 hour.

Punch down. On a lightly floured surface, roll out dough about 1/4 inch thick. Cut with a floured doughnut cutter. Place on prepared baking sheets. Cover and let rise until doubled in bulk, 30 to 40 minutes. In a deep-fryer or electric skillet, heat 1/2 inch of oil to 375F (190C). Fry doughnuts about 1 minute on each side until golden brown. Drain on paper towels. Brush warm doughnuts with Vanilla Glaze. Makes about 30 doughnuts.

PIZZA CRUST

Try partially baking the crust to save you time on a busy day.

**1 cup plus 2 tablespoons warm
  water 105F (40C)**
**1 tablespoon active dry yeast
  or 1 (1/4-oz.) package**
2 tablespoons vegetable oil
**3 to 3-1/4 cups HOT ROLL MIX,
  page 17**

Pour water in a large bowl. Sprinkle yeast over water; stir until dissolved. Let stand about 5 minutes. Stir in oil. Add 3 cups HOT ROLL MIX to make a soft dough. Sprinkle 1/4 cup additional HOT ROLL MIX on board. Turn out dough and knead 15 times. Clean and grease bowl. Place dough in bowl and turn to grease top. Cover and let rise in a warm place about 20 to 30 minutes or until doubled in size.

Preheat oven to 425F (220C). Punch down dough. Grease one 16-inch pizza baking pan. Pat dough on prepared pan forming a shallow rim around edge. Bake on lowest rack of oven for 3 to 6 minutes or until edges start to brown. Remove. Add sauce and topping. Bake 10 to 15 minutes until cheese is melted and sauce is hot. Makes 4 to 6 servings.

AEBLESKIVERS

You can also make these in muffin tins. Bake at 400F (205C) for 15 to 20 minutes.

2 eggs, separated
1-1/2 cups BUTTERMILK PAN-
  CAKE AND WAFFLE MIX,
  page 25
1/4 teaspoon ground
  cardamom, if desired
1 cup water
2 tablespoons melted butter
Butter for frying
Powdered sugar, for garnish,
  if desired

In a medium bowl, beat egg yolks until pale. Stir in BUTTERMILK PANCAKE AND WAFFLE MIX, cardamom, if desired, water and 2 tablespoons melted butter until blended. In a medium bowl, beat egg whites until stiff but not dry. Fold into egg yolk mixture.

Generously butter each Aebleskiver cup. Heat according to manufacturer's instructions. Fill each cup 3/4 full with batter. Cook until bubbly and set around edge, about 1-1/2 minutes. Turn 1/4 turn with a fork or wooden pick to brown other side. Continue 1/4 turns each 15 to 30 seconds until lightly browned and a wooden pick inserted in center comes out clean. Dust with powdered sugar for garnish, if desired. Serve warm. Makes about 20 Aebleskivers.

1. Butter each cup, heat until butter bubbles.

2. With wooden pick or fork, turn 1/4 turn until browned on all sides.

SUPER-DUPER DOUGHNUTS

The spice is nice!

Cooking oil for frying
2 cups QUICK MIX, page 21
1/4 cup sugar
1/4 teaspoon ground cinnamon
1/4 teaspoon ground nutmeg
1 teaspoon vanilla extract
1 egg, well beaten
1/3 cup milk or water
Vanilla Glaze, below

In a deep-fryer, heat oil to 375F (190C). In a medium bowl, combine QUICK MIX, sugar, cinnamon and nutmeg. Blend well. In a small bowl, mix together vanilla, egg and milk or water. Add all at once to dry ingredients. Stir until well blended. On a lightly floured surface, knead dough about 10 minutes. Roll out to 1/2-inch thickness and cut with a floured doughnut cutter.

Fry in hot oil about 1 minute on each side, until golden brown. Drain on paper towels. While doughnuts cool slightly, prepare Vanilla Glaze. Dip warm doughnuts in glaze. Makes about 12 doughnuts.

Vanilla Glaze
1-1/4 cups powdered sugar
2 teaspoons milk
1/2 teaspoon vanilla extract

Vanilla Glaze
Combine all ingredients.

ENGLISH GRIDDLE SCONES

You can also bake scones at 400F (205C) for 10 to 12 minutes.

3-1/2 cups QUICK MIX, page 21
2 eggs, room temperature
2 tablespoons honey
1/2 cup whipping cream
Peach Devonshire Cream, below

Put QUICK MIX in a large bowl. Add eggs, honey and whipping cream. Mix with fork just until blended and ball forms. Turn out dough onto a generously floured surface. Flour your hands and gently pat or press dough only until it holds together. Cut dough in half. Pat each half into a circle about 1/2-inch thick. Cut each circle into quarters.

Preheat an ungreased griddle or skillet over medium-low to low heat. Gently place scones on hot griddle. When bottoms are lightly browned and scones rise slightly, 8 to 10 minutes, turn and brown other side, 6 to 8 minutes. Serve hot with Peach Devonshire Cream. To preserve their tender texture, pull scones apart with a fork or your fingers. Do not cut with a knife. Makes 8 scones.

Peach Devonshire Cream
1/2 cup whipping cream, chilled
2 tablespoons brown sugar
1/2 cup dairy sour cream
1 cup diced, fresh peaches

Peach Devonshire Cream
In bowl of electric mixer, combine whipping cream and brown sugar. Let stand 2 or 3 minutes. Whip cream mixture until firm peaks form. Gently stir in sour cream and peaches. Spoon into a medium serving dish. Cover and refrigerate. Serve cold. Makes about 2-1/2 cups.

APPLE MUFFINS

The best way to have an apple a day.

**2-3/4 cups MUFFIN MIX,
    page 19**
1/2 cup chopped nuts
1/2 teaspoon ground cloves
2 cups grated apples
1 egg, beaten
**1/4 cup melted butter or
    margarine or oil**
1 cup milk

Preheat oven to 400F (205C). Spray muffin pans with vegetable cooking spray. In a medium bowl, combine MUFFIN MIX, nuts and cloves. Combine apples, egg and butter, margarine or oil and milk in a medium bowl. Add all at once to dry ingredients. Stir until just moistened; batter should be lumpy. Fill prepared muffin pans 3/4 full. Bake 18 to 20 minutes until golden brown. Makes 10 large muffins.

GRAN MUFFINS

Start your day right with hearty muffins made from granola.

2 cups MUFFIN MIX, page 19
**3/4 cup GRANOLA MIX,
    page 32**
1 egg, beaten
1/4 cup melted butter
1 cup milk

Preheat oven to 425F (220C). Spray muffin pans with vegetable cooking spray. In a bowl, combine MUFFIN MIX and GRANOLA MIX. In a bowl, combine egg, butter and milk. Add all at once to dry ingredients. Stir until moistened. Fill muffin pans 2/3 full. Bake 15 to 20 minutes. Makes 9 large muffins.

CAKES

Don't want the fuss and mess of making a cake from scratch? Try the ultimate dessert convenience—SNACK CAKE MIX. Although the recipes that use this mix describe two steps for the convenience of beginners, you can mix all of the ingredients in the baking pan to save time, effort and dishwashing. Most of the cakes do not need frosting or they create their own frosting while baking. The Carrot Snack Cake gives you the option of substituting a jar of baby-food carrots for the grated carrots in the recipe, making it even easier to prepare.

Boston Cream Pie is another old-time favorite that is always welcome. The tender yellow cake is accented with a cream filling and chocolate frosting. Special occasions require a fitting dessert. We often celebrate birthdays with Mom's Spumoni Cake.

When you long for a sinfully delicious, rich dessert make Mississippi Mud. It doesn't have great eye appeal, but the taste is unequaled.

Delicious as it is, topping each serving with a dollop of whipped cream is wonderful.

APPLESAUCE SNACK CAKE

This cake is even better the day after it's baked.

1 pkg. SNACK CAKE MIX,
  page 24
1 egg
1/3 cup vegetable oil
3/4 cup applesauce
1-1/2 teaspoons ground
  cinnamon
1/2 teaspoon ground allspice
1/8 teaspoon ground cloves
1/2 cup chopped nuts
1 cup raisins

Preheat oven to 325F (165C). Pour SNACK CAKE MIX into ungreased 8- or 9-inch-square baking pan; set aside.

In a small bowl, combine egg, oil, applesauce, cinnamon, allspice and cloves, beating with a fork to blend. Stir into SNACK CAKE MIX until smooth and blended. Stir in nuts and raisins. Bake 35 to 45 minutes until a wooden pick inserted in center comes out clean. Cool. Makes 9 servings.

BANANA-WALNUT SNACK CAKE

For a decorative look, place a paper doily on cooled cake, dust with powdered sugar, then remove doily.

**1 pkg. SNACK CAKE MIX,
   page 24**
1 egg
1/3 cup vegetable oil
1/2 cup mashed ripe banana
**1/2 cup buttermilk, milk
   or water**
1/2 cup chopped walnuts

Preheat oven to 350F (175C). Pour SNACK CAKE MIX into ungreased 8- or 9-inch-square baking pan.

In a small bowl, combine remaining ingredients, beating with a fork to blend. Stir into SNACK CAKE MIX until blended. Bake 35 to 45 minutes in preheated oven until a wooden pick inserted in center comes out clean. Cool. Makes 9 servings.

BANANA-SPLIT CAKE

And you thought banana splits were only made from ice cream!

2 cups GRAHAM-CRACKER-CRUST MIX, page 16

1/4 cup butter or margarine, melted

1 cup butter or margarine, softened

2 cups sifted powdered sugar

3 to 4 bananas

1-1/2 cups fresh crushed pineapple, drained or 1 (15-oz.) can crushed pineapple, drained

2 cups sweetened whipped cream or 1 (13-oz.) carton whipped topping

1/4 to 1/2 cup chopped nuts

In a medium bowl, combine GRAHAM-CRACKER-CRUST MIX and 1/4 cup melted butter or margarine. Press into an unbuttered 13"x 9" pan.

In a medium bowl, beat together 1 cup butter or margarine and powdered sugar until smooth. Spread over crust in pan. Slice bananas and place evenly over top of mixture. Spread pineapple over bananas. Top with whipped cream or whipped topping. Sprinkle with nuts. Refrigerate 3 to 4 hours. Makes about 12 servings.

1. Slice bananas over the mixture and spoon pineapple over bananas.

2. Top with whipped topping and nuts and refrigerate. Don't bake!

BOSTON CREAM PIE

For some reason this delicious cream-filled cake is known as a cream pie.

1/2 recipe Yellow Cake, page 289
Cream Filling, below
Chocolate Frosting, below

Cream Filling
1 egg yolk
1/3 cup VANILLA PUDDING & PIE-FILLING MIX, page 29
1-1/4 cups milk
1 tablespoon butter or margarine
1 teaspoon vanilla extract

Chocolate Frosting
1 cup sifted powdered sugar
2 tablespoons hot water
1 (1-oz.) square unsweetened chocolate, melted
1 teaspoon butter or margarine, melted

Preheat oven to 350F (175C). Prepare Yellow Cake as directed. Bake 30 minutes until cake is lightly browned and a wooden pick inserted in center comes out clean. Cool. Cut cake in half horizontally. Place bottom layer on a platter.

Prepare Cream Filling; cool. Prepare Chocolate Frosting; set aside. Spread cooled filling over bottom cake layer. Place top layer on top of filling. Spread frosting over top. Refrigerate 3 to 4 hours. Makes 8 servings.

Cream Filling
In a bowl, lightly beat egg yolk; set aside. In a saucepan, combine VANILLA PUDDING & PIE-FILLING MIX and milk. Cook and stir until mixture thickens, 3 to 5 minutes. Stirring vigorously, pour 1/2 hot milk mixture into beaten egg yolk. Slowly stir egg mixture into remaining hot milk mixture. Cook 1 minute longer. Remove from heat. Stir in butter or margarine and vanilla. Cover with plastic wrap; cool.

Chocolate Frosting
In a medium bowl, combine powdered sugar and water. Beat in chocolate and butter or margarine until smooth.

CARAMEL-NUT PUDDING CAKE

Delicate cake and scrumptious caramel pudding—what a combination!

1 cup QUICK MIX, page 21
1/2 cup brown sugar, packed
1/2 cup raisins, if desired
1/2 cup chopped nuts
1/2 cup milk
Brown-Sugar Topping, below

Brown-Sugar Topping
1 cup brown sugar, packed
1 tablespoon butter or
    margarine
2 cups boiling water

Preheat oven to 375F (190C). Lightly grease an 8-inch-square pan. In a medium bowl, combine QUICK MIX, brown sugar, raisins, if desired, and nuts. Mix well. Add milk and blend well. Pour into prepared pan.

Prepare Brown-Sugar Topping. Gently pour over top of cake mixture without stirring. Bake 30 to 40 minutes, until cake springs back when lightly touched in center. Cool in pan 15 minutes before serving. Makes one 8-inch cake.

Brown-Sugar Topping
Combine brown sugar, butter or margarine and boiling water. Blend.

CARROT SNACK CAKE

*For added convenience, substi-
tute a 7-ounce jar of junior baby-
food carrots for the grated carrots
and orange juice.*

**1 pkg. SNACK CAKE MIX,
  page 24**
1 egg
1/3 cup vegetable oil
1 cup grated carrots
3/4 cup orange juice
1 teaspoon ground cinnamon
1/2 cup chopped nuts
Cream-Cheese Frosting, below

Cream-Cheese Frosting
**3 tablespoons butter or
  margarine, softened**
**1 (3-oz.) pkg. cream cheese,
  softened**
**1-2/3 cups powdered sugar,
  sifted**
1/2 teaspoon vanilla extract

Preheat oven to 350F (175C). Pour
SNACK CAKE MIX into an ungreased
8- or 9-inch-square baking pan.

In a medium bowl, combine egg, oil,
carrots, orange juice and cinnamon,
beating with a fork to blend. Stir into
SNACK CAKE MIX until blended. Stir in
nuts. Bake 35 to 45 minutes until a
wooden pick inserted in center comes
out clean. Prepare Cream-Cheese
Frosting; set aside. Cool cake on a rack.
Spread frosting evenly over cooled cake.
Makes 9 servings.

Cream-Cheese Frosting
In a small bowl, cream butter or
margarine and cream cheese until light
and fluffy. Beat in powdered sugar and
vanilla until smooth.

DOUBLE-CHOCOLATE SNACK CAKE

We have demonstrated this cake before thousands of individuals throughout the country. Everyone loves it.

1 pkg. SNACK CAKE MIX, page 24
2 tablespoons unsweetened cocoa powder
3/4 cup water
1 egg
1/3 cup vegetable oil
1 teaspoon vanilla extract
1/2 cup semisweet mini-chocolate chips
1/2 cup chopped nuts

Variation

Bumpy-Road Snack Cake—Omit unsweetened cocoa powder. Substitute buttermilk for water.

Preheat oven to 350F (175C). In an ungreased 8- or 9-inch-square baking pan, combine SNACK CAKE MIX and cocoa powder. In a medium bowl, combine water, egg, vegetable oil and vanilla. Beat with a fork to blend. Stir into cocoa mixture until smooth and blended. Sprinkle chocolate chips and nuts evenly over top of batter. Bake 35 to 45 minutes in preheated oven until surface springs back when touched with your fingers. Makes 9 servings.

HOT-FUDGE PUDDING CAKE

Chocolate cake on top and a fudge pudding sauce below. Serve it à la mode!

1-1/2 cups QUICK MIX, page 21
1/2 cup granulated sugar
2 tablespoons cocoa
3/4 cup chopped nuts
1/2 cup milk
1 teaspoon vanilla extract
3/4 cup brown sugar, packed
1/4 cup cocoa
1-1/2 cups boiling water

Variation

Omit nuts and add 1 cup miniature marshmallows.

Preheat oven to 350F (175C). In an unbuttered, 8-inch-square pan, combine QUICK MIX, granulated sugar, 2 tablespoons cocoa, nuts, milk and vanilla. Blend well.

Combine brown sugar and 1/4 cup cocoa in a small bowl. Sprinkle over top of cake mixture. Gently pour boiling water over top of mixture. Do not stir. Bake 35 to 40 minutes, until edges separate from pan. Cool in pan 15 minutes before serving. Makes one 8-inch cake.

CRANBERRY CAKES WITH BUTTER SAUCE

Hot Butter Sauce complements the tart cranberries in this fall dessert. Use your food processor to chop cranberries.

1 cup raw cranberries, chopped
1/4 cup sugar
2-3/4 cups MUFFIN MIX,
   page 19
1 cup dairy sour cream
1 egg, beaten
1/4 cup butter or margarine
   or oil
Hot Butter Sauce, page 294

Preheat oven to 400F (205C). Generously grease muffin pans. In a medium bowl, combine cranberries and sugar. Let stand a few minutes.

Put MUFFIN MIX in a medium bowl. Combine sour cream, egg and butter or margarine or oil with cranberry mixture. Blend well. Add mixture all at once to MUFFIN MIX. Stir until just moistened; batter should be lumpy. Fill prepared muffin pans 3/4 full. Bake 18 to 20 minutes, until golden brown. Serve warm with Hot Butter Sauce. Makes about 10 cakes.

Welcome visitors with these pretty little cakes. For a more intense flavor add 1/3 cup dried cranberries to the batter.

MOM'S SPUMONI CAKE

This prize-winner was created by Karine's "Mom."

Rainbow Frosting, below
3-1/3 cups ALL-PURPOSE CAKE
 MIX, page 23
1/4 cup brown sugar, packed
3/4 cup cocoa powder
1/4 teaspoon baking soda
1-1/2 cups buttermilk
3 eggs
1 teaspoon vanilla extract
1/4 cup butter or margarine,
 melted

Rainbow Frosting
1 cup milk
2 tablespoons all-purpose flour
Pinch of salt
1/2 cup butter or margarine,
 softened
1/2 cup vegetable shortening
1 cup granulated sugar
2 to 3 drops each green, yellow
 and red food coloring
1/4 teaspoon each almond,
 lemon and peppermint
 flavorings
3 tablespoons cocoa powder
1/4 teaspoon vanilla extract

Prepare Rainbow Frosting; set aside. Preheat oven to 350F (175C). Grease and flour two 8- or 9-inch-round cake pans. Combine ALL-PURPOSE CAKE MIX, brown sugar, cocoa powder and soda. Mix well. Add buttermilk, eggs, vanilla and butter or margarine. Beat on high speed for 3 to 4 minutes. Pour into prepared pans. Bake 25 to 35 minutes, until a wooden pick inserted in center comes out clean.

Cool 10 minutes. When cool, cut each layer horizontally in 2. Frost each layer with a different color. Stack layers. Do not frost sides. Makes one 4-layer cake.

Rainbow Frosting
In a saucepan, combine milk, flour and salt. Stirring constantly cook 5 to 7 minutes, until thickened. Cool. Combine butter or margarine, shortening and sugar in a bowl. Beat well. Add to cooled milk mixture, beating constantly. Beat about 7 minutes, until smooth.

Divide among 4 bowls. In first bowl, add green food coloring and almond flavoring. In second, add yellow food coloring and lemon flavoring. In third, add red food coloring and peppermint flavoring. To fourth add cocoa powder and vanilla.

Mom's Spumoni Cake

GINGERBREAD SNACK CAKE

The smell of baking creates a wonderful aroma in your kitchen. Top with hot lemon sauce for an old-fashioned treat.

**1 pkg. SNACK CAKE MIX,
    page 24
3/4 cup hot water
1/3 cup molasses
1 egg
1/3 cup vegetable oil
1 teaspoon ground cinnamon
1 teaspoon ground ginger
1/2 teaspoon ground cloves
Hot Lemon Sauce, page 322**

Preheat oven to 350F (175C). Pour SNACK CAKE MIX into an ungreased 8- or 9-inch-square baking pan; set aside.

In a medium bowl, combine hot water, molasses, egg, vegetable oil, cinnamon, ginger and cloves. Beat with a fork to blend. Stir into SNACK CAKE MIX until blended. Bake 35 to 45 minutes in preheated oven until a wooden pick inserted in center comes out clean. Prepare Hot Lemon Sauce. Serve over warm gingerbread. Makes 9 servings.

One of our friends tops each serving with sliced peaches before spooning on the Lemon Sauce.

LEMON POUND CAKE

Served plain, glazed with a lemon glaze or dusted with powdered sugar.

5 cups ALL-PURPOSE CAKE MIX, page 23
1/4 cup vegetable shortening
1 cup sugar
1 cup milk
5 eggs
1/4 cup lemon juice
1-1/2 teaspoons lemon extract
1 teaspoon vanilla extract

Variation

Almond-Poppy Seed Pound Cake—Substitute 1/4 cup milk for lemon juice. Substitute almond extract for the lemon extract. Add 1/4 cup poppy seeds.

Preheat oven to 350F (175C). Generously grease and lightly flour one 12-cup Bundt pan; set aside.

In a large bowl, combine ALL-PURPOSE CAKE MIX, shortening and sugar. Beat with electric mixer. Gradually add milk and continue beating. Add eggs one at a time, beating well after each addition until batter is creamy. Beat in lemon juice, lemon extract and vanilla extract until well blended. Pour into prepared pan. Bake 1 hour and 20 to 25 minutes, until a wooden pick inserted in center comes out clean. Cool on a rack 15 minutes. Remove pan. Makes 12 to 16 servings.

MISSISSIPPI MUD

Appropriately named for its appearance—incredibly delicious.

2 eggs
1/3 cup butter or margarine, melted
2 cups BROWNIE MIX, page 14
1/2 teaspoon vanilla extract
1 cup chopped nuts
1 cup flaked coconut
1 (7-oz.) jar marshmallow creme
Chocolate Icing, below

Chocolate Icing
1-3/4 cups powdered sugar
1/4 cup butter or margarine
3 tablespoons evaporated milk
2 tablespoons unsweetened cocoa powder

Preheat oven to 350F (175C). Lightly grease and lightly flour an 11" x 7" pan. In a large bowl, beat eggs until foamy. Add melted butter or margarine and mix well. Add BROWNIE MIX and blend well. Stir in vanilla. Stir in nuts and coconut. Pour into prepared pan.

Bake about 30 minutes, until edges separate from pan. While still hot, carefully spread on marshmallow creme. When cool, frost with Chocolate Icing.

Chocolate Icing
Put powdered sugar in a medium bowl. In a small saucepan, combine butter or margarine, evaporated milk and cocoa. Bring to a boil, stirring constantly. Remove from heat. Immediately add to powdered sugar. Beat until smooth.

OATMEAL SPICE CAKE

The topping makes this cake extra special, but it's good plain too. It stays moist and is a great addition to picnics and potlucks.

3/4 cup rolled oats
1-1/4 cups boiling water
1 pkg. SNACK CAKE MIX,
   page 24
1 egg
1/3 cup vegetable oil
1 teaspoon ground cinnamon
1/2 teaspoon ground nutmeg
1 teaspoon vanilla extract
1/2 cup chopped nuts
1/2 cup raisins
Broiled Coconut Topping, below

Preheat oven to 325F (165C). Pour rolled oats into a small bowl. Stir in boiling water; set aside. Pour SNACK CAKE MIX in an ungreased 8- or 9-inch-square baking pan; set aside. In a medium bowl, combine egg, vegetable oil, cinnamon, nutmeg and vanilla. Stir in nuts and raisins. Beat with a fork to blend. Stir in softened rolled oats mixture. Stir into SNACK CAKE MIX until evenly distributed. Bake 45 minutes in preheated oven until a wooden pick inserted in center comes out clean.

Prepare Broiled Coconut Topping. Spread topping evenly over cake as it comes from oven. Turn oven to broil. Place cake in oven 3 inches below broiling element. Broil about 2 minutes until frosting bubbles. Makes 9 servings.

Broiled Coconut Topping
4 tablespoons butter or
   margarine
1/4 cup brown sugar, packed
2 tablespoons milk
1/2 teaspoon vanilla extract
1/2 cup shredded coconut
1/2 cup chopped nuts

Broiled Coconut Topping
In a small saucepan, melt butter or margarine. Stir in remaining ingredients.

PINEAPPLE UPSIDE-DOWN CAKE

A light, moist cake with a tangy fruit topping.

Brown-Sugar Topping, below
3 cups QUICK MIX, page 21
1-1/3 cups sugar
1 cup milk
3 eggs, slightly beaten
1-1/2 teaspoons vanilla extract
**1 (20-oz.) can crushed
    pineapple, drained**

Brown-Sugar Topping
1 cup brown sugar, packed
**1/2 cup butter or margarine,
    room temperature**

Variation

Substitute canned or frozen, thawed and drained fruit for pineapple. Try apples, apricots, peaches, or pears. If using strawberries or raspberries, substitute granulated sugar for brown sugar.

Lightly grease a 13" x 9" baking pan or two 8-inch-square pans. Prepare Brown-Sugar Topping and set aside. Preheat oven to 350F (175C). Combine QUICK MIX and sugar in a bowl. Mix well. In another bowl, combine milk, eggs and vanilla. Add half of milk mixture to dry ingredients. Beat 2 minutes until smooth. Add remaining milk mixture; beat 2 to 3 minutes.

Distribute Brown-Sugar Topping over bottom of pan. Spoon pineapple smoothly over topping. Spread batter over pineapple. Bake 35 to 45 minutes, until center springs back when lightly touched. Cool in pan 10 minutes. Invert onto a serving plate. Serve warm. Makes one large cake.

Brown-Sugar Topping
Combine ingredients.

Cool in pan 10 minutes Then invert onto a serving plate. Serve warm.

YELLOW CAKE

The secret to this moist, tender cake is to beat the batter until creamy.

5 cups ALL-PURPOSE CAKE MIX, page 23
1-1/4 cups milk
1 teaspoon vanilla extract
3 eggs

Variation

White Cake—Use only egg whites.

Preheat oven to 350F (175C). Generously grease and lightly flour two 8- or 9-inch-round cake pans or one 13" x 9" baking pan; set aside. In a large bowl, combine ALL-PURPOSE CAKE MIX, milk and vanilla. Beat with electric mixer on high speed 1 minute. Scrape batter from side of bowl with a rubber spatula. Beat on high 1 minute longer. Add eggs 1 at a time, beating well after each addition until batter is creamy. Pour into prepared pans.

Bake 30 to 35 minutes for 8- or 9-inch-round pans; bake 13" x 9" pan 35 to 40 minutes, until a wooden pick inserted in center comes out clean. Cool on a rack 10 minutes. Invert onto rack and remove pan, if desired. Frost, if desired, when cake is completely cool.
Makes 1 or 2 cakes.

Small Cake
Use half the ingredients (using 2 egg yolks or whites) and bake in 8-inch-square pan.

SUNDAY SHORTCAKE

Old-fashioned—with your choice of fruit.

3 cups QUICK MIX, page 21
2 tablespoons sugar
1/4 cup butter or margarine,
  melted
1/2 cup milk or water
1 egg, well-beaten
Fruit, as desired
Whipped cream

Preheat oven to 400F (205C). Combine QUICK MIX and sugar in a bowl. Mix well. In a small bowl, combine melted butter or margarine, milk or water and egg. Add to dry ingredients. Stir with a fork until just moistened.

On a lightly floured surface, knead 8 to 10 times. Roll out dough to 1/2-inch thickness. Cut with a lightly floured 3-inch-round cutter. Bake on an unbuttered baking sheet about 10 minutes, until golden brown. Cool. Top with fruit as desired and whipped cream. Makes 6 shortcakes.

We grew up thinking shortcake meant summer and fresh strawberries. With so many other berries and fresh fruits in our markets year-round, you can enjoy this treat whenever the urge strikes you.

TEXAS SHEET CAKE

A Bi-i-i-i-ig Brownie Cake. Super moist and stores well.

4 cups BROWNIE MIX,
    page 14
1/2 cup butter or margarine
1 cup water
1/2 cup dairy sour cream
2 eggs, slightly beaten
1 teaspoon baking soda
Cocoa Icing, below

Cocoa Icing
1/2 cup evaporated milk
1/2 cup butter or margarine
3 tablespoons unsweetened
    cocoa powder
3 cups powdered sugar
1 cup chopped nuts
1 teaspoon vanilla extract

Preheat oven to 375F (190C). Grease a 15" x 10" or larger baking pan. Put BROWNIE MIX in a large bowl. In a small saucepan, bring butter or margarine and water to a boil. Add to BROWNIE MIX. Add sour cream, eggs and baking soda. Blend well. Pour into prepared pan.

Bake 20 to 25 minutes, until a toothpick inserted in center comes out clean. Prepare Cocoa Icing. Frost cake while still hot. Makes one large cake.

Cocoa Icing
In a small saucepan, bring evaporated milk, butter or margarine and cocoa to a boil, stirring constantly. Remove from heat. Place powdered sugar in a bowl, add cocoa mixture. Beat. Stir in nuts and vanilla.

DATE-CHOCOLATE-CHIP SNACK CAKE

*A terrific picnic cake adapted
from Grandma Eliason's famous
cake. As important to our family
picnic as the people.*

1/2 cup chopped dates
3/4 cup boiling water
1 pkg. SNACK CAKE MIX,
  page 24
1/2 teaspoon ground cinnamon
1/3 cup vegetable oil
1 egg
1/2 teaspoon vanilla extract
1/2 cup brown sugar, packed
1/2 cup chopped nuts
1/2 cup chocolate chips

Preheat oven to 350F (175C). In a
small bowl, combine dates and boiling
water. Set aside.

Pour SNACK CAKE MIX into an
ungreased 8- or 9-inch-square baking
pan. Add cinnamon, vegetable oil, egg,
vanilla and cooled date mixture. Stir
with a fork until all ingredients are
blended. Top with brown sugar, nuts and
then chocolate chips. Bake 35 to 45
minutes until done. Cool on rack.
Makes 9 servings.

PIES

Ask your friends to name their favorite dessert and the answer will be apple pie. Our All-American Apple Pie will win you compliments each time it is served. Nevada's family always tops theirs with a Hot Butter Sauce.

We have taken the chore out of pie-making by giving you fail-proof recipes for FREEZER PIE-CRUST MIX and CREAM-CHEESE PASTRY MIX. To ensure a tender crust, handle the dough as little as possible. Roll the dough outward from the center, being careful to lift the rolling pin before it reaches the edge. This will keep the edge from becoming too thin.

Our cream pies are made from Chocolate and Vanilla Pudding & Pie Fillings. Although it sounds tart, you are in for a pleasant surprise with our Sour Cream & Orange Pie. A delightful filling hides under the Mile-High Meringue.

Tarts, those delectable individual pies, are especially popular in the South. For Pecan, Chess and Lime tarts we use CREAM-CHEESE PASTRY MIX. If you are looking for a spectacular dessert for a special occasion, try Cookie Crust Fruit Tart. Choose fruits of contrasting colors and shapes and create a masterpiece. Its beauty belies how easy it is to prepare.

ALL-AMERICAN APPLE PIE

One of Nevada's favorites and the most-requested pie we make. We use Granny Smith or Pippin apples and frequently throw in some Macintosh apples, too.

1 Double Freezer Pie Crust, unbaked, page 309
8 or 9 large tart cooking apples, pared, cored and sliced thin
Juice of 1 lemon (about 1/4 cup)
6 tablespoons all-purpose flour
3/4 cup sugar, more if desired
1 teaspoon ground cinnamon
1 teaspoon ground nutmeg
2 tablespoons butter

Hot Butter Sauce
1/2 cup butter
1 cup sugar
1 cup cream or evaporated milk
Dash of nutmeg

Prepare bottom crust in a 9-inch pie plate. Put apples in a large bowl. Toss with lemon juice. Set aside. Preheat oven to 400F (205C). In a small bowl, combine flour, sugar, cinnamon and nutmeg. Sprinkle about 1/4 cup of mixture on the bottom pie crust and add the rest to the apples. Stir to coat apples. Fill pie crust heaping full of apple mixture. Dot with butter.

Place top crust over filling. Press edges together and flute. Cut slits in top crust to let steam escape. Bake about 50 minutes, until crust is golden. Serve with Hot Butter Sauce. Makes one 9-inch double-crust pie.

Hot Butter Sauce
Combine butter, sugar and cream or evaporated milk in a small saucepan. Cook over medium heat 3 to 5 minutes, until butter melts and sugar dissolves. Do not boil. Remove from heat. Add nutmeg. Serve warm. Makes about 1-1/2 cups sauce.

All-American Apple Pie

CHOCOLATE CREAM PIE

Smooth, creamy and delicious

**Single Freezer Pie Crust, baked,
  page 309**
**1 cup CHOCOLATE PUDDING &
  PIE-FILLING MIX,
  page 27**
2-1/2 cups milk
**2 tablespoons butter or
  margarine**
1 teaspoon vanilla extract
**2 cups sweetened whipped
  cream, if desired**

Prepare pie crust in a 9-inch pie plate; set aside to cool. In a saucepan, combine CHOCOLATE PUDDING & PIE-FILLING MIX and milk. Cook and stir over medium heat until mixture thickens and begins to bubble, 3 to 5 minutes. Cook and stir 1 minute longer.

Remove from heat. Stir in butter or margarine and vanilla until blended. Cool slightly. Pour into pie crust; cover with plastic wrap. Refrigerate 2 to 3 hours. To serve, top with sweetened whipped cream, if desired. Makes 8 servings.

For a variation of this favorite, make Chocolate Banana Cream Pie by slicing 2 bananas into the baked pie crust. Garnish with chocolate curls and dust with powdered sugar.

CHERRY-ALMOND PIE

For special occasions, make a lattice-top crust by weaving strips of dough.

2 cups fresh tart cherries, pitted
1 (1-lb.) can pitted tart red cherries
1-1/4 cups sugar
1/3 cup all-purpose flour
1/4 teaspoon salt
1 tablespoon butter or margarine, melted
1/4 teaspoon almond extract
1/4 teaspoon red food coloring, if desired
Double Freezer Pie Crust, unbaked, page 309
Almond Glaze, below

Almond Glaze
1 cup powdered sugar
1/2 teaspoon almond extract
About 2 tablespoons cream or milk

Drain canned cherries, reserving 1/2 cup juice. In a medium bowl, combine fresh and canned cherries, sugar, flour, salt, butter or margarine, almond extract, 1/2 cup reserved cherry juice and food coloring, if desired. Let stand about 10 minutes.

Preheat oven to 425F (220C). Prepare bottom pie crust in a 9-inch pie plate. Pour cherry mixture into unbaked crust. Cover with top crust. Cut slits in crust to let steam escape. Trim and flute edges. Bake about 40 minutes until evenly browned. Prepare Almond Glaze. Brush top of hot pie with Almond Glaze. Makes about 8 servings.

Almond Glaze
In a small bowl, combine powdered sugar, almond extract and enough cream or milk to make a thin mixture.

297

IMPOSSIBLE PIE

Spicy pie forms its own custard on the bottom with a cake-like crust on top.

1/2 cup sugar
4 eggs
2 cups milk
1 teaspoon vanilla extract
3 tablespoons butter or
   margarine, melted
1/2 teaspoon ground cinnamon
1/4 teaspoon ground nutmeg
1/2 cup QUICK MIX, page 21

Preheat oven to 400F (205C). Butter a 9-inch pie plate. In a blender, combine sugar, eggs, milk, vanilla, melted butter or margarine, cinnamon and nutmeg. Blend until smooth. Add QUICK MIX and blend 30 more seconds. Pour into prepared pie pan. Bake 25 to 30 minutes until golden. Cool. Serve warm. Makes one 9-inch pie.

LUSCIOUS LEMON PIE

Tart and well worth the pucker!

**Single Freezer Pie Crust, baked,
   page 309**
**1-1/4 cups LEMON PIE-FILLING
   MIX, page 28**
2-1/2 cups water
3 egg yolks
**2 tablespoons butter or
   margarine**
Sweetened whipped cream

Variation

Meringue Topping—Omit
   whipped-cream topping. In a
   deep metal or glass bowl, beat
   3 egg whites until stiff, gradually adding 6 tablespoons
   sugar and 1/4 teaspoon
   cream of tartar. Spread on top
   of warm pie, sealing to edges.
   Preheat oven to 400F (205C).
   Bake 8 to 10 minutes, until
   meringue is lightly browned.
   Cool pie, then refrigerate.

Prepare pie crust. In a large saucepan,
combine LEMON PIE-FILLING MIX,
1/2 cup of the water and egg yolks. Mix
until smooth. Add remaining 2 cups
water. Cook over medium heat, 4 to 5
minutes, stirring constantly until mixture
is thick and bubbly.

Remove from heat. Add butter or margarine. Stir until melted. Cover and let
cool 5 minutes. Stir. Pour into baked pie
crust. Cover and refrigerate 3 hours.
Top with whipped cream before serving.
Makes one 9-inch single-crust pie.

FRESH PEACH PIE

When in season, use fresh straw-berries, blueberries, plums or nectarines.

**Single Freezer Pie Crust, baked,
    page 309**
1 cup fresh peaches, crushed
1/3 cup water
1 cup sugar
4 tablespoons cornstarch
Pinch of salt
1/4 cup water
1 tablespoon lemon juice
**1 tablespoon butter or
    margarine**
3 to 4 cups sliced fresh peaches
**2 cups sweetened whipped
    cream or 1 (8-oz.) container
    nondairy topping, thawed,
    for garnish**

Prepare pie crust in a 9-inch pie plate; set aside to cool. In a medium saucepan, combine 1 cup crushed peaches and 1/3 cup water. Stir constantly over medium heat until mixture begins to boil. Cook and stir about 2 minutes longer. Remove from heat.

In a medium bowl, combine sugar, cornstarch, salt, 1/4 cup water and lemon juice, beating with a wire whisk to blend. Stir into cooked-peach mixture. Cook and stir over medium heat until slightly thickened. Stir in butter or margarine until melted. Set aside to cool.

Arrange 3 to 4 cups sliced peaches in prepared pie crust. Spoon cooled mixture over peaches. Cover and refrigerate 2 hours. To serve, cut in wedges and garnish each wedge with a dollop of whipped cream or topping. Makes about 8 servings.

*If you want the filling a bit
more colorful, add 1 or 2 drops
of red food coloring to water.*

SOUR CREAM & RAISIN PIE

To change the pie, top it with Mile-High Meringue, page 310.

Single Freezer Pie Crust, baked, page 309

2/3 cup VANILLA PUDDING & PIE-FILLING MIX, page 29

2-1/2 cups milk

1/4 teaspoon ground nutmeg

1/4 teaspoon ground cinnamon

1/3 cup raisins

2 tablespoons butter or margarine

1 teaspoon vanilla extract

1 cup dairy sour cream

2 cups sweetened whipped cream or 1 (8-oz.) container nondairy whipped topping, thawed

Prepare pie crust in a 9-inch pie plate; set aside to cool. In a medium saucepan, combine VANILLA PUDDING & PIE-FILLING MIX, milk, nutmeg, cinnamon and raisins. Cook and stir over medium heat until mixture thickens and begins to bubble, 3 to 5 minutes. Remove from heat.

Stir in butter or margarine and vanilla until blended. Cover with plastic wrap. Cool. Fold in sour cream. Pour into baked pie crust. Cover and refrigerate about 2 hours. Top with sweetened whipped cream or topping. Makes about 8 servings.

VANILLA CREAM PIE

Creamy pie filling has no eggs—reducing the fat content.

Single Freezer Pie Crust, baked, page 309
2/3 cup VANILLA PUDDING & PIE-FILLING MIX, page 29
2-1/2 cups milk
2 tablespoons butter or margarine
1-1/2 teaspoons vanilla extract

Variations

Banana Cream Pie—Slice 2 ripe bananas into pie crust before adding filling.

Strawberry Cream Pie—Stir 2 to 4 tablespoons sugar into 2 cups sliced strawberries. Let stand 1 hour. Drain off juice. Spoon sweetened strawberries into baked pie crust. Pour chilled filling over strawberries. Top with whipped cream.

Coconut Cream Pie—Fold 3/4 cup shredded coconut into cooled filling. Garnish with whipped cream and 1/4 cup toasted shredded coconut.

Prepare crust in a 9-inch pie plate; set aside to cool. In a medium saucepan, combine VANILLA PUDDING & PIE-FILLING MIX and milk. Cook and stir over medium heat until mixture thickens and begins to bubble, 3 to 5 minutes. Remove from heat. Stir in butter or margarine and vanilla until blended. Cover with plastic wrap. Cool.

Pour into baked pie crust. Cover and refrigerate about 2 hours. Makes about 8 servings.

CHESS TARTS

Serve these Southern favorites at a holiday buffet.

1 pkg. **CREAM-CHEESE PASTRY MIX**, page 50, thawed
1/2 cup **butter or margarine**, softened
1-1/4 cups **sugar**
3 **eggs**, separated
3/4 cup **raisins**
3/4 cup **chopped nuts**
1 teaspoon **vanilla extract**

Preheat oven to 400F (205C). Divide CREAM-CHEESE PASTRY MIX into 10 pieces. Shape into balls. Place each ball in a medium muffin cup. With your thumbs press dough over bottom and sides of each cup, keeping dough at an even thickness; set aside. In a large bowl, cream butter or margarine and sugar. Add egg yolks, 1 at a time, beating thoroughly after each addition. Stir in raisins, nuts and vanilla.

In a medium bowl, beat egg whites until soft peaks form. Fold into creamed mixture. Fill each pastry shell about 3/4 full with batter. Bake 15 minutes in preheated oven. Reduce temperature to 325F (165C). Bake 10 to 15 minutes longer until golden brown. Makes 10 tarts.

LIME TARTS SUPREME

Creamy chiffon filling is topped with a dollop of whipped cream and grated lime peel.

1 pkg. CREAM-CHEESE PASTRY
MIX, page 50, thawed
Lime Filling, below

Lime Filling
2 eggs
1/2 cup sugar
1/4 cup lime juice
1 teaspoon grated lime peel
1/4 cup butter or margarine
2 drops green food coloring,
if desired
1 cup whipping cream,
whipped

Preheat oven to 400F (205C). Divide CREAM-CHEESE PASTRY MIX into 10 pieces. Shape into balls. Place each ball in a medium muffin cup. With your thumbs press dough over the bottom and sides of each cup, keeping dough at an even thickness. Bake in preheated oven 10 minutes or until lightly browned. Cool.

Prepare Lime Filling. Carefully remove cooled tart shells. Spoon filling into shells. Garnish with reserved whipped cream and reserved lime peel from filling. Makes 10 tarts.

Lime Filling
In a small bowl, beat eggs until light and pale. Beat in sugar, lime juice and half of lime peel. Pour into top of double boiler. Add butter or margarine. Cook and stir over hot water until thickened. Remove from heat. Stir in food coloring. Refrigerate 1 hour.

Reserve 3 tablespoons whipped cream. Fold remaining whipped cream into chilled egg mixture.

*For a tropical treat:
Omit pecans and
vanilla extract.
Substitute macadamia
nuts and orange or
coconut extract.*

PECAN TARTS

Miniature pecan pies are always a welcome treat.

**1 pkg. CREAM-CHEESE PASTRY
  MIX, page 50, thawed**
2 eggs, slightly beaten
**2 tablespoons butter or
  margarine, melted**
1-1/2 cups brown sugar, packed
1/8 teaspoon salt
2 teaspoons vanilla extract
1-1/4 cups chopped pecans

Preheat oven to 325F (165C). Divide CREAM-CHEESE PASTRY MIX into 10 pieces. Shape into balls. Place each ball in a medium muffin cup. With your thumbs press dough over bottom and sides of each cup, keeping dough at an even thickness; set aside.

In a large bowl, combine eggs, butter or margarine, brown sugar, salt and vanilla, beating with a wire whisk until blended. Stir in pecans. Fill each pastry shell about 3/4 full. Bake 25 minutes in preheated oven until golden brown. Makes 10 tarts.

COOKIE CRUST FRUIT TART

A colorful presentation.

**1 roll SLICE-&-BAKE SUGAR
   COOKIES, page 60, thawed**
Cream-Cheese Filling, below
Fruit Glaze, below
**2 to 3 cups fresh or canned
   fruits, drained (berries, kiwi,
   bananas, etc.)**

Preheat oven to 350F (175C). Press thawed dough into a 12-inch quiche pan with removable bottom or pizza pan to 1/4-inch thickness. Make rim around edge of cookie. Bake 15 to 20 minutes until edges brown. Cool. Prepare Cream-Cheese Filling. Spread on top to within 1/2 inch of edge. Prepare Fruit Glaze; set aside. Top filling with concentric circles of assorted fruits. Brush fruit with Fruit Glaze. Cover with plastic wrap and chill. Makes 8 to 12 servings.

Cream-Cheese Filling
**1 (8-oz.) pkg. cream cheese,
   softened**
1/2 cup sugar
1 teaspoon vanilla extract

Cream-Cheese Filling
In a small bowl, mix all ingredients until smooth.

Fruit Glaze
1 tablespoon cornstarch
1/2 cup orange juice
1/4 cup water
2 tablespoons sugar
2 tablespoons fresh lemon juice

Fruit Glaze
In a saucepan, combine all ingredients and boil 1 minute. Cool.

MINI FRUIT TARTS

Eye-appealing tarts make a wonderful addition to any buffet table. Attractively fill and decorate with any fruit in season or a variety of canned pie fillings.

2 pkgs. **CREAM-CHEESE PAS-TRY MIX, page 50, thawed**
3 cups fresh fruit in season
(kiwi, strawberries, raspber-ries, blackberries, green or red grapes, bananas, nec-tarines or peaches. Canned fruits such as mandarin oranges can be added.)
Fruit Glaze, page 306

Variation

Cream-Cheese Fruit Tarts—In a small bowl combine 2 (3-oz.) pkgs. cream cheese and 2 tablespoons sugar until smooth. Stir in 1 (6-oz.) con-tainer fruit-flavored yogurt. Put a spoonful of filling into each shell before adding fruit and brushing with glaze.

Preheat oven to 400F (205C). Divide CREAM-CHEESE PASTRY MIX into about 40 pieces. Shape into balls. Place each ball in a mini-muffin cup. With your thumb, press dough over bottom and sides of each cup, keeping dough an even thickness. Bake in preheated oven 10 minutes or until lightly browned. Cool.

Cut fresh fruit into various shapes—fans, slices, or wedges, as desired.

Prepare Fruit Glaze. Cool. Arrange fruits in decorative designs in each tart shell. You can mix fruits or keep them all the same. Brush with glaze to prevent dark-ening or drying. Chill until ready to serve. Makes about 40 tarts.

CREAM-CHEESE PASTRY

For a change of pace try this rich tasting pastry.

CREAM-CHEESE PASTRY MIX,
page 50, thawed

To make tart shells: Thaw two packages CREAM-CHEESE PASTRY MIX. Divide each package into 10 pieces. Roll each piece into a ball. Preheat oven to 400F (205C). Place each ball in a muffin cup. Use your thumbs to press dough over bottom and sides, keeping dough at an even thickness. Bake 10 to 12 minutes until lightly browned. Cool and remove. Fill as desired.

To make a single pie crust or baked pie shell: Thaw 1 package CREAM-CHEESE PASTRY MIX. On a floured pastry cloth or between pieces of floured plastic wrap, roll out dough to an 11-inch circle. Dough will be quite thin. Remove plastic wrap. Fit dough into an 8- or 9-inch pie pan without stretching. Trim and flute edge. For baked shell, prick bottom and sides with fork tines; bake as for tart shells at left. Or add filling and bake according to filling directions.

To make double-crust pie: Completely thaw 2 packages CREAM-CHEESE PASTRY MIX. Prepare 1 ball of dough according to directions above; do not prick crust or flute edges. Turn filling into shell. Roll out top crust. Place over filling. Press edges together; flute pressed edges. Cut small slits in top crust to let steam escape. Bake according to directions for filling.

FREEZER PIE CRUST

Minimal handling of the dough ensures great results.

**FREEZER PIE-CRUST MIX,
page 51, thawed**

To make tart shells: Thaw two packages FREEZER PIE-CRUST MIX. Divide each package into 10 pieces. Roll each piece into a ball. Preheat oven to 400F (205C). Place each ball in a muffin cup. Use your thumbs to press dough over bottom and sides, keeping dough at an even thickness. Bake 10 to 12 minutes until lightly browned. Cool and remove. Fill as desired.

To make a single pie crust or baked pie shell: Thaw 1 package FREEZER PIE-CRUST MIX. On a floured pastry cloth or between two pieces of floured plastic wrap or wax paper, roll dough to an 11-inch circle. Dough will be thin. Remove plastic wrap. Fit dough into an 8- or 9-inch pie pan without stretching. Trim and flute edge. For shell, prick bottom and sides with fork tines. Bake as for tart shells at left. Or add filling and bake according to filling directions.

To make double-crust pie: Thaw two packages FREEZER PIE-CRUST MIX. Prepare as directed above; do not prick or flute edge. Place filling in shell. Roll out top crust and place over filling. Press edges together and flute or crimp. Cut slits in top crust to let steam escape. Bake according to directions for filling.

1. Roll dough between 2 sheets of floured wax paper.

2. Do not strech pie dough. Place top crust over filling and flute edges.

SOUR CREAM & ORANGE PIE

This meringue will not stick to your fork.

Single Freezer Pie Crust, baked, page 309
1 cup sugar
5 tablespoons cornstarch
Pinch of salt
1 cup milk
3 egg yolks
4 tablespoons butter or margarine
1 teaspoon grated orange peel
1/3 cup fresh orange juice
1 cup dairy sour cream
Mile-High Meringue, below

Prepare pie crust in a 9-inch pie plate; set aside to cool. In a saucepan, combine sugar, cornstarch and salt. Gradually stir in milk. Cook and stir over medium heat until smooth and slightly thickened; set aside. In a small bowl, beat egg yolks. Beating vigorously, add about half of hot mixture. Slowly stir egg mixture into remaining hot mixture. Cook and stir 2 minutes; set aside. Stir in butter or margarine, orange peel and orange juice. Cover with plastic wrap. Cool.

Fold in sour cream. Pour into pie crust; set aside. Preheat oven to 325F (165C). Prepare Mile-High Meringue. Spoon meringue on top of pie, spreading to seal completely. Bake 20 to 30 minutes until golden brown. Makes 8 servings.

Mile-High Meringue
1 tablespoon cornstarch
3 tablespoons sugar
Pinch of salt
1 teaspoon orange juice
1/2 cup water
3 egg whites, room temperature
6 tablespoons sugar

Mile-High Meringue
In a saucepan, combine cornstarch, 3 tablespoons sugar, salt, orange juice and water. Cook and stir over medium heat until clear and thickened. Set aside to cool. In a bowl, beat egg whites until soft peaks form. Gradually add cooled cornstarch mixture, beating until mixture thickens. Gradually add 6 tablespoons sugar, beating until soft peaks form, 5 to 8 minutes.

DESSERTS

Be a "Supermom" by filling your home with the tempting aroma of freshly baked cookies. The smell says "welcome." In this chapter you'll find chewy cookies, bar cookies and many others. Our favorites, however are in the Master Mixes section—SLICE & BAKE COOKIES in a variety of flavors.

If you're looking for a way to introduce cooking to your children, COOKIE MIX is made to order. Success right from the beginning will motivate them to move on to more challenging mixes. And there will be very little mess!

Children might have the right idea when they eat main dishes sparingly to save room for the finishing touch—dessert! A meal without a dessert is like a kitchen without a sink. Desserts such as puddings or fruit-filled desserts even add nutrition to a meal.

When planning your menus, include desserts that will complement the meal. For example, serve a light dessert such as Lemonade Ice Cream Dessert with pasta or another substantial food.

Need a spectacular dessert for a special occasion? Try the Cookie Crust Fruit Tart. In addition to being beautiful, it is delicious and easy. Check the Cakes and Pies sections for other great finales.

APPLE-WALNUT COBBLER

*Real "comfort" food—especially
if you top it with ice cream.*

**4 cups peeled, cored and sliced
    apples**
1/2 cup sugar
1/2 teaspoon cinnamon
**3/4 cup coarsely chopped
    walnuts**
2 cups QUICK MIX, page 21
3 tablespoons sugar
1 egg, slightly beaten
1 cup milk or water

Variation

Cherry Cobbler—Omit apples,
    sugar, cinnamon and walnuts.
    Drain and reserve liquid from
    1 (16-oz.) can red, sour, pitted
    cherries. Combine 2 table-
    spoons flour, 3/4 cup sugar
    and 1/8 teaspoon salt. Stir in
    reserved cherry juice. Fold in
    cherries and 1 teaspoon
    almond extract. Make cobbler
    mixture, reducing milk or water
    to 6 tablespoons; add 1 tea-
    spoon almond extract. Bake at
    425F (220C) 25 minutes.

Preheat oven to 325F (165C). Grease
an 8-inch-square pan. Place apples in
bottom of pan. Combine sugar, cinnamon and walnuts in a bowl. Sprinkle
over apples in pan, reserving 1/4 cup
for topping.

In a bowl, thoroughly combine QUICK
MIX and sugar. Combine egg and milk
or water in a small bowl. Add all at
once to dry ingredients. Blend. Spread
dough evenly over top of apple mixture.
Top with remaining cinnamon-sugar
mixture. Bake about 45 minutes, until
light brown. Cut into squares. Makes
8 to 10 servings.

PEACH COBBLER

*Try other fruits in this basic cob-
bler as they are in season or
according to your personal taste.*

**1/4 cup butter or margarine,
    melted**
**3 cups fresh peaches, sliced or
    1 (28-oz.) can peaches,
    drained**
1/2 teaspoon nutmeg
**1 pkg. SNACK CAKE MIX,
    page 24**
1 teaspoon cinnamon
3/4 cup milk
1/3 cup vegetable oil
1 egg
**1 teaspoon vanilla or
    almond extract**

Preheat oven to 350F (175C). In an
11" x 7" baking pan put melted butter
or margarine, peaches and nutmeg. Stir
to coat peaches. In a medium mixing
bowl, combine SNACK CAKE MIX, cinnamon, milk, vegetable oil, egg and
vanilla or almond extract. Pour over fruit
mixture in pan. Bake for about 30 minutes or until cake is set. Makes 8
servings.

*We've used most
fresh fruit in season,
including nectarines,
plums, and berries.*

OUR BEST BROWNIES

We had no trouble getting our family to test this recipe.

1/4 cup butter or margarine, melted
2 eggs, beaten
1 teaspoon vanilla extract
2-1/4 cups BROWNIE MIX, page 14
1/2 cup chopped nuts
Brownie Toppers, below

Preheat oven to 350F (175C). Grease and flour an 8-inch-square pan. Combine melted butter or margarine, eggs, vanilla and BROWNIE MIX. Beat until smooth. Stir in nuts. Pour into prepared pan. Bake 30 to 35 minutes, until edges separate from pan. Sprinkle or frost with Brownie Topper of your choice. Cut into 2-inch bars when cool. Makes 16 brownies.

Brownie Toppers

Chocolate Topper
Sprinkle 1 (6-oz.) package chocolate chips over warm brownies. Warm in oven until melted. Spread evenly. Sprinkle with more chopped nuts.

Coconut-Pecan Topping
Combine 1/3 cup sugar, 1/3 cup evaporated milk, 1 beaten egg yolk and 3 tablespoons butter or margarine. Stirring constantly, cook 5 minutes, until mixture comes to a boil. Remove and stir in 1/4 teaspoon vanilla, 2/3 cup coconut and 1/2 cup chopped pecans. Cool 10 minutes. Spread on cooled brownies.

Bittersweet Frosting
Combine 1-1/2 cups powdered sugar, 1/2 cup butter and 1/2 cup evaporated milk. Cook 7 to 10 minutes, until temperature reaches 230F (110C). Cool. Beat until stiff; spread on cooled brownies. Melt 2 (1-oz.) squares unsweetened chocolate and spread over topping.

Marshmallow Surprise
Prepare 1/2 recipe Chocolate Icing, page 286. Sprinkle 1-1/2 cups miniature marshmallows over warm brownies. Warm until melted, about 2 to 3 minutes. Cool. Frost with icing.

BROWNIE ALASKA

Prepare it ahead of time for a spectacular but simple dessert.

1 quart vanilla ice cream, softened slightly
2 cups BROWNIE MIX, page 14
4 eggs, separated
2 tablespoons water
2 tablespoons butter or margarine, melted
1 teaspoon vanilla extract
1/2 cup coarsely chopped walnuts
1/2 cup sugar

Variation

Substitute mint chocolate chip or peppermint ice cream for vanilla ice cream.

Line an 8-inch bowl with foil. Pack ice cream into bowl and freeze until very firm. Preheat oven to 350F (175C). Grease an 8-inch-round cake pan. Line pan with wax paper. Grease wax paper. In another medium bowl, combine BROWNIE MIX, egg yolks, water, butter or margarine, vanilla and nuts. Spread in prepared pan. Bake about 25 minutes, until edges separate from pan. Cool in pan 10 minutes, then cool. Peel off wax paper. Place cake on a wooden cutting board or baking sheet lined with heavy brown paper. Cover with plastic wrap. Freeze about 1 hour until hard.

Beat egg whites until foamy. Gradually add sugar and beat until stiff peaks form. Set aside. Quickly invert bowl of ice cream over cake. Remove bowl and foil. Quickly spread meringue over ice cream and brownie, sealing meringue to cutting board or paper. Return to freezer for at least 30 minutes.

Just before serving, preheat oven to 500F (260C). Bake about 3 minutes, until meringue is browned. Cut in wedges with a knife dipped in water. Refreeze leftover Brownie Alaska, if desired. Makes 10 to 12 servings.

CHEWY CHOCOLATE COOKIES

Crown each one with a nut.

1/4 cup butter or margarine, melted
2 eggs, slightly beaten
1/4 cup water, more if needed
2-1/4 cups BROWNIE MIX, page 14
1/2 teaspoon baking soda
3/4 cup all-purpose flour
1 teaspoon vanilla extract
Walnut or pecan halves

Preheat oven to 375F (190C). Grease baking sheets. Combine butter or margarine, eggs and water in a medium bowl. Beat with a fork until blended. Stir in BROWNIE MIX, baking soda, flour and vanilla. Add additional water, if needed. Blend well.

Drop by teaspoonfuls 2 inches apart on prepared baking sheets. Put a walnut or pecan half in center of each cookie Bake 10 to 12 minutes, until edges are browned. Cool. Makes 36 cookies.

CHOCOLATE-CHIP COOKIES

Rich-chocolate flavor in every bite.

3 cups COOKIE MIX, page 30
3 tablespoons milk, more if necessary
1 teaspoon vanilla extract
1 egg
1/2 cup nuts or coconut
1 cup chocolate chips or sugar-coated chocolate candies

Preheat oven to 375F (190C). Grease baking sheets. In a large bowl, combine COOKIE MIX, milk, vanilla and egg. Blend well. Stir in nuts or coconut and chocolate chips or candies.

Drop by teaspoonfuls onto prepared baking sheets. Bake 10 to 15 minutes, until golden brown. Makes 24 cookies.

ENERGY BARS

A crunchy snack to be enjoyed any time of the day.

1/2 cup dark-brown sugar, packed
1/2 cup light corn syrup
1/2 cup peanut butter
3-1/2 cups GRANOLA MIX, page 32
1/2 cup Spanish peanuts

Butter a 9-inch-square baking pan; set aside. In a saucepan, combine brown sugar and corn syrup. Cook and stir over medium heat until mixture comes to a boil. Remove from heat. Stir in peanut butter until blended. Stir in GRANOLA MIX and peanuts until coated.

Press into prepared pan. Cool to room temperature. Cut into 3" x 1" pieces. Makes 27 bars.

MOLASSES COOKIES

A soft, chewy and delicious cookie.

2 cups QUICK MIX, page 21
1/4 cup sugar
1/2 teaspoon ground cinnamon
1/2 teaspoon ground ginger
1/4 teaspoon ground cloves
1 egg yolk
1/2 cup molasses
Sugar

In a medium bowl, combine QUICK MIX, 1/4 cup sugar, cinnamon, ginger and cloves. Mix well. Combine egg yolk and molasses in a small bowl. Add to dry mixture. Blend well. Refrigerate at least one hour.

Preheat oven to 375F (190C). Lightly grease baking sheets. Shape dough into 1-1/2-inch balls. Place on prepared baking sheets. Flatten balls with the bottom of a glass dipped in sugar. Bake 8 to 10 minutes, until edges are browned. Makes about 30 cookies.

PEANUT-BUTTER COOKIES

A better peanut-butter batter.

3 cups COOKIE MIX, page 30
1/4 cup brown sugar, packed
1 teaspoon vanilla extract
2 eggs
**1/2 cup chunky-style peanut
  butter**

Variation

Peanut-Butter & Jelly Cookies—
  On baking sheets, make
  indentation with thumb in
  center of balls. Do not flatten.
  Fill with grape jelly.

Preheat oven to 375F (190C). Lightly
grease baking sheets. Combine all
ingredients in a medium bowl. Blend
well. Shape dough into 1-inch balls.
Place on prepared baking sheets and
flatten with fork tines. Bake 10 to 12
minutes, until edges are browned.
Makes 30 to 36 cookies.

SNICKERDOODLES

Soft when they're warm—snappy when they're cool!

2-1/2 cups COOKIE MIX,
  page 30
1/4 teaspoon baking soda
1 teaspoon cream of tartar
1 egg
2 tablespoons sugar
1 teaspoon ground cinnamon

Preheat oven to 400F (205C). In a medium bowl, combine COOKIE MIX, baking soda, cream of tartar and egg. Mix well. Combine sugar and cinnamon in a small dish.

Shape dough into 1-1/2-inch balls. Roll in sugar-cinnamon mixture and place 2 inches apart on unbuttered baking sheets. Flatten balls slightly. Bake 8 to 10 minutes, until lightly browned with cracked tops. Do not overbake. Makes about 24 cookies.

TROPIC MACAROONS

A tropical South Seas adventure in cookies.

2 cups COOKIE MIX, page 30
2 egg yolks
1 (8.5-oz.) can crushed
  pineapple, drained
1-1/4 cups shredded coconut,
  more if desired
Maraschino cherries,
  for garnish

Preheat oven to 350F (175C). Lightly grease baking sheets. In a medium bowl, combine COOKIE MIX, egg yolks, pineapple and coconut. Stir until well-blended. Drop by teaspoonfuls onto prepared baking sheets. Top with maraschino cherries. Bake 12 to 15 minutes, until edges are golden. Makes 30 to 36 cookies.

OUR FAVORITE CHEESECAKE

To guarantee a creamier texture, place a pan of water below cheesecake while it bakes.

Graham-Cracker Crust, baked, page 16
4 (8-oz.) pkgs. cream cheese, room temperature
1-1/2 cups sugar
4 eggs, beaten
4 teaspoons vanilla extract
2 teaspoons fresh lemon juice
2 teaspoons grated lemon peel
Sour Cream Topping, below
1 (21-oz.) can blueberry, raspberry, cherry or other fruit pie filling, if desired

Sour Cream Topping
1 cup dairy sour cream
1/4 cup sugar
1 teaspoon vanilla extract

Prepare Graham-Cracker Crust in springform pan, set aside to cool. Preheat oven to 325F (165C). Beat together cream cheese, sugar, eggs, vanilla, lemon juice and lemon peel until very smooth. Spoon into cooled crust in springform pan. Place in preheated oven and bake 1 hour 10 to 1 hour 20 minutes.

Prepare Sour Cream Topping. Spread topping on cheesecake and continue to bake 7 to 10 more minutes or until topping is set. Cool. When completely cool cover with plastic wrap and refrigerate 8 to 24 hours. To serve, remove pan side. Top cheesecake with pie filling. Makes about 15 servings.

Sour Cream Topping
Combine sour cream, sugar and vanilla. Blend well.

You can omit the Sour Cream Topping. Crown your cheesecake with fresh fruit and your favorite whipped topping.

Our Favorite Cheesecake

QUICK FUDGE SAUCE

To prevent scorching, stir continuously over low heat.

1-1/2 cups CHOCOLATE SYRUP MIX, page 64
6 tablespoons butter or margarine
1 teaspoon vanilla extract or other flavoring

In a small saucepan, combine CHOCOLATE SYRUP MIX and butter or margarine. Cook over low heat until smooth, thick and shiny, 5 to 7 minutes. Stir in extract or flavoring. Makes about 1-1/2 cups.

HOT LEMON SAUCE

A great addition to many desserts.

1 cup water
1/4 cup LEMON PIE-FILLING MIX, page 28
2 tablespoons butter or margarine

Combine water and LEMON PIE-FILLING MIX in a small saucepan. Bring to a boil over high heat, stirring constantly. Remove from heat. Add butter or margarine and stir to melt. Serve warm over gingerbread, pound cake, apple pie, steamed pudding and other desserts.

ORANGE-LIGHT DESSERT

A refreshing light dessert that's welcome after a hearty meal.

**Graham-Cracker Crust,
  unbaked, page 16**
3 eggs, beaten
6 tablespoons orange juice
**Grated peel of 1 orange
  (about 1 tablespoon)**
3/4 cup sugar
**1 (13-oz.) can evaporated milk,
  partially frozen**

Prepare Graham-Cracker Crust in 9-inch-square baking pan; set aside. In top of a double boiler, combine eggs, orange juice, orange peel and sugar. Cook and stir over hot water until thickened. Cool.

In a large bowl, whip chilled evaporated milk until thick. Fold into cooled orange mixture. Spoon evenly over crust in pan. Refrigerate 3 to 4 hours. To serve, cut in squares. Makes about 9 servings.

CREAMY VANILLA PUDDING

If you prefer a lighter pudding, omit egg yolks and substitute egg whites.

2 egg yolks
2/3 cup VANILLA PUDDING &
**   PIE-FILLING MIX, page 29**
2-3/4 cups milk
2 tablespoons butter or
**   margarine**
1-1/2 teaspoons vanilla extract

Variation

Creamy Chocolate Pudding—
    Substitute 1 cup CHOCOLATE
    PUDDING & PIE-FILLING MIX,
    page 27, for VANILLA PUD-
    DING & PIE-FILLING MIX.

In a medium bowl, beat egg yolks; set aside. In a medium saucepan, combine VANILLA PUDDING & PIE-FILLING MIX and milk. Cook and stir over medium heat until mixture thickens and begins to bubble. Stirring vigorously, pour about half of the hot mixture into beaten egg yolks. Stir egg-yolk mixture into remaining hot mixture. Cook and stir 1 minute longer.

Remove from heat. Stir in butter or margarine and vanilla until blended. Pour cooked pudding into 6 dessert or custard cups. Cover each with plastic wrap. Refrigerate 1 hour. Makes 6 servings.

LAYERED VANILLA CREAM

You'll like this French-style dessert as much as we do. It tastes like a chocolate eclair.

1-1/4 cups **VANILLA PUDDING & PIE-FILLING MIX, page 29**
3-2/3 cups milk
3 tablespoons butter or margarine
1-1/2 teaspoons vanilla extract
Chocolate Glaze Topping, below
1 cup whipping cream
45 single graham crackers (do not crush)

Chocolate Glaze Topping
2 (1-oz.) squares semisweet chocolate
6 tablespoons butter or margarine
2 tablespoons white corn syrup
2 teaspoons vanilla extract
1-1/2 cups powdered sugar
3 tablespoons milk

In a saucepan, combine VANILLA PUDDING & PIE-FILLING MIX and milk. Cook and stir over medium heat until mixture bubbles, 3 to 5 minutes. Remove from heat. Stir in butter or margarine and vanilla until blended. Cover with plastic wrap. Cool.

Prepare Chocolate Glaze Topping; set aside. In a bowl, whip cream until stiff peaks form. Fold into cooled pudding mixture. Arrange 15 single graham crackers in bottom of a 13" x 9" baking dish. Spread half of pudding mixture over crackers. Repeat layers. Arrange remaining graham crackers on top.

Pour Chocolate Glaze Topping over top layer of crackers. Cover with plastic wrap. Refrigerate at least 10 hours. Makes 12 servings.

Chocolate Glaze Topping
In a small saucepan, melt chocolate and butter or margarine. Stir in corn syrup, vanilla, powdered sugar and milk, beating until smooth.

Omit peppermint and marshmallows, then substitute sliced fresh fruits in season. Nectarines, plums, and berries work well in this recipe.

CHOCOLATE-PEPPERMINT SUPREME

Pretty as a picture

**Graham-Cracker Crust,
   unbaked, page 16**
1/2 cup butter or margarine
1 cup powdered sugar
**1 (1-oz.) square unsweetened
   chocolate, melted**
1/2 cup chopped nuts
1 cup whipping cream
**1 (3-oz.) pkg. hard peppermint
   candy, crushed**
1/2 cup mini marshmallows
1/2 cup chopped nuts
**3/4 cup GRAHAM-CRACKER-
   CRUST MIX, page 16**

Prepare Graham-Cracker Crust in an 8-inch-square baking pan; set aside. In a bowl, cream butter or margarine and powdered sugar. Stir in melted chocolate and 1/2 cup nuts. Spoon chocolate mixture over crust. Refrigerate 1 hour.

Whip cream until stiff peaks form. Fold in peppermint candy, marshmallows and 1/2 cup nuts. Spoon over chilled chocolate mixture. Sprinkle with GRAHAM-CRACKER-CRUST MIX. Refrigerate at least 1 hour. Makes about 12 servings.

LEMONADE ICE CREAM DESSERT

A light and cool dessert to top off any meal.

3 cups GRAHAM-CRACKER-CRUST MIX, page 16
1/2 gallon vanilla ice cream, softened
1 (6-oz.) can frozen lemonade concentrate, unthawed
1 cup whipping cream
12 maraschino cherries, for garnish

Variations

Pineapple-Orange—Omit lemonade and substitute pineapple-orange-passion fruit concentrate and garnish with mandarin oranges and pineapple.

Lime-Coconut—Omit lemonade and substitute frozen limeade. Add 1/2 cup shredded coconut. Sprinkle chopped nuts over whipped cream. Or try any frozen fruit drink concentrates that appeal to you.

Press 2 cups of GRAHAM-CRACKER-CRUST MIX into an 11" x 7" baking pan. Put softened ice cream and frozen lemonade concentrate in a large bowl. Beat with an electric mixer until well blended. Quickly spoon ice-cream mixture into crumb-lined pan.

Top with remaining 1 cup crumbs. Whip cream until stiff. Pipe or spread over crumbs, top with cherries. Freeze. Slice and serve. Makes about 12 servings.

BANANA-COCONUT DELIGHTS

Serve these giant-size treats for breakfast with a glass of milk.

2 cups COOKIE MIX, page 30
1 cup flaked coconut
1 medium banana, mashed
1 teaspoon vanilla extract
1 egg, beaten
1/2 cup chopped nuts
1/2 cup rolled oats

Preheat oven to 375F (190C). Lightly grease baking sheets. In a medium bowl, combine COOKIE MIX, coconut, banana, vanilla and egg. Beat well. Stir in chopped nuts and oats.

Drop by teaspoonfuls onto prepared baking sheets. Bake 10 to 12 minutes, until edges are browned. Makes about 36 cookies.

INDEX

A

Aebleskivers 268
All-American Apple Pie 294
All-Purpose Cake Mix 23
All-Purpose Ground-Meat Mix 38
Almond Glaze 297
Almond Kringle 211
Almond-Poppy Seed Pound Cake 285
Appetizers & Snacks 82-92
Apple Muffins 271
Apple-Walnut Cobbler 312
Applesauce Bread, Spicy 245
Applesauce Snack Cake 273
Apricot Chicken 169

B

Bagels 264
Baked Beef Brisket 127
Baked Pork Chops 200
Baking & cooking with mixes 3
Banana-Coconut Delights 328
Banana Cream Pie 302
Banana-Nut Bread 236
Banana-Split Cake 275
Banana-Walnut Snack Cake 274
Bars, Energy 317
Basic White Sauce 101
Bean Soup, Calico 114
Beans, Fat-Free Refried 119
Beans, Molasses-Baked 116
Beef & Vegetables, Teriyaki 140
Beef Gravy and Mix 61
BEEF
  Baked Beef Brisket 127
  Bread Basket Stew 130
  Country Casserole 137
  Deep-Dish Pot Pie 147
  Dinner In A Pumpkin 138
  Enchilada Casserole 136
  Hurry-Up Curry 139
  Meat & Potato Pie 141
  Mexican Haystack 142
  No-Fuss Swiss-Steak Stew 134
  Onion Pot Roast 128
  Oriental-Style Skillet Dinner 143
  Saturday Stroganoff 132
  Skillet Enchiladas 133
  Slumgullion 148
  Smothered Hamburger Patties 131
  Tasty Beef Birds 129
  Teriyaki Beef & Vegetables 140
  Three-Layer Casserole 145
  Vegetable Cheese Casserole 135
  Wintry-Day Chili 146
Best-Ever Minestrone Soup 103
Big Soft Pretzels 92
Biscuits 255
Biscuits, Never-Fail Rolled 256
Blueberry Muffins 250, 252
Boston Cream Pie 276
BREADS, QUICK
  Applesauce, Spicy 245
  Banana-Nut 236
  Carrot-Orange 237
  Corn, Golden 238
  Cranberry 241
  Crispy Breadsticks 253
  Date-Nut 240
  Poppy Seed-Lemon 242
  Pumpkin 243
  Zucchini 246

BREAD, YEAST
  Basket Bowls 244
  Country French 247
  French 230
  Homemade White 231
  Mary's Honey-Walnut Swirl 234
  Raisin-Cinnamon 231
  Savory Tomato-Rosemary 232
  Swedish Rye 233
Breadmaker Mix and Recipes 13
Breadsticks, Crispy 253
Breakfast & Brunch 210-228
Broccoli & Ham Rolls 199
Broiled Coconut Topping 287
Brown-Sugar Topping 277, 288
Brownie Alaska 315
Brownie Mix 14
Brownies, Our Best 314
Buns, Hamburger 260
Burgers, Chicken 151
Burros, Green-Chile 174
Burros, Whole-Bean Veggie 198
BUTTERS
  Cinnamon 214
  Honey 238
  Orange 261
BUTTERMILK
  Pancake & Waffle Mix 25
  Pancakes 222
  Waffles 220
Butterscotch Butter Balls 212

C

Caesar Salad Dressing and Mix 66
Cake Mix, All-Purpose 23
Cakes 272-292
CAKES
  Almond-Poppy Seed 285
  Applesauce Snack 273
  Banana-Split 275
  Banana-Walnut Snack 274
  Carrot Snack 278
  Double-Chocolate Snack 279
  Cranberry Cakes with Butter Sauce 281
  Date-Chocolate-Chip Snack 292
  Gingerbread Snack 284
  Mississippi Mud 286
  Mom's Spumoni 282
  Oatmeal Spice 287
  Pineapple Upside-Down 288
  Sunday Shortcake 290
  Texas Sheet 291
  White 289
  Yellow 289
Calico Bean Soup 114
Caramel Topping 214
Caramel-Nut Pudding Cake 277
Carrot Snack Cake 278
Carrot-Orange Loaf 237
Cashew Chicken, Stir-Fry 161
CASSEROLES
  Chicken-Zucchini 120
  Club Chicken 152
  Enchilada 136
  Scallop 194
  Spaghetti 179
  Three-Layer 145
  Vegetable-Cheese 135
Cathy's Meatball Sandwiches 177
Cauliflower Fritters in Cheese Sauce 117
Celery Sauce 101
Chalupa 171

CHEESE
  Breakfast Strata, Sausage- 224
  Casserole, Vegetable- 135
  Fondue 86
  Sauce 101
  Sauce, Freezer 54
  Soup in Bread Bowls, Broccoli- 99
  Tart, Self-Crust 208
Cheesecake, Our Favorite 320
Cherry-Almond Pie 297
Cherry Cobbler 312
Chess Tarts 303
Chewy Chocolate Cookies 316
Chicken Gravy and Mix 62
Chicken Mix 39
Chicken Noodle Salad, Oriental 107
Chicken Continental Rice Seasoning Mix 76
Chicken Salad, Gayle's 105
Chicken Salad, Hot 106
Chicken Soup, Corn-Tortilla 94
Chicken Soup, Cream-of- 100
CHICKEN
  Apricot Chicken 169
  Chicken & Ham Foldovers 156
  Chicken À La King 157
  Chicken Breasts En Croûte 150
  Chicken Burgers 151
  Chicken Cacciatore 151
  Chicken Continental 153
  Chicken in Mushroom Sauce 167
  Chicken Oahu 160
  Chicken Strata 163
  Chicken-Zucchini Casserole 120
  Club Chicken Casserole 152
  Creamy Chicken Enchiladas 155
  Crunchy-Crust Chicken 154
  Hawaiian Haystack 158
  Mexican Chicken Bake 168
  Stir-Fry Cashew Chicken 161
  Sunday Chicken 162
  Sweet & Sour Chicken 161
  Soft Chicken Taco 176
  Turkey Dinner Pie 165
  White Chili 166
Chili 67
Chili Con Carne 187
Chili & Seasoning Mix 67
Chili, Wintry-Day 146
Chimichangas 172
CHOCOLATE
  Chip Cookies 55, 316
  Cream Pie 295
  Double-Chocolate Snack Cake 279
  Date-Chocolate-Chip Snack Cake 292
  Frosting 276
  Glaze Topping 325
  Icing 286
  Pudding, Creamy 27, 324
  Pudding & Pie-Filling Mix 27
  Syrup Mix 64
  Wafer Cookies 56
  Peppermint Supreme 326
Chow Mein, Quick 204
CHOWDERS
  Eastern Corn 95
  Hearty 112
  Hearty New England Clam 98
CINNAMON
  Butter 214
  Crumble Topping 218
  Filling 216

Rolls 213, 256
Rolls, Whole-Wheat 214
Twists, Swedish 216
Whipped Topping 243
Club Chicken Casserole 152
Coating Mix, Crisp 253
Cobbler, Apple-Walnut 312
Cobbler, Peach 313
Cocktail Meatballs 88
Cocoa Icing 291
Coconut Cream Pie 302
Coconut Delights, Banana- 328
Cookie Crust Fruit Tart 306
Cookie Mix 30
COOKIES
Banana-Coconut Delights 328
Chewy Chocolate 316
Chocolate-Chip 55, 316
Chocolate Wafer 56
Energy Bars 317
Gingersnap 57
Molasses 317
Oatmeal 58
Peanut-Butter 59, 318
Snickerdoodles 319
Sugar 60
Tropic Macaroons 319
Corn Bread and Mix 15
Corn Bread, Golden 238
Corn Bread, Mexican 238
Corn Chowder, Eastern 95
Corn Dogs 206
Corn-Tortilla Chicken Soup 94
Country Casserole 137
Country French Bread 247
Cranberry Bread 241
Cranberry Cakes with Butter Sauce 281
Cream-Cheese Fruit Tarts 307
Cream-Cheese Swirls 257
Cream Filling 276
Cream, Peach Devonshire 270
CREAM-CHEESE
Filling 257, 306
Frosting 278
Pastry 308
Pastry Mix 50
Cream-of-Chicken Soup 100
Creamy Chicken Enchiladas 155
Creamy Chocolate Pudding 27, 324
Creamy Crudité Dip and Mix 68
Creamy Mushroom Sauce 101
Creamy Sauce 160
Creamy Vanilla Pudding 324
Crescent Rolls 258
Crisp Coating Mix 31
Crispy Breadsticks 253
Crunchy Fish Bake 209
Crunchy-Crust Chicken 154
Crust, Cream Cheese 308
Crust, Freezer Pie 309
Crust, Pizza 267
Cubed Pork Mix 47
Curried Shrimp Rounds 83
Curry Sauce 101
Curry, Hurry-Up 139
D
Date-Chocolate-Chip Snack Cake 292
Date-Nut Bread 240
Deep-Dish Pot Pie 147
Desserts 311-328
Dinner In A Pumpkin 138

Dip, Quick Taco 85
Doughnuts, Super-Duper 269
DRESSINGS
Caesar Salad 66
French 69
Home-Style 70
Low-Calorie 71
Orange 108
Priscilla's Salad 72
Sweet Italian 69
Sweet Salad 80
Dried Calico Bean Soup Mix 37
E
Eastern Corn Chowder 95
Eggplant Parmesan 178
Eggs Florentine 225
Enchilada Casserole 136
Enchiladas, Skillet 133
Enchiladas, Sour-Cream 173
Energy Bars 317
English Griddle Scones 270
English Muffins 259
English Poached Eggs & Ham 225
Equipment & Procedures 10-12
F
Fat-Free Refried Beans 119
Fiesta Fruit Topping 223
FILLINGS
Cinnamon 216
Cream 276
Cream-Cheese 257, 306
Honey-Nut 234
Lime 304
Taco 36
Fish Bake, Crunchy 209
Five-Way Beef Mix 40
Fondue, Cheese 86
Freezer Cheese-Sauce Mix 54
Freezer Pie Crust 309
Freezer Pie-Crust Mix 51
French Bread 230
French Bread, Country 247
French Dressing and Mix 69
French Onion Soup Gratiné 96
Fresh Peach Pie 300
FROSTINGS
Chocolate 276
Cream-Cheese 278
Rainbow 282
Fruit Glaze 306
Fruit Slush and Mix 53
Fruit Topping, Fiesta 223
Fudge Sauce, Quick 322
G
Gayle's Chicken Salad 105
Gingerbread Snack Cake 284
Gingersnap Cookies 57
GLAZES
Almond 297
Fruit 306
Lemon 242
Orange 261
Powdered-Sugar 216
Sweet 257
Vanilla 269
Golden Corn Bread 238
Graham-Cracker-Crust Mix 16
Gran Muffins 271
Grandma's Hamburger Soup 109
Granola and Mix 32

Gravy, Beef 61
Gravy, Chicken 62
Green Peppers Mediterranean-Style 123
Green Peppers, Stuffed 186
Green-Chile Burros 174
Ground-Meat Mix, All-Purpose 38
Guacamole 174
H
Ham Foldovers, Chicken & 156
Ham Rolls, Broccoli & 199
Hamburger Buns 260
Hamburger Soup, Grandma's 109
Hamburger Soup, Swiss 113
Hamburger Trio Skillet 188
Hamburger-Noodle Skillet 188
Hawaiian Haystack 158
Hearty Chowder 112
Hearty New Englad Clam Chowder 98
Herbed Stuffing Mix 33
Home-Style Dressing and Mix 70
Homemade White Bread 231
Honey Butter 238
Honey-Nut Filling 234
Honey-Walnut Swirl, Mary's 234
Hot Butter Sauce 294
Hot Chicken Salad 106
Hot Chocolate and Mix 78
Hot Lemon Sauce 322
Hot Roll Mix 17
Hot-Fudge Pudding Cake 280
Hurry-Up Curry 139
I
Ice Cream Dessert, Lemonade 327
ICINGS
Chocolate 286
Cocoa 291
Kringle 211
Impossible Pie 298
Ingredients 6-8
Italian Cooking Sauce Mix 41
Italian Dishes, see
Mexican & Italian Dishes
Italian-Style Meat Mix 42
Italian-Style Zucchini 124
K
Kringle Icing 211
L
Last-Minute Lasagna 207
Layered Vanilla Cream 325
Lemon Bread, Poppy Seed- 242
Lemon Glaze 242
Lemon Pie-Filling Mix 28
Lemon Pound Cake 285
Lemon Sauce, Hot 322
Lemon-Poppy Seed Muffins 249
Lemonade Ice Cream Dessert 327
Lime Filling 304
Lime Tarts Supreme 304
Loaf, Carrot-Orange 237
Low-Calorie Dressing and Mix 71
Luscious Lemon Pie 299
M
Macaroons, Tropic 319
Main Dishes - Beef 126-148
Main Dishes - Chicken 149-169
Main Dishes - Mexican & Italian 170-188
Main Dishes - Other 189-209
Manicotti Shells, Stuffed 182
Marie's Fruit Cocktail and Mix 52
Mary's Honey-Walnut Swirl 234

Meat & Potato Pie 141
Meat Loaf Mix 43
Meat Loaf with Tangy Topper Sauce 185
Meat Pinwheels 256
Meat Sauce Mix 45
Meatball Mix 44
MEATBALLS
   Cocktail 88
   Sandwiches, Cathy's 177
   Stew 183
   Swedish 196
   Sweet & Sour 184
Melt-In-Your-Mouth Muffins 250
Meringue, Mile-High 310
Mexican Chicken Bake 168
Mexican Corn Bread 238
Mexican Delight 91
Mexican Haystack 142
Mexican Meat Mix 46
Mexican & Italian Dishes 170-188
   Cathy's Meatball Sandwiches 177
   Chalupa 171
   Chili Con Carne 187
   Chimichangas 172
   Eggplant Parmesan 178
   Green-Chile Burros 174
   Hamburger Trio Skillet 188
   Hamburger-Noodle Skillet 188
   Meat Loaf with Tangy Topper Sauce 185
   Meatball Stew 183
   Rancher's Sloppy Joes 187
   Soft Chicken Taco 176
   Sour-Cream Enchiladas 173
   Spaghetti Casserole 179
   Spaghetti Royale 180
   Stuffed Green Peppers 186
   Stuffed Manicotti Shells 182
   Sweet & Sour Meatballs 184
   Taco Supreme 175
Mile-High Meringue 310
Minestrone Soup, Best-Ever 103
Mini Fruit Tarts 307
Mini-Chimis 89
Mississippi Mud 286
MIXES, DRY AND SEMI-DRY 1, 13-37
   All-Purpose Cake 23
   Breadmaker 13
   Brownie 14
   Buttermilk Pancake & Waffle 25
   Chocolate Pudding and Pie-Filling 27
   Cookie 30
   Corn Bread 15
   Crisp Coating 31
   Dried Calico Bean Soup 37
   Graham-Cracker-Crust 16
   Granola 32
   Herbed Stuffing 33
   Hot Roll 17
   Lemon Pie-Filling 28
   Mueseli Oatmeal 34
   Muffin 19
   Onion Seasoning 35
   Quick 21
   Snack Cake 24
   Sweet Quick-Bread 20
   Taco Seasoning 36
   Vanilla Pudding & Pie-Filling 29
   Whole-Grain Pancake 26
   Whole-Wheat Hot-Roll 18
MIXES, FREEZER-REFRIGERATOR 1, 38-53
   All-Purpose Ground-Meat 38

Beef Gravy 61
Chicken 39
Chicken Gravy 62
Chocolate Syrup 64
Cream-Cheese Pastry 50
Cubed Pork 47
Five-Way Beef 40
Freezer Cheese-Sauce 54
Freezer Pie-Crust 51
Fruit Slush 53
Italian Cooking Sauce 41
Italian-Style Meat 42
Marie's Fruit Cocktail 52
Meat Loaf 43
Meat Sauce 45
Meatball 44
Mexican Meat 46
Navy Bean 48
Oriental Stir-Fry 65
Pinto Bean 49
Slice & Bake Chocoate-Chip Cookies 55
Slice & Bake Chocolate-Wafer Cookies 56
Slice & Bake Gingersnap Cookies 57
Slice & Bake Peanut-Butter Cookies 59
Slice & Bake Sugar Cookies 60
Slice & Bake Oatmeal Cookies 58
White Sauce 63
MIXES, SPECIAL 2, 66-81
   Caesar Salad Dressing 66
   Chicken Oriental Rice Seasoning 76
   Chili Seasoning 67
   Creamy Crudité Dip 68
   French Dressing 69
   Home-Style Dressing 70
   Hot Chocolate Mix 78
   Low-Calorie Dressing 71
   Priscilla's Salad Dressing 72
   Russian Refresher 81
   Sloppy Joe Seasoning 74
   Spaghetti Seasoning 75
   Spanish Rice Seasoning 77
   Spice Bundles 79
   Sweet Salad Dressing Mix 80
Molasses Bran Muffins 251
Molasses Cookies 317
Molasses-Baked Beans 116
Mom's Spumoni Cake 282
Monte Cristo Sandwiches 190
Morning Muffins 252
Mueseli Oatmeal Mix 34
Muffin Mix 19
Muffins & Rolls 248-271
MUFFINS
   Apple 271
   English 259
   Gran 271
   Lemon-Poppy Seed 249
   Melt-In-Your-Mouth 250
   Molasses Bran 251
   Morning 252
   Variations 250, 252
   Zucchini 253
Mushroom Sauce, Chicken in 167
N
Navy Bean Mix 48
Never-Fail Rolled Biscuits 256
New England Clam Chowder, Hearty 98
No-Fuss Swiss-Steak Stew 134
Noodle Soup, Oriental 102
O
Oatmeal Cookies 58

Oatmeal Mix, Mueseli 34
Oatmeal Spice Cake 287
Old-Fashioned Vegetable Platter 122
Omelet, Puffy 226
Onion Pot Roast 128
Onion Seasoning Mix 35
Onion Soup Gratiné, French 96
Orange Butter 261
Orange Butterflake Rolls 261
Orange Dressing 108
Orange Glaze 261
Orange Loaf, Carrot- 237
Orange-Light Dessert 323
Oriental Chicken Noodle Salad 107
Oriental Noodle Soup 102
Oriental Stir-Fry Mix 65
Oriental-Style Skillet Dinner 143
Our Best Brownies 314
Our Favorite Cheesecake 320
P
Pan Rolls 262
PANCAKES
   Buttermilk 222
   Puff 223
   Quick 221
   Whole-Grain 221
Pasta e Fagioli 97
Pastry, Cream-Cheese 308
Peach Cobbler 313
Peach Devonshire Cream 270
Peanut-Butter Cookies 59, 318
Pecan Tarts 305
Peppermint Supreme, Chocolate 326
Pies 293-310
PIES
   All-American Apple 294
   Banana Cream 302
   Boston Cream 276
   Cherry-Almond 297
   Chocolate Cream 295
   Coconut Cream 302
   Deep-Dish Pot Pie 147
   Fresh Peach 300
   Impossible 298
   Luscious Lemon 299
   Meat & Potato 141
   Sour Cream & Orange 310
   Sour Cream & Raisin 301
   Spanish Cheese 193
   Strawberry Cream 302
   Turkey Dinner 165
   Vanilla Cream Pie 302
Pineapple Upside-Down Cake 288
Pinto Bean Mix 49
Pizza Crust 256, 267
Pizza, Speedy 87
Pluckit 215
Poached Eggs & Ham, English 225
Pound Cake, Almond-Poppy Seed 285
Pound Cake, Lemon 285
Poppy Seed-Lemon Bread 242
Pork Chops, Baked 200
Pork Chops, Stuffed 201
Pork Chow Mein 202
Pork, Sweet & Sour 203
Porridge, Swiss 229
Pot Pie, Deep-Dish 147
Pot Roast, Onion 128
Potato Pie, Meat & 141
Potatoes Au Gratin 118
Pound Cake, Almond-Poppy Seed 285

Pound Cake, Lemon 285
Powdered-Sugar Glaze 216
Pretzels, Big Soft 92
Priscilla's Salad Dressing and Mix 72
Pudding Cake, Caramel-Nut 277
Pudding Cake, Hot-Fudge 280
Pudding, Creamy Vanilla 324
Puff Pancakes 223
Puffy Omelet 226
Pumpkin Bread 243

Q
Quiche, Simplified 227
Quick Chow Mein 204
Quick Fudge Sauce 322
Quick Mix 21
Quick Pancakes 221
Quick Taco Dip 85

R
Rainbow Frosting 282
Raisin-Cinnamon Bread 231
Rancher's Sloppy Joes 187
Refried Beans, Fat-Free 119
Rice, Chicken Continental 76
Rice, Spanish 77
ROLLS
   Cinnamon 213, 256
   Crescent 258
   Orange Butterflake 261
   Pan 262
   Pluckit 215
   Squash 263
   Whole-Wheat Cinnamon 214
Rosemary Bread, Savory Tomato- 232
Russian Refresher and Mix 81
Rye Bread, Swedish 233

S
SALADS
   Gayle's Chicken 105
   Hot Chicken 106
   Oriental Chicken Noodle 107
   Strawberry-Spinach 108
   Taco 111
Sandwiches, Cathy's Meatball 177
Sandwiches, Monte Cristo 190
Saturday Stroganoff 132
SAUCES
   Celery 101
   Cheese 101
   Creamy 160
   Creamy Mushroom 101
   Curry 101
   Freezer Cheese 54
   Hot Butter 294
   Hot Lemon 322
   Quick Fudge 322
   Spaghetti 75
   Sweet & Sour 90
   Tangy Topper 185
Sausage-Cheese Breakfast Strata 224
Savory Tomato-Rosemary Bread 232
Scallop Casserole 194
Scones, English Griddle 270
Self-Crust Cheese Tart 208
Semi-dry mixes 1
Shrimp & Vegetable Stir-Fry 195
Shrimp Rounds, Curried 83
Simplified Quiche 227
Skillet Enchiladas 133
SLICE & BAKE COOKIES
   Chocolate-Chip 55

Chocolate-Wafer 56
Gingersnap 57
Oatmeal 58
Peanut-Butter 59
Sugar 60
Sloppy Joes and Seasoning Mix 74
Sloppy Joes, Rancher's 187
Slumgullion 148
Smothered Hamburger Patties 131
Snack Cake Mix 24
Snickerdoodles 319
Soft Chicken Taco 176
SOUPS
   Best-Ever Minestrone 103
   Calico Bean 114
   Corn-Tortilla Chicken 100
   Cream-of-Chicken 100
   Grandma's Hamburger 109
   Oriental Noodle 102
   Pasta e Fagioli 97
   Swiss Hamburger 113
Soups & Salads 93-114
Sour Cream & Orange Pie 310
Sour Cream & Raisin Pie 301
Sour Cream Topping 320
Sour-Cream Enchiladas 173
South of the Border Vegetarian Bake 192
Spaghetti Casserole 179
Spaghetti Royale 180
Spaghetti Sauce 75
Spaghetti Seasoning Mix 75
Spanish Cheese Pie 193
Spanish Rice and Seasoning Mix 77
Speedy Pizza 87
Spice Bundles 79
Spicy Applesauce Bread 245
Spinach Salad, Strawberry- 108
Spumoni Cake, Mom's 282
Squash Rolls 263
Stew, Bread Basket 130
Stew, Meatball 183
Stew, No-Fuss Swiss-Steak 134
Stir-Fry Cashew Chicken 161
Strata, Sausage-Cheese Breakfast 224
Strawberry Cream Pie 302
Strawberry-Spinach Salad 108
Stuffed Green Peppers 186
Stuffed Manicotti Shells 182
Stuffed Pork Chops 201
Stuffing, Supper 125
Sugar Cookies 60
Sunday Chicken 162
Sunday Shortcake 290
Sunshine Coffee Cake 218
Super-Duper Doughnuts 269
Supper Stuffing 125
Swedish Cinnamon Twists 216
Swedish Meatballs 196
Swedish Rye Bread 233
SWEET & SOUR
   Chicken 163
   Meatballs 184
   Pork 203
   Sauce 90
Sweet Glaze 213, 257
Sweet Italian Dressing 69
Sweet Quick-Bread Mix 20
Sweet Salad Dressing and Mix 80
Swiss Hamburger Soup 113
Swiss Porridge 228
Swiss-Steak Stew, No-Fuss 134

T
Taco Dip, Quick 85
Taco Filling 36
Taco Salad 111
Taco Seasoning Mix 36
Taco Supreme 175
Tangy Topper Sauce 185
TARTS
   Chess 303
   Cookie Crust Fruit 306
   Lime Tarts Supreme 304
   Mini Fruit 307
   Pecan 305
   Self-Crust Cheese 208
Tasty Beef Birds 129
Tatonuts 266
Teriyaki Beef & Vegetables 140
Texas Sheet Cake 291
Three-Layer Casserole 145
Tips For Lowering Fat 9
Tomato-Rosemary Bread, Savory 232
TOPPINGS
   Broiled Coconut 287
   Brown-Sugar 277, 288
   Caramel 214
   Chocolate Glaze 325
   Cinnamon Crumble 218
   Fiesta Fruit 223
   Sour Cream 320
Tropic Macaroons 319
Tuna-Cheese Swirls 197
Turkey Dinner Pie 165

V
Vanilla Cream Pie 302
Vanilla Cream, Layered 325
Vanilla Glaze 269
Vanilla Pudding & Pie-Filling Mix 29
Veal Parmigiana 205
Vegetable Cheese Casserole 135
Vegetable Platter, Old-Fashioned 122
Vegetable Stir-Fry, Shrimp & 195
Vegetables & Side Dishes 115-125
Vegetables, Teriyaki Beef & 140
Vegetarian Bake, South of the Border 192
Veggie Burros, Whole-Bean 198

W
Waffles, Buttermilk 220
Waffles, Whole-Grain 220
Whipped Topping, Cinnamon 243
White Bread, Homemade 231
White Cake 289
White Chili 166
White Sauce Mix 63
White Sauce 101
Whole-Bean Veggie Burros 198
Whole-Grain Pancake Mix 26
Whole-Grain Pancakes 221
Whole-Grain Waffles 220
Whole-Wheat Cinnamon Rolls 214
Whole-Wheat Hot-Roll Mix 18
Wintry-Day Chili 146
Won Tons 90

Y
Yeast Breads & Quick Breads 229-247
Yellow Cake 289

Z
ZUCCHINI
   Bread 246
   Casserole 120
   Italian-Style 124